MARK
TWAIN:
THE FATE
OF
HUMOR

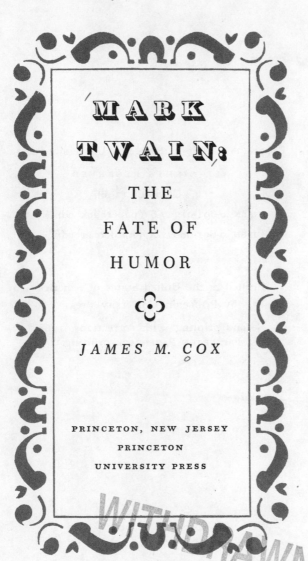

MARK TWAIN:
THE
FATE OF
HUMOR

JAMES M. COX

PRINCETON, NEW JERSEY
PRINCETON
UNIVERSITY PRESS

PREFACE

Books on Mark Twain abound, but Mark Twain criticism remains chiefly indebted to three writers: Albert Bigelow Paine, whose biography, for all its genteel protection of its subject, remains after more than fifty years the standard work; Van Wyck Brooks, whose critical attack on Mark Twain took the shape of a coherent theory of Mark Twain's personality and art; and Bernard De Voto, whose spirited defense constituted a counter theory. Although many critics and scholars have challenged the interpretations of Paine, Brooks, and De Voto, their challenges have resulted at best in revision, not displacement, of the earlier work. That is why the work of Paine, Brooks, and De Voto remains decisive—and therefore indispensable.

Indispensable, but surely not insurmountable. Every critic of Mark Twain, at some point in his work, hopes not merely to argue with or to depend upon but to displace their work. Certainly this was the hope in which much of my book was written. As I look upon the finished book, my hope seems only a hope. Yet all will not have been lost if my ambition has saved the reader from being subjected to one more laborious study of Mark Twain.

The other writer whose work I found indispensable was Freud, who did for the Comic what Aristotle had done for the Tragic. He sought to describe, analyze, and define it. By developing critical categories—wit, the comic, and humor—Freud established distinctions which are absolutely essential for anyone wishing really to think about humor. For Freud, humor was the "highest" joke, and the only regret a student of humor must have in reading his work is that he did not give as much space to humor as he did to wit and the comic. Yet because he had defined the nature of jokes and the comic, Freud was able in brief space to treat humor more analytically and suggestively than anyone who has written on the subject.

Freud not only understood humor; he understood that Mark Twain was a master humorist and used his art as an example par excellence of the humor he was defining. This should not be surprising to any student of cultural history, since Freud's psychoanalytic theory was itself a culmination of nineteenth-century thought and sensibility, of which Mark Twain was so conspicuous a part. Indeed, if one sees the century in terms of evolution, as it often inclined to see itself, then Freud is one of its highest developments. He fulfilled the innumerable impulses and struggles of nineteenth-century writers and thinkers to develop a theory of consciousness. Thus, just when Mark Twain's line on the Moral Sense was hardening (*The Mysterious Stranger*) and when Henry James's drama about it was maturing (*What Maisie Knew*), Freud was initiating a theory of repression which would eventuate in the concept of the superego. And when Freud cited Mark Twain's humor as a perfect example of the economy of expenditure of affection, he was not being merely Freudian but was reaching the heart of Mark Twain's humor, which had been so pervasively concerned with repression, censorship, dreams, the conscience, and self-approval.

To have said so much does not mean, I hope, that my study of Mark Twain will be tagged as Freudian, that adjective so conveniently employed faintly to damn and faintly praise. It does mean that my thought could not have taken the direction it took without my consciousness of Freud's achievement.

Work on this book began longer ago than I like to think, and in the process of completing it I have received more help than I can remember. Yet I have received much that I cannot forget.

First of all, I wish to thank the American Council of Learned Societies for granting me the fellowship which enabled me to spend a year in Berkeley, California, in 1960-61. There and then I was able to begin writing the book. I also wish to thank the Indiana University Graduate School, the Indiana University Foundation, and the Dartmouth Faculty Research Committee for generously providing funds for summer research, research assistance, travel, and typing.

I particularly wish to express my debt to the late James A. Work—that rarest of persons, an ideal English Department chairman—who was always encouraging, generous, and true.

Two teachers made a difference in my life. First, there was Kenneth Burke. Going to school to him was indeed learning to read, and I could not begin to estimate how much I learned from his teaching and writing. Then there was Leslie Fiedler, whose preparation, organization, and performance as a lecturer were an inspiration when I first heard him fifteen years ago and remain for me a standard of excellence to this day.

Two friends—Robert Y. Turner and Alan Hollingsworth —have also made a difference in my life. Their friendship, thought, and criticism have been invaluable not only in helping me think about Mark Twain but in enabling me to understand literature and the teaching of literature.

I wish especially to thank Justin Kaplan, whose recent biography of Mark Twain seems to me the decisive work on Mark Twain in our time. He gave my manuscript a careful reading and made many suggestions, every one of which was valuable. My thanks also go to Henry Nash Smith, who has been a critic of my work probably longer than even he remembers. His characteristically thorough reading of my manuscript pointed out weaknesses which made revision both necessary and possible. I owe much to John S. Tuckey, who, by disclosing a crucial contradiction in my conception of Mark Twain's late works, provided the fine resistance which drove me to find a real conclusion. I must also thank Richard Lanham, whose exhaustive criticism of my style and thought helped me on almost every page. Finally, I wish to thank Frederick Anderson, Editor of the Mark Twain Papers, for offering helpful and prompt answers to all the questions I could ask him.

I am delighted to acknowledge the encouragement and help of Herbert S. Bailey, Jr., Miriam Brokaw, and Eve Hanle of the Princeton University Press. Their concern, apt criticism, and sound advice have assisted me at more points and in more ways than I could begin to recount.

I take special pleasure in thanking Carol Moffatt, who—as critical reader, experienced proofreader, and willing researcher—helped my manuscript in a hundred ways. Both Dorothy Beck, who did the index, and Jennie Wells, who did the typing, deserve and have my thanks for their excellent contributions.

Finally, I wish to thank the many students—and particularly Grace Brown—who have contributed more than they or I know to my thoughts about literature, criticism, humor, and Mark Twain.

CONTENTS

MARK
TWAIN:
THE FATE
OF
HUMOR

CHAPTER

I

DISCOVERY

FOR the biographer, the life of Mark Twain begins on November 30, 1835, in Florida, Missouri, with the birth of Samuel Clemens. But for the critic it begins on February 3, 1863, with Samuel Clemens' discovery of his pseudonym "Mark Twain" in the Nevada Territory. On that date, in the Virginia City *Territorial Enterprise*, the name was affixed to a humorous travel letter describing an "exciting" trip with a talkative companion named Joe Goodman, who in the course of four hours managed to utter three or four words. The Joe Goodman of the sketch was the impassive foil to the suffering traveler Mark Twain; he was the first of a long line of buffoons who were to encumber the pilgrimage of the deadpan Mark Twain, who would in turn become one of the world's great travelers.

The two figures in the sketch—a pair created for the purposes of comedy—had their counterparts in reality. Joseph Goodman was the immensely capable editor of the *Enterprise*; Mark Twain was his star reporter. It is possible that Samuel Clemens had used the pseudonym in earlier letters—this "first" letter alludes to prior experiences, as if Mark Twain were no neophyte making his debut. But if Mark Twain had a recorded comic past, it is not likely ever to emerge, for the files of the *Enterprise* have been lost. The chief reason, and a good one, for believing the February 3 exercise to be the first appearance of Mark Twain is that Goodman, whose entire life reveals a rare integrity, remembered the event as having occurred on February 2, 1863, which is only one day off.[1]

Mark Twain is hardly more than a name at first; he scarcely possesses a personality in any sense of the word. All that the first brief and somewhat crudely funny letter reveals is a minimal humorous perspective. Yet it was to the development and fulfillment of this perspective that the entire imaginative powers of Samuel Clemens were to address themselves. In the name Mark Twain, Clemens had discovered much more than a mere pseudonym. He had discovered his genius, his authentic signature; and his discovery, though he could not have known it at the time, became the event around which his life was to be reorganized.

Precisely because it was such an event, it is also the point at which to begin critical discussion of Mark Twain. With another writer the logical point might be the first book, but with Mark Twain it is the signature itself which constitutes the first distinct *work*. The moment such a decision is made, certain striking significances assert themselves and Mark Twain is disclosed in a new light which, though it may not illuminate all recesses, reveals a new writer against a new background. Instead of beginning with the culture of the Midwest frontier, or with the scars of childhood, we begin with a writer who is "born" at the age of twenty-eight. And instead of beginning with the society of Hannibal, Missouri, in the age of Jackson, we begin with the Nevada Territory at the height of the Civil War. Finally, instead of examining the genealogy of the Clemens family, we begin with the pseudonym "Mark Twain" and all the meanings it had and came to have. The aim of such a beginning is neither to evade the complex issues of Samuel Clemens' early life nor to ignore the frontier literary tradition he exploited, but to

[1] For an authoritative account of the first appearance of the pseudonym, see *Mark Twain of the Enterprise,* ed. Henry Nash Smith (Berkeley, 1957), pp. 47-49.

discover how Mark Twain reorganized his past and how he triumphed over the traditions he inherited.

Mark Twain was "born" in the territory of Nevada, one month after the Emancipation Proclamation. "I feel," writes this territorial figure in the first sentence of his career, "very much as if I had just awakened out of a long sleep."[2] Thus, almost as if he were Rip Van Winkle, Mark Twain makes his debut in American literature. And there is a sense in which Mark Twain is the true progeny of Rip. Rip had slept through the American Revolution, returning to the new America to find his whole identity in jeopardy; Mark Twain had slept through the Civil War— had slept through the inner division of his country—and he would ultimately return to a different America from the one Samuel Clemens had known on the west bank of the Mississippi River before the war.

It would be easy to say he slept because the war was remote from Virginia City, but the fact is that Nevada, from within as well as from without, was defined by the Civil War. From without, Abraham Lincoln was engaging in overt political maneuvers in an effort to accelerate Nevada's admission to the Union and thus add another pro-Union state legislature which would in turn make possible the ratification of the Thirteenth Amendment abolishing slavery. From within, the populace was split on the matter of the Civil War. Although Union sentiment prevailed, there was widespread secession sympathy. The name of the chief metropolis, Virginia City, attested the territory's Southern past. Prominent Southerners such as William Gavin, Henry S. Foote, Colonel Davis S. Terry, and General William Walker had been struggling to swing neighboring California to the Southern side. Terry became governor of the newly created Nevada Territory in March, 1860. Though Lincoln's election diminished Secessionist power in Nevada, there were open demonstrations on the part of the "Secesh" after the battle of Bull Run;

[2] *Ibid.*, p. 49.

and though the battles of Virginia were remote from Virginia City, the issues of the Civil War cut directly across the entire territory, at once determining and defining territorial politics.[3]

More important than the Civil War in Nevada was the discovery of silver. If the national issue of slavery gave Nevada political significance, silver gave it substance. Without the silver there would have been no population, no territory, no statehood, no community. Nevada would have remained no more than a vast and desolate extension of Brigham Young's Utah Territory. But with the discovery of the Comstock Lode in 1859, settlers and investors poured into Washoe—as the territory was called—and by 1861, despite Young's attempt to thwart secession, what had been Carson County, Utah, became the Nevada Territory, and Virginia City became the second great city of the West.

The entire economic reality of Nevada lay in its mines. California had become great because of its gold, but it had many other assets—good land, timber, water power, and a magnificent coast—to sustain it after the gold rush abated. Nevada had nothing but desert. True, the Mormons had made agricultural settlements in the few river valleys in an effort to remain a political force capable of contending with the gold seekers flooding into Carson County, but they abruptly departed when Brigham Young recalled them to aid him against the assembling forces of the Federal Government. After their departure, only the mines and sporadic industries remained.

This was the territory into which Samuel Clemens came in the summer of 1861. In a sense he was admirably suited to the nature of the place. If it was not fully committed to the Civil War, neither was he. He had been a lieutenant in the Confederate Army in the spring of 1861 and had retreated for two hectic weeks before "resigning"—as he drolly referred to his desertion. Later in the

[3] Paul Fatout, *Mark Twain in Virginia City* (Bloomington, 1964), pp. 61-72.

summer he came West with his brother Orion, a strong Union man who had been appointed Territorial Secretary for Nevada by Lincoln in return for active aid in the campaign of 1860. Though it is inaccurate to say that Samuel Clemens fled from the war, it is inadequate to insist that he was an innocent child who had no mind of his own, that he did not realize the seriousness of the slavery issue, and, having entered boyishly and thoughtlessly into the war, just as innocently deserted when he realized that the war led to killing his fellow men. This is the explanation Mark Twain was to give 24 years later in "The Private History of a Campaign that Failed." But Mark Twain's "private" history of Samuel Clemens' experience in the war is as much a burlesque of all the public histories then appearing in the *Century Magazine* as it is a confession of Samuel Clemens' behavior in the war.

Samuel Clemens' actual response to the Civil War will perhaps never be known, but it is absurd to think that a twenty-five-year-old able-bodied young man who had held the exacting and responsible position of steamboat pilot on the great Mississippi had no knowledge about the slavery issue. Nor is it enough to say that Samuel Clemens really did not want to be a Southerner but simply went along with the heavy pressures of society. After all, his brother Orion had freed himself to become an active abolitionist. Samuel Clemens' early letters home from New York and Philadelphia show that he was actively Southern in his sympathies. He deplores the rise of the black man in the North and on the whole sounds little like the desouthernized Southerner William Dean Howells was later to know. "I reckon I had better black my face," he wrote to his mother from New York, "for in these Eastern States niggers are considerably better than white people."[4]

[4] This letter, written August 24, 1853, was first published in the Hannibal *Journal*. Minnie M. Brashear reprinted it in full in her *Mark Twain, Son of Missouri* (Chapel Hill, 1934), pp. 153-55.

Clemens' reconstruction as a Union man took place in Nevada, but it was no sudden conversion. Henry Nash Smith has convincingly shown that the realignment did not begin to be complete until late 1862. As late as February 28, 1862—six months after arriving in Nevada—Clemens was still referring to Union forces as "they." On March 8, he sarcastically observed to his friend William Claggett of a gentleman named Sewall, "He is a Yankee,—and I naturally love a Yankee." Not until September 9, 1862, did his pronoun designating Union forces become "we," and even when he identified himself with the North, he scathingly criticized Union braggadoccio.[5] It was during this period of realignment from Southerner to Union man that "Mark Twain" was discovered. Yet through all the territorial discord generated by war issues Mark Twain remained essentially silent. This silence would be relatively inconsequential if slavery and the Civil War past played no major part in the world Mark Twain was to reconstruct; but slavery becomes one of his major—perhaps *the* major—concern in *Huckleberry Finn, A Connecticut Yankee*, and *Pudd'nhead Wilson*.

The confrontation of slavery lay far ahead. At the time Mark Twain was discovered, Samuel Clemens was essentially evading the issues of the Civil War. In that early and confusing time, the pseudonym may have provided, among other things, a means of evasion and escape, just as, much later, it would constitute a means of confrontation. Certainly the territory, though it might feel the issues of the war, was an excellent realm in which to sidestep the public pressure of the war. The territory, though a legal organization under protection of the Federal Government, did not pay taxes to the Government. Carl Sandburg observes that the reason Nebraska did not join the Union earlier was that the territorial legislature did not wish to pay taxes. Admission cost too much.[6] Beyond all

[5] *Mark Twain of the Enterprise*, pp. 18-19.
[6] Carl Sandburg, *Abraham Lincoln: The War Years* (4 vols.; New York, 1939), III, 3.

this, the territory was an uncommitted region which had the geographical shape of a state without the character and responsibilities of statehood. The territories had been the safety valves which released mounting pressure for Civil War. They were, historically speaking, the means by which the entire nation was able to delay the growing conflict between North and South. As the territories diminished with the admission of new states, the unresolved differences between North and South became more and more acute, and the means of compromise became less and less available.

If Samuel Clemens avoided the slavery issue, he by no means avoided the silver fields. He might have to wait until much later to discover how he actually had felt about slavery and the Civil War, but his speculative sense of adventure, excitement, and a world of possibility came quickly and vigorously to the surface. Not surprisingly, his first distinctive humorous quality emerges out of a commitment to the extravagant and grandiose dream of territorial glory. It is evident in the first letter he wrote to his mother from Nevada. Refusing to invite her until she can be received in "style," he sets out to detail the quality of the area, first by an inclusive list of Nevada's riches—a list which begins with gold and ends with jackass rabbits. After describing the desolation by faintly burlesquing Biblical language, he expands into this fantasy:

> I said we are situated in a flat, sandy desert. True. And surrounded on all sides by such prodigious mountains that when you stand at a distance from Carson and gaze at them awhile,—until, by mentally measuring them, and comparing them with things of smaller size, you begin to conceive of their grandeur, and next to feel their vastness expanding your soul like a balloon, and ultimately find yourself growing, and swelling, and spreading into a colossus,—I say when this point is reached, you look disdainfully down upon the insignificant village of

Carson, reposing like a cheap print away yonder at the foot of the big hills, and in that instant you are seized with a burning desire to stretch forth your hand, put the city in your pocket, and walk off with it.[7]

Although there is nothing particularly original in the substance of the fantasy, there is an impulse to dramatize, to *play*. The fantasy takes its departure not in the form of a vernacular character's actions—as in the case of Davy Crockett—but from the literary mind's activity under the pressure of a particular kind of space. The result is the invention of a Brobdingnagian figure who at once expresses and burlesques the romantic attitude of identification with nature. The comic impulse of the letter exploits the inadequacy of the clichés of travel literature to describe the desolation of a new landscape. But the humor, the emotional quality of the letter, emerges from the point of view. The person writing the letter is not angry or disillusioned by the discrepancy; he discharges both anger and disillusion by exaggerating the discrepancy, thereby converting it into an imaginative playground—a field for invention.

The subsequent letters to his mother during the winter and spring of 1861-62 show beyond a doubt that Samuel Clemens' quest for gold and his discovery of himself were one and the same thing. These letters chronicle his travels over the great vacant stretches of Nevada in search of gold and silver. They are not private letters describing suffering and doubt, but public travel letters—many of them were published in the Keokuk *Gate City* almost as soon as they were received—transforming the futility of the journey into the humor of excessive suffering. In two of them, the writer, referring to himself as the bard, begins by burlesquing poetry. Inventing his reader—in this case his mother—in the role of an innocent Aunt Polly

[7] *The Pattern for Mark Twain's* Roughing It: *Letters from Nevada by Samuel and Orion Clemens 1861-1862*, ed. Franklin R. Rogers (Berkeley and Los Angeles, 1961), p. 24.

relying on literary and travel-book tradition, he good-naturedly undertakes to tease her out of her clichés and ignorance in the process of educating her. In order to dramatize his correspondent, he has to dramatize himself as the prodigal son who will one day entertain his mother in the grand style. His generosity is predicated upon the boundless hope of discovering wealth; the gold is always the illusion which sustains his generous and audacious idea of himself.

His humor arises from his awareness that he is the fool of his illusion, but the awareness is no direct communication of disillusion or despair; instead it is a conversion of the futility of the quest into a comic odyssey in which landscape, inhabitants, and the journey itself become the absurd resistances to the illusion. In such a humorous vision, the mere device of investing an animal with elaborate human psychology becomes a genuinely imaginative event. Clemens' description of the horse Bunker and the dog Curney reveal a rapidly maturing writer. Of Bunker, who had accompanied the prospecting party on the Nevada expedition, he wrote:

> But it was on Bunker's account, principally, that we pushed behind the wagon. For whenever we came to a hard piece of road, that poor, lean, infatuated cuss would fall into a deep reverie about something or other, and stop perfectly still, and it would generally take a vast amount of black-snaking and shoving and profanity to get him started again; and as soon as he was fairly under way, he would take up the thread of his reflections where he left off, and go on thinking, and pondering, and getting himself more and more mixed up and tangled in his subject, until he would get regularly stuck again, and stop to review the question.[8]

By transferring to the horse what would otherwise be, and no doubt were, the narrator's feelings and thoughts

[8] *Ibid.*, p. 30.

of futility, Samuel Clemens was investing the world with an absurd humanity it had hitherto lacked.

His humor arises from the act of exploiting the discrepancy between futile illusion—not merely his own, but those of society and history—and "reality." The humorist's creative role lay in inventing a "reality" which would define the inadequacy of the given traditions, clichés, and illusions. Thus in these early letters to his mother he already shows a mastery of this technique of invention. Asserting that she has asked him to tell her about the "lordly sons of the forest sweeping over the plains on their fiery steeds," he devotes an entire letter *not* to demolishing the illusion of the Indian but to the creation of a grotesque Indian who will seem more "real" than the cliché. Asking her to imagine an Indian called Hoop-de-doodle-doo, he first outlines his ignoble red man's appearance—slouched and slovenly in the cast-off clothes he has been given by whites—and continues:

> Now, Ma, you know what the warrior, Hoop-de-doodle-doo looks like—and if you desire to know what he smells like, let him stand by the stove a moment, but have your harts-horn handy, for I tell you he could give the stink-pots of Sebastopol four in the game and skunk them. Follow him too, when he goes out and burn gun powder in his footsteps; because wherever he walks he sheds vermin of such prodigious size that the smallest specimen could swallow a grain of wheat without straining at it, and still feel hungry. You must not suppose that the warrior drops these vermin from choice, though. By no means, Madam—for he knows something about them which you don't; viz, that they are good to eat. There now. Can you find anything like that in Cooper? Perhaps not. Yet I could go before a magistrate and testify that the portrait is correct in every particular. Old Hoop himself would say it was "heap good."[9]

[9] *Ibid.*, p. 38.

Clemens' Indian is no more real or realistic than Cooper's. The truth of the vision depends not upon its accuracy but upon its commitment to exaggeration and contrast. In that commitment, which so exceeds the reader's expectations, lies the authority of Samuel Clemens' imagination and the distinction of his humor. Cooper is not being attacked so much as he is being belittled by the exaggerative play of the humorous imagination.

In the same way that he used Cooper, Clemens used his whole futile quest for gold. His discovery of himself as a writer depended upon the failure, not the success, of his quest. He had to fail as a prospector and later as a speculator so that he could succeed as a writer, for his very invention of himself as a writer is based not upon finding the proverbial pot of gold but upon discovering *nothing*—nothing but the resources of the comic imagination which can elaborate the futility of the territory into the material of humor. Thus, after utterly failing to find gold or silver in the Nevada Territory, Samuel Clemens became a reporter on the Virginia City *Territorial Enterprise*. From that seemingly unpromising claim in the literary world, he went on to discover Mark Twain and fortune.

The discovery of Mark Twain was not a radical redefinition of personality so much as a gesture, the meaning of which was to continue emerging throughout Samuel Clemens' life. There is no evidence that young Sam Clemens became suddenly a different person upon finding Mark Twain; instead he had discovered a style as well as a structure by means of which he could express as well as expose himself. As Samuel Clemens he continued to be a reporter for the *Enterprise*, devoting himself to covering the territorial scene—its killings, law suits, personalities, and above all, its mines. He was now writing about the very world in which he had so lately invested his speculative energies. He himself saw how closely the writing was related to the speculation itself because by mentioning property he could influence its value; in this way he could and did acquire for himself properties from parties who were benefited. His reporting and his speculation were thus intimately related. As long as he remained a reporter in Nevada and California, he maintained a relationship with the mines. Even after he left Virginia City and went on to San Francisco, he continued to write his brother giving advice about mining properties, offering to handle particular investments, and asking for money to launch speculative enterprises.

But if he did not commit himself fully to the personality of Mark Twain, the emergence of the personality defined certain areas of writing upon which he could concentrate: the humorously imaginative elaborations of Mark Twain. Mark Twain's humorous reporting falls into three categories.[10] First there is the hoax, which reports fantasy in the guise of fact in such a way as to invite the reader's belief. "The Empire City Massacre" and "The Petrified Man" are the best known hoaxes of these early years. The first described in such a direct, reportorial manner the totally imaginary incident of a citizen's having slaughtered his family that the preposterous nature of the event only gradually emerged from the plausible guise in which it appeared.

Then there is the humorous travel letter, the most important form of the three. It had been the convention which Samuel Clemens had adopted as early as 1856 when he wrote *The Adventures of Thomas Jefferson Snodgrass*. The Snodgrass letters are merely conventional, however; any humorist might have written them. They are meaningful only in the sense that they disclose the form through which Clemens instinctively chose to reveal himself: the pseudonymous personality writing a letter

[10] Henry Nash Smith (*Mark Twain of the Enterprise*, p. 7) breaks it into four categories: (1) routine "local" items; (2) occasional unsigned pieces; (3) letters sent to the paper from other places; (4) reports of the Territorial Legislature and the Constitutional Convention of 1863 in Carson.

"home." But the Snodgrass letters confined Clemens to the ignorant and illiterate utterance of Snodgrass, whereas the literate Mark Twain allowed him a full range of style and expression. As in the letters he wrote to his mother, he could invent accompanying characters to represent various styles, he could burlesque the clichés and traditions of polite travelers, and he could interpolate fantasies and narratives which expanded the personality of the narrator at the same time they enriched his themes and substance.

Next there are the specific political burlesques in which Mark Twain parodied legislative proceedings of the territorial legislature. He was, in fact, a prominent member of a burlesque Third House of the legislature, reported its proceedings in dispatches to the *Enterprise*, was eventually "elected" Governor and duly delivered his annual message. This election to Governor, in addition to showing Mark Twain's stature among his contemporaries, forecasts the burlesque and satiric relation to government he was to have throughout his career. "Governor" Mark Twain of Nevada is a prefiguration of the author of *The Gilded Age*, *A Connecticut Yankee*, and "To the Person Sitting in Darkness."

But beyond the hoax, the travel letter, and the political burlesque there is a mode of discourse which, if not a form, constitutes a style not to be overlooked. I refer to personal invective. As a form of public discourse, personal invective flourishes only under certain conditions. First of all, there must be the tension requiring such relief; there must be the individual willing to "publish" himself; and there must be a relatively closed society which will appreciate the barb and recognize the victim; finally there must be a standard of honor in the society before which the assailant heaps scorn and behind which the victim must cower in shame. If the practical joke is the social analogue of the hoax, the duel is the analogue of personal invective, for invective is actually a duel of words. These were the representative forms of discourse through which Mark Twain found himself in Nevada. All of them—particularly the hoax, political burlesque, and personal invective—were relatively direct ways of discharging aggression. Their very style carried with them the risk that they would be taken seriously and precipitate the kind of violence they were presumably displacing. If they were the means by which a man could win a name for himself, they could also spell trouble for the person who became too effective with them, which is precisely what happened to Mark Twain after a fierce verbal exchange with one James Laird, a writer for a rival paper.

The affair began with an unsigned editorial by Mark Twain charging that proceeds from a fancy dress ball given by the ladies of Carson City were to be "sent to aid a Miscegenation Society somewhere in the East." Laird of the Virginia City *Union* so viciously attacked the editorial that Mark Twain dropped the mask of anonymity, apologized to the ladies on the one hand and published a reply to Laird on the other, challenging him to a duel if he did not retract his insults. The two continued to exchange public insults preparatory to their duel, until Mark Twain abruptly left the territory without fighting the duel. To be sure, there is in Mark Twain's *Autobiography* an account of the duel's having taken place, but the account is simply one of Mark Twain's reconstructions of experience written in that late time when, as he himself said, he could remember only what *didn't* happen.

That it didn't happen probably indicates how much the invective was itself a kind of substitute for the duel. Duels were, after all, illegal in the territory, and journalistic invective was no doubt one legal way of retaining the satisfaction of a forbidden ritual. Looked at in another way, however, the bombastic exchange of published threats and challenges promising a duel which never took place is a burlesque of the duel itself. Thus the "publication" provided amusement for *Enterprise* readers who understood that no duel was going to take place and that the solemn accusations, the vicious insults, and the affirmations of honor would lead to nothing. The reality of the running battle with Laird no doubt lies somewhere between genuine antagonism and burlesque, for Mark Twain did depart from the territory, which means that the writing, no matter how "humorous," had either failed to resolve the crisis or was being used as a pretext for leaving.[11]

In the larger context of Mark Twain's career this departure from the territory is doubly significant. It points backward to his resignation from the Confederate Army— a resignation which if not ignominious was yet not wholly honorable. Moreover, the editorial which precipitated the affair was the somewhat "confederate" accusation that the sanitary fund was going to a miscegenation society, revealing that Mark Twain's humor still showed a native if not a partisan Southern cast. Finally, his departure from Nevada reflects the same evasive action which characterized the resignation from the Confederacy. But there is an important difference. The Civil War had been someone else's war and Samuel Clemens had been caught in circumstances largely beyond his control, whereas in Nevada he had done much to create the situation he adroitly side-stepped. If he had failed to establish dominion over circumstance, he had managed to create in writing the dilemma which he evaded.

But the departure from the territory points forward. Again Samuel Clemens had, by ordinary standards, failed in courage and honor. First there had been the war; now there was the duel. The duel was the ritual evolved by a society in order to institutionalize revenge and to codify the behavior of gentlemen in violence. It was the ritual Henry James's Christopher Newman first patronized, only to find himself about to take a meaner revenge than the field of honor allowed. Mark Twain was not

---

[11] For an extensive account of Mark Twain's altercation with Laird, see Fatout, *Mark Twain in Virginia City*, pp. 196-213.

Christopher Newman; and having considerably more indignation to control and channel than his fictional contemporary, he would need a great deal of literary time and space to deal with it.

When Samuel Clemens left Nevada for California, he had not discovered silver; but in the signature of Mark Twain he had discovered his genius, that rich vein he would ceaselessly exploit to gain the fortune he never found. He did not immediately strike it rich, did not fully work his claim. Though he wrote items which showed genuine promise under his new signature, none surpassed the letters written to his mother before his discovery. But the name remained. To comprehend its significance requires seeing it in relation to two realities—the reality of the convention of the pseudonym and the reality of Mark Twain's career.

As for the pseudonym in general, it falls into at least three categories. First there is the pseudonym which totally conceals the author's identity. Henry Adams' use of Francis Snow Compton is a good example of such concealment, for not even Adams' most intimate friends knew of his authorship of *Esther*. Then there is the pseudonym which does not conceal so much as it displaces the original identity. Poquelin's Molière, Arouet's Voltaire, and Mary Ann Evans' George Eliot each in its separate way effects such a displacement. Finally there is the pseudonym which either denotatively or absurdly exposes itself as pseudonym. Irving's Geoffrey Crayon, Dickens' Boz, and Samuel Clemens' Mark Twain exemplify such exposure. The absurdity of the comic pseudonym as it was employed in the nineteenth century, particularly by the American humorists with whom Mark Twain was familiar, designated a "character," a personality marked by special eccentricities and predilections. This character was not so much a creature of action as of language and attitude. Thus, Petroleum V. Nasby, Josh Billings, and Artemus Ward depended for their individuality on an orthography which, by phonetically mimicking the sounds of unlettered speech, gave oral and provincial identity to the character. The illiteracy could be, and usually was, employed to double effect—to reveal the gullibility and naïveté of the character in the face of urbanity, and to release a certain amount of horse sense through the innocence of the pose. Despite the freshness of their mock innocence and the frequent penetration of their shrewd "philosophy," the characters were severely limited. Unless sufficient stylistic latitude was allowed them, they could not develop but had to move from subject to subject until their act was thoroughly routinized. If too much latitude was allowed, the salient aspects of the character were threatened. The careers of Petroleum V. Nasby (David Ross Locke), Josh Billings (Henry Wheeler Shaw), John Phoenix (George Horatio Derby), Orpheus C. Kerr (Robert Henry Newell), Bill Arp (Charles Henry Smith), and even Artemus Ward (Charles Farrar Browne), all display the rigid restriction of comic journalism.

In choosing the pseudonym Mark Twain, Samuel Clemens was following the convention of the comic journalists, but instead of casting himself as a character, parodying a particular form or personality, or indulging in hoaxes, Mark Twain was left free to perform all these assignments. He remained the true reporter whose direct force and clarity were gravely deployed to fetch in the freaks and absurdities from the world of humor. Though it is tempting to see in this early variety of stances the naïve beginner's uncertainty about his art, Mark Twain's freedom is a result of knowledge—not ignorance—of pseudonymic identity, for Samuel Clemens was no rank beginner but a seasoned veteran in the use of the pseudonym, having used at least four and possibly five before he hit upon Mark Twain. As W. Epaminondas Adrastus Blab, he had played the pompous and pretentious politician; as Sergeant Fathom, the mocking parodist; as Thomas Jefferson Snodgrass, the illiterate bumpkin; as Quintus Curtius Snodgrass, the overrefined observer of vulgar pretenders; and as Josh, the anecdotist. In those earlier incarnations, Samuel Clemens had indeed been merely conventional. Under the signature of Mark Twain, however, he was never to be merely conventional. If he failed to make an astonishing achievement immediately upon assuming his sobriquet, he succeeded in avoiding the fixed identity of his contemporaries. This does not mean that Mark Twain had a Jamesian consciousness about the career which lay before him; it simply emphasizes that the innocence of his poses and the uncertainty of his maneuvers rested not upon ignorance and naïveté but upon extensive apprenticeship and experience.

Yet if Mark Twain remained free from the limiting restrictions of his predecessors—Blab, Snodgrass, Fathom, and Josh—he was by no means free in the way that Henry James or William Dean Howells was free. Though the name Mark Twain implied greater freedom than such pseudonyms as Orpheus C. Kerr and Petroleum V. Nasby, it was nonetheless a humorous pseudonym. To adopt and keep the name was to be committed to the fate of a humorist, a fate which Samuel Clemens lived through to the end. Though he came more and more to resent the fate, he never really cast off the identity. Dickens abandoned Boz because Boz would have prevented Dickens from making the transformation into a novelist. He could never, for example, have written *David Copperfield* under the name of Boz. For Samuel Clemens, Mark Twain became the means of realizing himself. The pseudonym neither concealed, obliterated, nor narrowed his identity, but exposed and freed it. Choosing it did not involve a modification of the self or a revolt against the father. Had this been the deep intention of the choice, Samuel Clemens might have become Samuel Clement, as Hathorne became Hawthorne, Walter Whitman Walt Whitman, Falkner Faulkner. Nor did the pseudonym, world famous though it was to become, obliterate the reality of Samuel Clemens. The general reader who does not recognize Jean Baptiste Poquelin, François Marie

Arouet, or Mary Ann Evans, will certainly know who Samuel Langhorne Clemens was.

For Mark Twain was neither a character who seized reality from Samuel Clemens, nor a persona which masked his identity; rather he was an extension, an addition, by means of which Samuel Clemens was able to enlarge and fulfill himself. True, there would be times when Mark Twain and Samuel Clemens seemed almost in conflict, when the world would be dramatized in terms of Siamese twins not so much antagonistic to each other as going in opposite directions.[12] But even Samuel Clemens' most restive relations with his pen name did not bring him to abandon it or to assert himself above it. The two times he went so far as to conceal Mark Twain as author, he produced in *Joan of Arc* and *What Is Man?* his most lifeless extended performances. The reason was not at all that Mark Twain had repressed Samuel Clemens, but that in denying Mark Twain, Samuel Clemens was blocking the creative channels through which his imagination achieved its distinct expression. Far from losing his identity in his new name, Samuel Clemens had found it. Thus, the life of Mark Twain which was to be written was the imaginative life of Samuel Clemens.

The essence of that imagination is its humorous nature, the chief "humor" of which is that it represents an exaggeration of the actual life of Samuel Clemens. That is why the adventures of Mark Twain cannot be reliably taken as the adventures of Samuel Clemens. It is, after

[12] One of Mark Twain's most recurrent strategies plays upon twins and pairs. There are the Siamese Twins Chang and Eng, Tom and Huck, Huck and Jim, the Prince and the Pauper, the King and the Duke, Those extraordinary Twins Angelo and Luigi Capello, and those other extraordinary twins Thomas à Becket Driscoll and Valet de Chambre. The repeated emergence of twins, the plots developed around and by means of balanced dualities, and the thematic emphasis placed upon dual personality and mistaken identity, in addition to being aspects of universal comic convention, go back to the primal creative act of inventing Mark Twain. Though the very pen name implies the presence of a division, it neither denotes nor requires one and can equally well be seen as a means of containing the very division it marks.

all, Mark Twain's nature to refract, exaggerate, misremember, or forget the experiences of Samuel Clemens. These distortions are not, however, fictions in the literary meaning of that term; they pivot always upon the world of actuality and are in a certain respect dependent upon it. They may show the deceptions of that world, may call it into question, but they never transcend it. That is why, if Mark Twain's world is a reconstruction of Samuel Clemens' experience, the reader is constantly in the process of reconstructing Samuel Clemens out of Mark Twain. The "humor" of Mark Twain, in the sense of a characterizing trait, is just this inevitable tendency to enlarge upon the facts—not to depreciate them so much as to be free with them. The enlargements are the "stretchers" of Mark Twain—those remarkable fictions whose whole intention is to evoke the reader's suspicion of their veracity. What becomes certain for the reader, even as the dubious character of narrator and narrative becomes evident, is that both narrator and narrative are humorous. That is the inescapable *fact* for us, and surely it was the inescapable fact for Samuel Clemens. In Mark Twain he had at once named and defined his identity—named it with a term out of his past, and defined it as irrevocably humorous. That fate, inherent in the pseudonym, could never be evaded as long as the name should stand. It was the certainty which was to sustain all Mark Twain's bitter doubts, dreams, frustrations, vacillations, indignation, and anger. Indeed, all the pathos, hostility, and tragedy which Samuel Clemens could possibly feel were to be converted under the sign of his genius into the form of humor.

The most graphic illustration of this humorous process is to be found in our relation to the name Mark Twain. Samuel Clemens' discovery of the pseudonym, his later remarks about it, and his use of it have all given rise to a host of doubts about where it came from, when it was used, what it means, and how to use it ourselves. We do not really know when Mark Twain first appeared. Samuel

Clemens later said that it had been the *nom de plume* of one "Isaiah Sellers, who used to write river news over for the New Orleans *Picayune*," but patient research has disclosed that this, in all probability, is false. Nor is there unanimous agreement about the origin of the name. Though it clearly is a leadsman's cry meaning two fathoms, Paul Fatout has recently accumulated telling evidence that the name was first applied to Samuel Clemens by saloon keepers as a means of keeping tally of the inevitable two drinks he took on credit.[13] If we are not sure about the origin of the name and its meaning, we are equally in doubt about what name to use in writing about the man. Howells called him Clemens, because the pseudonym, he said, seemed to mask his friend, but then Howells *was* a personal friend. He was also exceedingly genteel, and though some scholars and biographers have followed Howells in using the original name, it seems excessively formal. At the other extreme are those who write familiarly of "Mark," but this seems excessively familiar. As for "Twain," many rightly reject it on the ground that it is not a patronym but half of a particular term which cannot logically be divided. The uncertainty fully manifests itself in indexes, where three possibilities —"Clemens," "Mark Twain," and "Twain, Mark"—must be checked if one is to be *sure* of Mark Twain's absence.

Even old certainties dissolve in the process of humorous doubt. Thus, every schoolboy knows that "Mark Twain" is a leadsman's cry meaning two fathoms. He knows it because Mark Twain himself made the term famous. And because Mark Twain much later said so, every schoolboy has been led to believe that the term was the welcome cry meaning "safe water"—which it does, of course, if the steamboat is coming out of shallows. If, however, it is heading into them, "Mark Twain" is hardly a comforting call. The term literally means *barely* safe water—a message which might bring either relief or fear to the pilot, depending on the circumstances. Of course,

---

[13] Fatout, *Mark Twain in Virginia City*, pp. 34-39.

Mark Twain much later in his career—in *Life on the Mississippi*—was to construct an elaborate tall tale about how he acquired the sobriquet; but that was a development an accretion, which constitutes simply one of the multiple meanings the name would come to have. Like the Scarlet Letter, Samuel Clemens' pseudonym was to be incarnated into the most complex of personalities. And though it would always, mean "barely safe water," it would come to mean much more.

Samuel Clemens had discovered Mark Twain in Nevada; Mark Twain in turn discovered Simon Wheeler and the Notorious Jumping Frog in California. During the more than two years—May, 1864 to December, 1866—he spent in California, he discovered little else. Certainly the effort to prove that he discovered much more is hard to sustain amid the pedestrian newspaper items which mark his production. After "The Jumping Frog," he made a few interesting attempts at sketches in Bret Harte's *Californian*, particularly in "The Story of the Bad Little Boy Who Did Not Come to Grief." But his entire production in California aside from "The Jumping Frog" is characterized by an impulse toward reflexive burlesque. Properly speaking, his publications are *acts* by a comedian intent on fulfilling expectations he imagines his audience to have. There are burlesques of George Washington's life and Benjamin Franklin's proverbs, there are parodies of spiritualistic mediums, and there is a vaguely amusing account of a trial in which slang confutes the court.

All of these efforts, though they deal with subjects of permanent and recurrent interest to students of Mark Twain, fail to go beyond the mechanism of burlesque. They impersonate a cliché and parody it—no more. But there is "The Jumping Frog." The one piece which Mark Twain fully executed, it was precisely the kind of success which invited him to repeat it in a series of failures. At the same time, this story was the kind of success which forced him to go beyond it toward his unrealized future, and the circumstances out of which it grew are as important as those surrounding the birth of his pseudonym.

First of all, there are the actual facts of his discovery. He had not been long in San Francisco before he began to repeat the pattern of behavior which had led to his departure from Virginia City. This time, however, his indignation paralleled the terms of a feud rather than a duel, and his victim was the chief of police rather than a rival editor. Attacking the police department for its inhumanity and stupidity, he is supposed to have roused its ire to the point that it was out to get him and his friend Steve Gillis—who had accompanied him to California from Washoe. But here again the feud with the police department begins to assume such legendary proportions that it is difficult to distinguish actual event from tall tale. Even so, in December, 1864, Mark Twain left San Francisco—presumably a fugitive from the law— in much the same manner that he had departed from Missouri and Nevada.[14]

His flight led him to the cabin of Jim Gillis on Jackass Hill in Tuolomne County, California. There, in what seemed such unpromising literary surroundings, he first heard the story of the frog he was to celebrate. After returning to San Francisco in February, 1865, he told the story to Artemus Ward who in turn encouraged him to write it and send it East to be included in a book of Western sketches Ward was compiling. Mark Twain did write it, but it arrived in New York too late for inclusion in Ward's book, and ultimately found its way to publication in the final issue of the New York *Saturday Press* on November 18, 1865.[15] Although its publication made the

[14] See Albert Bigelow Paine, *Mark Twain: A Biography* (3 vols.; New York, 1912), I, 253-69, for an account of Mark Twain's San Francisco experience. For a specialized and elaborate discussion of the San Francisco literary scene, see Franklin Walker, *San Francisco's Literary Frontier* (New York, 1939).

[15] Paine, *A Biography*, I, 270-73. See also Margaret Duckett, *Mark Twain and Bret Harte* (Norman, 1964), pp. 24-26.

jumping frog more famous than its celebrator, Samue
Clemens had touched a remote audience and broken free
of the region in which he had found his identity.

These are the facts which, coupled with the action o
the story, constitute an enactment of Mark Twain'
experience in the West. For Mark Twain in the role o
fugitive had literally discovered the story in abandonec
mining country. It is the experience remaining amid the
decay after all the gold has been removed and only the
memory of speculation is left behind. And it is the
memory of speculation which Mark Twain incarnated i
the inimitable voice of Simon Wheeler. Wheeler was
after all, Mark Twain's chief means of transforming the
story into art, for in its original form the Jumping Frog
story was no more than a crude account of a practica
joke in which one gambler takes the measure of another

Mark Twain did not change the original joke so mucl
as he enfolded it in the consciousness—which is to sa
the *style*—of Simon Wheeler.[16] Thus, as everyone knows
the greatness of "The Jumping Frog" is in its telling
in the creation of a powerful illusion that the story i
being told instead of written. In the classic Henry Jame
or Hawthorne story the illusion that the story is being
told by a narrator drops away because the narrator'
consciousness is so urbanely literary. The same is tru
in Washington Irving's sketches. But in "The Jumping
Frog," the fact that the story is written—in the earlies
version the story was an epistle addressed to Artemu
Ward—is lost amid the sound of Wheeler's voice. Th
illusion of the story's being told is produced by Mar
Twain's use of two narrators: one, "Mark Twain," wh
uses literary or written language in the frame aroun
the story; the other, Wheeler, who counters with th
nonliterary or spoken language, the dialect.

[16] The fullest account of the various forms of the original jok
and Mark Twain's elaboration of them is in Oscar Lewis, *Th
Origin of the Celebrated Jumping Frog of Calaveras County* (Sa
Francisco, 1931).

Such a structure, instead of recalling the urbane sketch which Irving perfected, rises out of the traditions developed by Southwestern humorists. By means of fully styled literary frames, such artists—and they were artists— as A. B. Longstreet, Thomas Bangs Thorpe, Johnson J. Hooper, and George W. Harris were able to condescend to the dialect they skillfully mimicked. The truth of their form lay in their adherence to the very class distinctions their form mirrored. Thus they were to a man, as Kenneth Lynn has wisely observed, Whigs in politics who felt no egalitarian guilt in treating dialect characters as the bumpkins, gulls, rogues, and low comedy characters the superior literary language defined them to be.[17] To be sure, there is a cruelty in the humor of Longstreet, Hooper, and Harris, but there is not the sentimentality which characterizes the work of such literary exploiters of dialect as Cooper and Harriet Beecher Stowe. For although both Cooper and Mrs. Stowe tried to use dialect, in the very act of asserting the "nobility" of dialect characters, they invariably relied upon literary language for analysis and "elevated" description. Thus their dialect could convey only picturesque utterance and quaint or crackerbarrel rural identities, at best giving conventional wisdom a fresh turn. Southwestern humorists, on the other hand, being freed of a sentiment which contradicted their form, were able to discover much more vitality in their humorous creations. At their best, as in Harris' Sut Lovingood, the dialect becomes so extreme that it threatens to be a language in itself; or in Thorpe's "The Big Bear of Arkansas," the frontier hunter's story of the legendary bear becomes the vehicle for disclosures at once broadly—even crudely—humorous and strikingly imaginative.

The form of "The Jumping Frog," like that of "The Big Bear of Arkansas," sets the oral story inside a literary frame. But unlike Thorpe, Mark Twain never interrupts

[17] Kenneth S. Lynn, *Mark Twain and Southwestern Humor* (Boston, 1959), Chapters 3 and 4.

Wheeler's story once it begins, until the very end of the sketch. And whereas the nub of Thorpe's story covertly revolves around the old masculine joke of being caught with one's breeches down—the hunter is surprised by the looming bear at the inopportune moment of his morning defecation—Mark Twain's humor is open and utterly innocent in this respect.

It is, in fact, Wheeler's total innocence which sets him apart from Thorpe's bragging and freewheeling frontiersman. Thus Mark Twain, the literary narrator, consciously and overtly describes Wheeler's manner and method of narration:

> He never smiled, he never frowned, he never changed his voice from the gentle-flowing key to which he tuned his initial sentence, he never betrayed the slightest suspicion of enthusiasm; but all through the interminable narrative there ran a vein of impressive earnestness and sincerity, which showed me plainly that, so far from his imagining that there was anything ridiculous or funny about his story, he regarded it as a really important matter, and admired its two heroes as men of transcendent genius in *finesse*. I let him go on in his own way, and never interrupted him once.[18]

While Mark Twain painfully condescends to suffer the boredom of listening to Wheeler's interminable narrative, Wheeler is apparently so absorbed in his own story that he is utterly unaware of his listener's attitude. He is, after all, the deadpan narrator; and if he suspects the condescension, he betrays no hint of his suspicion, being

---

[18] Samuel L. Clemens, *The Writings of Mark Twain*, Author's National Edition (25 vols.; New York, 1907-18), XIX, 17. Hereafter referred to as *Writings*. I have used this edition rather than the so-called Definitive Edition (37 vols.; New York, 1923-25) because of its much greater availability and also because the Definitive Edition is not really definitive at all in matters of text—no more definitive, in fact, than the Author's National Edition. A new edition of Mark Twain's works, which presumably will be definitive, is currently being undertaken.

content to blockade Mark Twain and force him to undergo the role of listener.

This structure, revealing two contrasting styles, imitates the action of Wheeler's story. Smiley, who had consciously trained his animals, fostering their genius and lying in wait for gullible souls willing to bet on the merely natural animals to beat them, is "taken in" by a deadpan stranger. Innocently refusing to see the virtue of Smiley's frog, the mysterious stranger dupes him into fetching a mere ordinary, unpedigreed, and unnamed frog with which he defeats the celebrated Dan'l Webster. The stranger is not innocent, of course, but the first of a long line of mock-innocents to people Mark Twain's world, and his victory over Smiley comes by virtue of his having weighted Dan'l Webster with so much birdshot that the frog's incomparable style is reduced to no more than an impotent strain against its recently acquired sense of gravity. The stranger's secret act of "fixing" the jumping contest corresponds to the artist's "secret" structure which becomes apparent to the reader only after he has been taken in.

In much the same way that the stranger's deadpan takes in Smiley, Wheeler's style is "taking in" the literary language which introduces it. The literary "Mark Twain" quite appropriately suspects that he has been taken in as he recounts the story, but he obtusely attributes the trick to his friend from the remote East, not to the beguiling Wheeler. Yet it would be a distortion to attribute a sly trickery to Wheeler. He is no mere Western confidence man taking his revenge on the superior Easterner.[19] Such

[19] Paul Schmidt, in "The Deadpan on Simon Wheeler," *Southwestern Review*, XLI (Summer, 1956), 270-77, sees Wheeler as a Western confidence man outwitting the supercilious Easterner. Paul Baender, in "The Jumping Frog as a Comedian's First Virtue," *Modern Philology*, LX (February, 1963), 192-200, has demonstrated that Mark Twain's technique transcended such a regional posture. Edgar Branch's analysis of the story, in *The Literary Apprenticeship of Mark Twain* (Urbana, 1950), pp. 120-29, remains the most balanced extended discussion. Branch rightly recognizes that nothing Mark Twain had done either equaled or forecast

an interpretation reduces the story to the familiar East-versus-West regionalism, which is precisely the dimension "The Jumping Frog" at once exploited and transcended. The comic force of the story lies in the unwitting collaboration between the two narrators, and the impossibility of being sure of Wheeler's deadpan. The literary narrator is bored and abruptly interrupts the inveterate Wheeler who is about to launch into another anecdotal episode concerning the unforgettable Smiley. Wheeler presumably neither recognizes nor resents the condescension. He betrays no suspicion, and the reader who would have him guileful must read in his own distrust, for Wheeler apparently moves forward in serene oblivion. His obliviousness, his total self-absorption, both defines his character and constitutes his humor. Brooding over the decaying mining camp almost like a tutelary deity, Wheeler's memory, moving irresistibly backward in an associative recovery of the past, converts all the speculation, deception, and disillusion in the very scene of the mining camp into the rich recollection of Jim Smiley and his frog.

The full force of that conversion lies in the astonishing fullness of Wheeler's memory, which yields a return far exceeding the mere necessity of the tale he recalls. Wheeler's invariable digressions constitute the excess of pleasure his remarkable narrative produces. Take for example the description of Smiley's dog, a gratuitous miracle that the apparently absent-minded Wheeler can't help remembering:

> And he had a little small bull-pup, that to look at
> him you'd think he warn't worth a cent but to set
> around and look ornery and lay for a chance to

"The Jumping Frog," but he perceptively demonstrates that it was most similar to Samuel Clemens' first published work, "The Dandy Frightening the Squatter," which had appeared in 1853. "The Jumping Frog," according to Branch, constitutes a coming full circle for Samuel Clemens, a consummation in art of his initial effort toward literary form.

steal something. But as soon as money was up on him he was a different dog; his under-jaw'd begin to stick out like the fo'castle of a steamboat, and his teeth would uncover and shine like the furnaces. And a dog might tackle him and bully-rag him, and bite him, and throw him over his shoulder two or three times, and Andrew Jackson—which was the name of the pup—Andrew Jackson would never let on but what *he* was satisfied, and hadn't expected nothing else—and the bets being doubled and doubled on the other side all the time, till the money was all up; and then all of a sudden he would grab that other dog jest by the j'int of his hind leg and freeze to it—not chaw, you understand, but only just grip and hang on till they throwed up the sponge, if it was a year. Smiley always come out winner on that pup, till he harnessed a dog once that didn't have no hind legs, because they'd been sawed off in a circular saw, and when the thing had gone along far enough, and the money was all up, and he come to make a snatch for his pet holt, he see in a minute how he'd been imposed on, and how the other dog had him in the door, so to speak, and he 'peared surprised, and then he looked sorter discouraged-like, and didn't try no more to win the fight, and so he got shucked out bad. He give Smiley a look, as much as to say his heart was broke, and it was *his* fault, for putting up a dog that hadn't no hind legs for him to take holt of, which was his main dependence in a fight, and then he limped off a piece and laid down and died. It was a good pup, was that Andrew Jackson, and would have made a name for hisself if he'd lived, for the stuff was in him and he had genius—I know it, because he hadn't no opportunities to speak of, and it don't stand to reason that a dog could make such a fight as he could under them circumstances if he hadn't no talent. It always makes me feel sorry when I think of that last fight of his'n, and the way it turned out.[20]

[20] *Writings*, XIX, 19-20.

Here the speaker's similes and metaphors—his comparison of the dog with a steamboat, and his description of the dog "freezing" to his victim—not only reveal an easy appropriation of diverse experiences; the sustained commitment with which he "humanizes" the dog reveals the capacity and intensity of his investment in the experience he narrates. This investment executes the superb humorous reversal, making Andrew Jackson and not the two-legged dog the object of sympathy, and in the very process converting the clichés of sympathy into a transcendent humorous synthesis.

The character of Wheeler provided both the style and structure for Mark Twain's first masterpiece. Wheeler was as essential to the humor of the sketch as "Mark Twain" was to Samuel Clemens. His grave and pained earnestness, the equivalent in narrative to Mark Twain's deadpan on the lecture platform, was the very embodiment of the humorist's version of the original seriousness from which the tale originated. His voice in the story seems interminable because Mark Twain's interruption of that voice, which constitutes the end of the story, creates the illusion that the voice goes on forever. Mark Twain himself evidently thought that it continued, for he attempted at later times to call on Wheeler again, but never successfully. The reason was that Simon Wheeler had said all he could say—all he *had* to say. The virtue of the ending lay in preserving the illusion that Wheeler was long-winded and endlessly digressive when in reality the tale he tells is a masterpiece of compression and economy.

Given such a discovery, Samuel Clemens could well feel that his humorous career had fatally begun. To his brother Orion he wrote on October 19, 1865—almost immediately after he had completed "The Jumping Frog" but before it was published—what is one of his most important letters. Beginning with that heightened gravity faintly suggesting parody, he declared that Orion had the genius for preaching. As for himself, he had had two powerful ambitions—to be a pilot and to be a preacher.

One he had realized, but the other had eluded him because of his deficiency of religion. Orion, he confidently declared, should leave the pursuit of law and yield to the prompting of his true genius. He himself had accepted his own call:

> I *have* had a "call" to literature, of a low order—*i.e.* humorous. It is nothing to be proud of, but it is my strongest suit, & if I were to listen to that maxim of stern *duty* which says that to do right you *must* multiply the one or the two or the three talents which the Almighty entrusts to your keeping, I would long ago have ceased to meddle with things for which I was by nature unfitted & turned my attention to seriously scribbling to excite the *laughter* of God's creatures. Poor, pitiful business! Though the Almighty did His part by me—for the talent is a mighty engine when supplied with the steam of *education*—which I have not got, & so its pistons & cylinders & shafts move feebly & for a holiday show & are useless for any good purpose.[21]

To excite the laughter of God's creatures! That is the unmistakable intention shining through the assumed stateliness, the ponderous gravity, the elaborate mechanical analogy, and the pervasive self-depreciation. It does not merely shine through but assimilates these solemnities in such a way that they become part of the intention itself. This conversion, mirroring Samuel Clemens' conversion from would-be preacher to low humorist, was both the act and fate to which he would give his life.

[21] *My Dear Bro, A Letter from Samuel Clemens to His Brother Orion*, ed. with a foreword by Frederick Anderson (Berkeley, 1961), pp. 6-7.

CHAPTER

II

PROFESSIONAL

TRAVELER

THE fame which Mark Twain received upon publication
of "The Jumping Frog" brought with it the opportunity
to move beyond the range of California and Nevada.
Asked by the Sacramento *Union* to accompany the
steamer *Ajax* to the Sandwich Islands on its maiden
voyage, he at first refused; but then changing his mind,
he persuaded the publishers to commission him special
correspondent reporting on trade, agriculture, and general interest. With his acceptance of this position, he
began to fulfill himself in the role of professional traveler.
In a sense he had always been a traveler and would always be one. His first interesting letters home were
travel letters to his mother during his first trip East in
1853-54, and his first attempts at professional humor
were conventional "travel" letters of the bumpkin Thomas Jefferson Snodgrass reporting his urban adventures.
In Nevada his mature style began appearing in his letters
to his mother—letters which were obviously intended for
publication as reports from the prodigal son in the West.
And one of Mark Twain's chief occupations as reporter
for the *Enterprise* was to write letters to the editors
chronicling his travels.

But for all the travel writing he had done, not until he
became special correspondent for the Sacramento *Union*

did he officially launch his career as a professional traveler. It was not his whole career, this touring in the role of literary journeyman, but it was to become a major part, and thus much of his work goes under the heading of the commercial travel book. *A Tramp Abroad*, *Life on the Mississippi*, "Some Rambling Notes of an Idle Excursion," and *Following the Equator* are all travel books in the strictest sense of the term—accounts of real journeys taken largely for the purpose of producing precisely such accounts. In the early trips—to the Sandwich Islands and to the Holy Land—Mark Twain was the special correspondent of a paper, writing periodic dispatches, assimilating and integrating them into book form. As a final means of exploiting the business of traveling, he transformed his written accounts into public lectures. After he became thoroughly established as a writer, he dropped the drudgery of contributing to papers, thereby gaining opportunity to enjoy himself more regally during the journeys, and waiting until things were over before settling down to the laborious task of transforming his extensive notes into a book that would entertain his public.

The Innocents Abroad was the book in which Mark Twain defined himself as humorous traveler. Though his later travel books reflected some changes in attitude, they added practically nothing to the shape of the personality which emerged so powerfully in *The Innocents Abroad*. The subsequent travel books suffer when compared to *The Innocents* because, although they have the characteristic perspective, they lack the sense of confidence and conquest. The burlesque personality, instead of being emergent, is busy meeting expectations already defined; and therefore, this first travel book stands in the same relation to Mark Twain's experience as traveler that "The Jumping Frog" occupies in relation to his life as a miner. It is a great summarizing performance, realizing in a single creative act all the implications and tendencies which had been in a process of tentative expression for twenty years.

The genesis of *The Innocents Abroad* needs little rehearsal. Having returned to California from a four-month sojourn in the Sandwich Islands and completed a successful lecture tour in California and Nevada, Mark Twain took a position as special traveling correspondent for the San Francisco daily *Alta California*. Setting sail from San Francisco on December 15, 1866, he came to New York via the Isthmus, writing letters on the way and dispatching them at various ports of call. The trip afforded its own interest in both its phases; first, in the person of Captain Ned Wakeman who commanded the ship from San Francisco to the Isthmus and was, as the prototype for Captain Stormfield, to be a ruling figure in Mark Twain's imagination; and second, in the form of a cholera epidemic which broke out aboard ship between Panama and Key West, causing near panic among the passengers. Arriving in New York about the middle of January, Mark Twain dispatched letters to the *Alta* describing for San Franciscans the life and society of Gotham. In the spring of 1867 he returned to the Middle West and the Mississippi for a brief visit, duly recording his impressions of the postwar world which confronted him.[1]

Even before returning to the Mississippi, Mark Twain had heard of the impending pleasure excursion aboard the *Quaker City* and had persuaded the *Alta* editors to pay his fare and to retain him as their traveling correspondent. He sailed on June 8, 1867, and during the *Quaker City*'s 5-month cruise, he wrote 58 travel letters for the *Alta*.[2] These letters form the basis or, better still, the substance of *The Innocents Abroad*. Shortly after his return,

[1] The early *Alta* letters have been collected and edited by Franklin Walker and G. Ezra Dane in *Mark Twain's Travels with Mr. Brown* (New York, 1940).

[2] Daniel M. McKeithan (ed.), *Traveling with the Innocents Abroad* (Norman, 1958), p. ix. This book contains all 58 of the travel letters.

he was asked by Elisha Bliss, manager of the American Publishing Company in Hartford, about the possibility of publishing a book based upon the *Alta* letters. *The Innocents Abroad* was Mark Twain's ultimate response to Bliss's query. But the book was by no means an edition or mere incorporation of the letters; rather, it was a revision and integration of these letters into a larger, more ambitious design.[3]

The Innocents Abroad was Mark Twain's first great public entertainment. Before he wrote it, he had a reputation as a Western humorist, the "Wild Humorist of the Pacific Slope"; with its appearance—though he retained his identity as a Westerner—he clearly established himself as a national writer. Thus, whatever difficulties might arise in describing the book, it would never be considered a book by a Westerner or even a Western American; rather, it is a book by an American who, among other things, had been in the West. One of the chief distinctions

[3] Mark Twain did most of the writing of the book in San Francisco. He had completed about one-fourth of the book in Washington, but, learning that editors of the *Alta* were planning to publish his travel letters in book form, he hurried by ship to California in an effort to forestall publication. Though he persuaded the *Alta* editors to abandon their plans, he remained in California for three months. When he returned in July, 1868, he had all but completed his manuscript, and was able to turn it over to Bliss in August. Mark Twain thus wrote his first book in the city from which he had launched himself two years earlier. In that span of time he had gone to the Sandwich Islands, traveled extensively there before returning to San Francisco in August, 1866; had taken to the lecture platform, touring his way to Virginia City, Carson City, and back to San Francisco; had sailed to New York via the Isthmus after a harrowing voyage on a cholera-swept ship; had taken a two-month trip from New York to Saint Louis, Hannibal, and Keokuk; and had finally made the *Quaker City* Pilgrimage to Europe and the Holy Land. This "official" travel coupled with the vast unofficial travel of his youth—travel in the East, on the great Mississippi, on the overland stage, and in Nevada—constituted the experience which sustained the mask of innocence in *The Innocents Abroad*. For a reliable account of his life during the period of writing *The Innocents Abroad*, see DeLancey Ferguson, *Mark Twain, Man and Legend* (Indianapolis, 1943), pp. 114-38.

of *The Innocents* is that it established an American point of view toward Europe as opposed to a Southern, Western, or New England point of view. Following hard upon the Civil War, it represented an attitude of national assurance and confidence which neither the nation nor its travelers had had before the war. At the moment in American history when postwar nostalgia was begetting the regional and local color movement in American literature, Mark Twain, going in an opposite direction, returned from the territory into the Union and moved beyond, to survey Europe with American eyes.

They are new American eyes, of course. To read the book in relation to American literature is to be struck by the departure it signals. There had been criticisms of Europe by earlier travelers; Cooper, Hawthorne, and Emerson, to name but three, had all shown a disposition toward vigorous criticism. They had seen and lamented the American tendency to stand in impotent awe of Europe, and they had particularly resented the European affectation of superiority to Americans. There had also been the American brag, not merely in folklore and the frontier West, but in the persons of writers as great as Melville and Whitman. All of these attitudes—the assertive democratic individualism, the resentment toward Europe and the past, and the spirited American brag—are so apparent in *The Innocents Abroad* that any one might be singled out to define Mark Twain's point of view. Yet what makes Mark Twain a powerful writer, and what makes *The Innocents Abroad* genuinely new, is not the attitudes but their coordination into the character of his stance, the character of humor.

But because the humor proves so difficult to define and the attitudes so readily available, they usually become the primary rather than the secondary concern in critical discussion. Such a failure of discrimination, which is responsible for the large body of inadequate criticism of the book, results in dismantling the character, the personality, the *humor* of Mark Twain into a number of contradictory attitudes. Thus, if the critic decides that the point of view is against Europe, he encounters rigorous attacks on the American tourist; if he sees the book as an attack upon the tourist, he is surprised by the criticism not simply of the Europe found in the guidebook, but the one which is not found there; if he sees the book as an attack upon the past, he reads dozens of apostrophes to the grandeur of time and its ruins. In this process, Mark Twain becomes in turn an iconoclastic American; a defender of gentility; a rowdy tourist sneering at the values of the past; an ignorant philistine, who, incapable of appreciating art, laughs complacently at the old masters; a militant frontiersman stripping off the sham of Europe; a fearless democrat attacking the crimes of Pope and King; an essentially conservative capitalist praising European technology, the Czar, and Napoleon III. Small wonder that once this kind of criticism begins, the book no longer has "unity" and "integrity."

Yet there is unity in *The Innocents Abroad*, and the best place to begin our search for it is in the Preface, for the Preface itself is the briefest and probably the best description of the book that has been written:

> This book is a record of a pleasure trip. If it were a record of a solemn scientific expedition it would have about it that gravity, that profundity, and that impressive incomprehensibility which are so proper to works of that kind, and withal so attractive. Yet not withstanding it is only a record of a picnic, it has a purpose, which is, to suggest to the reader how *he* would be likely to see Europe and the East if he looked at them with his own eyes instead of the eyes of those who traveled in those countries before him. I make small pretense of showing anyone how he *ought* to look at objects of interest beyond the sea—other books do that, and therefore, even if I were competent to do it, there is no need.
>
> I offer no apologies for any departures from the usual style of travel-writing that may be charged against me—for I think I have seen with impartial

eyes, and I am sure I have written at least honestly, whether wisely or not.[4]

The most striking characteristic of the Preface—and indeed of Mark Twain's entire travel narrative—is the utter clarity of the prose. It is a clarity which, more than being merely striking, is so masterful as to be the very essence of the style. That is why Mark Twain never seems to have acquired clarity but to be possessed of it. And possessed of clarity so decisively as to be in a new relationship with all the style that preceded him. In "The Jumping Frog" he had shown himself a master of vernacular; in *The Innocents Abroad* he proved himself a master of the English language.

With the heavy emphasis currently being placed on Mark Twain's vernacular, it is easy to overlook this equally important achievement. Yet just as Mark Twain's humor defined his identity and just as total experience formed the background for his mock innocence, utter clarity lay at the heart of his burlesque impersonation. Unless these realities are recognized at the outset, Mark Twain invariably eludes definition. His pseudonym becomes a mask, his humor an appearance, and his style a guise. The perfect clarity of style is what enables Mark Twain to be confident of his honesty. Lacking it, he would have been no more than an impersonator with no genuine identity of his own; possessing it, he effortlessly exposed the mustiness and strained formality of every style he faced. That exposure is the visible effect of Mark Twain's *presence* as a writer. His purity of diction and total clarity are the invisible constituents of style which make his prose seem effortless and wonderfully natural.

This new relationship with language signals a new relationship with the reader, a relationship immediately disclosed in the Preface. For Mark Twain not only defines his book as the record of a pleasure trip, but states his purpose: "to suggest to the reader how *he* would be likely

[4] *Writings*, I, ix.

to see Europe and the East if he looked at them with his own eyes instead of the eyes of those who traveled in those countries before him." The central assumption of this sentence, likely to be overlooked, defines the relation between book and reader. The book is not, according to the Preface, an attempt to guide the reader; rather it is a suggestion to the reader predicated on the assumption that as long as the narrator is honest, there is no real distinction between narrator and reader. The narrator's feelings and vision stand for the reader's own.

I do not mean that Mark Twain thought this out; instead he took it for granted in a way that Walt Whitman, who had articulated the notion fifteen years earlier, never could take it for granted. Mark Twain apparently never asked himself who this hypothetical reader was, but assuming that whoever he was he would have precisely the same reactions as "Mark Twain," he went about the business of recording his impressions.

The Innocents Abroad is that record. Its unity derives from the narrator's humorous discovery and assimilation of Europe. It is not surprising that the change in narrative method should have been the chief dimension added to the original *Alta* letters. In those letters Mark Twain had employed a simple burlesque form involving a dramatization of himself as a refined character traveling in company with a rather disreputable vernacular figure called Mr. Brown. "Mr. Twain" would provide the well-bred and romantic response to experience whereas Mr. Brown erupted with repressed, "realistic" reactions. Mark Twain had used Mr. Brown in the Sandwich Islands letters and in the letters to the *Alta* which told of his trip to New York via Panama.[5] His method in the letters was to intersperse the Mr. Twain-Mr. Brown exchanges with chapters of straight reporting, thus retaining a narrative illusion and at the same time providing information. The major revision Mark Twain made in assimilating the *Alta* let-

[5] See Walker and Dane, *Travels with Mr. Brown.*

ters for *The Innocents Abroad* was to eliminate both "Mr. Twain" and Mr. Brown and replace them with the single narrator, Mark Twain. Noting these changes, Franklin Rogers observes that they tend "toward a sharper focus upon the narrator and his consciousness as the unifying aspect of the book."[6] Actually the focus is toward the narrator's consciousness rather than his character, the primary effect of Mark Twain's revision being to displace characterization with narrative and episode with experience.

There are two aspects of the narrator's experience: the static and the emergent. The static aspect animates Mark Twain's perspective, equipping him with a burlesque stance toward experience which gives unity of vision to the immense variety of scenes and experiences he encounters. This burlesque perspective is established at the beginning. The actual trip of the *Quaker City* was a planned excursion to the Holy Land—the first planned American excursion ever made, revealing a certain pioneering aspect of the venture itself. Mark Twain could have underplayed this aspect of the journey by concentrating upon a single country, a single experience, or he could have organized the book around a series of theses and antitheses. He chose instead to organize it around the very nature of the trip and at the outset of the book reproduced in full the text of the advertisement and itinerary of the excursion, prefacing the document with these remarks: "Who could read the program of the excursion without longing to make one of the party? I will insert it here. It is almost as good as a map. As a text for this book, nothing could be better."[7]

This initial gesture does much to define the organization of the entire book, for the Captain's advertisement represents in its impotently anonymous language (it begins, "The undersigned will make an excursion as above

[6] Franklin R. Rogers, *Mark Twain's Burlesque Patterns as Seen in the Novels and Narratives 1855-1885* (Dallas, 1960), p. 43.
[7] *Writings*, I, 2.

during the coming season and begs to submit to you the following program")[8] a whole set of expectations promising a particular kind of experience. The experience is, of course, essentially that of a guided tour; its language is that of a guidebook. It is—as Mark Twain so rightly puts it—the basic *text* on which all that follows becomes a burlesque commentary.

One of the most remarkable features of the book is the extent to which parody and burlesque are carried. The parody comes to include all those forms which tell the tourist how to react or how he *ought* to react to a given scene or object. Thus legends, such as those of Heloise and Abelard and the Seven Sleepers of Ephesus, are rendered absurd by imitations which reveal their inadequacy to depict what really happened. Art criticism which provides the tourist with ready-made emotional responses is challenged by an assertion about what the paintings actually look like; guidebooks are travestied for their failure to describe the European world "as it is." All forms of discourse which have been employed to control the visitor's responses by creating reverent attitudes are subject to ridicule. Historical legend, government propaganda, literature connected with religious worship— lives of the saints, histories of miracles, and the Bible itself—are all parodied at one time or another.

Against this world created by various forms of literature and legend, the burlesque narrator constructs a world of "reality" to measure the discrepancy between what the tour promised and what it produced. Thus what is advertised as an excursion takes on under the rationale of burlesque the character of a funeral procession. "Reality"—which has no more metaphysical reality but much more operative reality than the romance it ridicules—unfolds against the pious backdrop of extravagant advertisements, guidebook formulae, false expectations, and poor advice. Denying validity to the host of literary and historical associations, the burlesque strips

8 *Ibid.*

away the past as if it were a null. The result is a reduction or, more accurately, a belittling of Europe.

But criticism is not so much the end as the means of burlesque. The end of burlesque must be entertainment. If burlesque fails to amuse it has failed, no matter how brilliantly it has criticized, no matter how much sham it has penetrated, for the sermon also criticizes and penetrates sham. Like its related forms—comedy, satire, and parody—burlesque is parasitic in a way that epic and tragedy are not, because its reality depends upon a double vision, half of which imitates the parent form, the other half which mocks it. This twin vision constitutes the totality of burlesque in much the same way that the twin aspects of Samuel Clemens came to constitute the unity of Mark Twain.

The distortion is in a genuine sense a re-forming of the parent form. Though this reformation does not have to be from a moral motive, it is not difficult to see that, by the necessities of art, the burlesque personality is a reformer. Nor is it surprising that throughout his life Mark Twain impersonated the gravity of preacher and moralist, formed friendships with the clergy, and had for his most intimate friend Joseph Twichell, minister of the Asylum Hill Congregational Church in Hartford. But if the motive of the burlesque artist's "reform" may be indignation, his performance must culminate in laughter instead of outrage. The sermon, not unlike *The Innocents Abroad*, takes a text, comments upon it, often shows indignantly how reality fails to conform to the text—particularly if the text happens to be the Bible—and ends by raising the guilt of the congregation for being a party to the failure. Although much of Mark Twain's burlesque has its roots in indignation, it moves the reader not toward guilt but toward a laughter arising from recognition of the absurdity of the world; and the laughter is not an acceptance of, or a guilt toward, but a relief *from* responsibility.

The achievement of Mark Twain's burlesque is thus to redeem or at least to recover the journey from the condition of funeral procession and make it a genuine pleasure trip. Bunyan in his *Pilgrim's Progress* had given an account of the Pilgrim's attempt to regain the joy of the divine way from which the betrayals of the earthly life have led him. *The New Pilgrim's Progress*, as *The Innocents Abroad* was subtitled, was Mark Twain's account of an attempt to recover the joy of the earthly life which the betrayals of the spirit have almost annihilated. His pilgrims in their own way encounter all the frauds and deceits and disappointments which the original Pilgrim faced. But whereas all the disappointed hopes and righteousness are transformed by Bunyan into the agonies and grotesque obstacles along the Pilgrim's arduous way, they are the pious absurdities in Mark Twain's world. What he must constantly do in order to restore the threatened excursion is to invent burlesque distortions which literally make fun of the various forms of piety.

If the static aspect of Mark Twain's experience constitutes the style of the book, it is the emergent aspect that constitutes the action. For at the same time Mark Twain has a static slant upon experience, he also seems to undergo experience, finding himself constantly involved in painfully learning about Europe and the Holy Land. But this process of suffering and learning, far from being a genuine initiation, is a mock-initiation. The burlesquing Mark Twain and the suffering Mark Twain are thus not divergent but twin aspects of the humorous narrator who realizes himself in Europe.

This realization is managed by making Europe not only a bill of goods sold to a tourist, but an illusion which the narrator has built up out of years of reading—a cherished illusion which is being progressively stripped away as he proceeds toward the Holy Land. The comic aspect of the discovery lies in the narrator's insistence on being the fool of his illusions. The innocence which gives him the capacity to see what *is* there has also given him in the past the gullibility to believe what he has been told. The book intersects his experience at the point where false expectations accumulated during a lifetime of fatuous belief are being peeled away faster than new ones can be supplied.

Thus the illusion he indulges concerning the "select" nature of the touring group is exploded first when General Sherman, Henry Ward Beecher, and other celebrities who were to have gone fail to appear; and second when he sees the shabby group which does appear. A characteristic example of this type of humor is his experience with Parisian barbers. Mark Twain prepares for the situation by elaborately describing his long-standing dream of being barbered in Paris:

> From earliest infancy it had been a cherished ambition of mine to be shaved some day in a palatial barber shop of Paris. I wished to recline at full length in a cushioned invalid-chair with pictures about me, and sumptuous furniture; with frescoed walls and gilded arches above me, and vistas of Corinthian columns stretching far before me, with perfumes of Araby to intoxicate my senses, and the slumbrous drone of distant noises to soothe me to sleep. At the end of an hour, I would wake up regretfully and find my face as smooth and as soft as an infant's. Departing, I would lift my hands above that barber's head and say, "Heaven bless you, my son!"[9]

Here the clichés of romantic travel are used to elaborate fantasy; the whole experience is envisioned as an immense indulgence, culminating in the contentment of well-being. The "reality" which concludes the episode is as elaborately developed in the opposite direction. First there is no shop to be found, only wig-making establishments with "shocks of dead and repulsive hair bound upon the heads of painted waxen brigands." Reluctantly

[9] *Ibid.*, pp. 106-107.

deciding that the wig-makers must be barbers, he finally enters a grimy room where his "old old dream of bliss vanished into thin air!"

> I sat bolt upright, silent, sad, and solemn. One of the wig-making villains lathered my face for ten terrible minutes and finished by plastering a mass of suds into my mouth. I expelled the nasty stuff with a strong English expletive and said, "Foreigner, beware!" Then this outlaw strapped his razor on his boot, hovered over me ominously for six fearful seconds, and then swooped down upon me like the genius of destruction. The first rake of his razor loosened the very hide from my face and lifted me out of the chair. . . . Then the incipient assassin held a basin of water under my chin and slopped its contents over my face, and into my bosom, and down the back of my neck, with a mean pretense of washing away the soap and blood. He dried my features with a towel, and was going to comb my hair; but I asked to be excused. I said, with withering irony, that it was sufficient to be skinned—I declined to be scalped.[10]

The "reality" which deflates the expectation is clearly not actuality, but an extravagant invention which, poised against the clichés, displaces them. The language of illusion is compounded of clichés, all of which are characterized by their having a certain literary and romantic quality. The language of disillusion, while it clearly avoids vernacular, constructs an image of barbarity which nevertheless has its sources in the folklore of American experience. Thus the Parisian barber, the greasy room, the slopping water, and finally the reference to scalping, all suggest a frontier condition prevailing in a land where luxurious enchantment had been envisioned.

This process of illusion followed by disillusion is so recurrent as to be the very mechanism of the narrator's behavior. Over and over again he undergoes the "dis-

[10] *Ibid.*, p. 108.

covery" that he has been deceived either by his own inventions or by those of others. Considered in relation to this process, Europe and the Holy Land become at once the disenchanting and the disenchanted. "I can see easily enough," observes Mark Twain in Palestine, "that if I wish to profit by this tour and come to a correct understanding of the matters of interest connected with it, I must studiously and faithfully unlearn a great many things I have somehow absorbed concerning Palestine."[11] It is not only the guidebooks which deceive—they merely perpetuate and foster the deceptions and illusions to which the imagination is always prey. At the Jordan River, Mark Twain puts the matter succinctly: "When I was a boy I somehow got the impression that the river Jordan was four thousand miles long and thirty-five miles wide. It is only ninety miles long, and so crooked that a man does not know which side of it he is on half the time."[12]

Mark Twain's narrative is therefore a fusion of burlesque and mock innocence. Though Mark Twain seems to learn and to change, he really does not. Neither do the other passengers, whether they be Pilgrims or Sinners. The Pilgrims are the pious fools whose ignorance and piety are burlesqued in the persons of the dialect fools—the Oracle, the Poet, and Interrogation Point. Thus the Oracle, upon approaching Gibraltar, remarks: "Do you see that there hill out there on that African coast? It's one of them Pillows of Herkewls, I should say—and there's the ultimate one alongside of it."[13]

Against the pious and dialect Pilgrims, Mark Twain sets the Sinners—the "boys," Jack, Dan, Moult, and the Youth. Though he identifies himself with them, they do no more than serve as companions of the carefree expeditions he wishes to make. Their identity and reality come from their desire to make fun of the Pilgrims; in fact, seeing in the Paris Zoological Gardens a "long-

[11] *Ibid.*, II, 214.   [12] *Ibid.*, p. 345.   [13] *Ibid.*, I, 57-58.

legged bird with a beak like a powder-horn, and close fitting wings like the tails of a dress-coat," the Sinners—with Mark Twain among them—call it "The Pilgrim."[14] As a society they have a good time in a relatively uninhibited, boyish American way, but there is practically no indication that as a group they discover anything.

These two aspects—the static and the emergent—combine to form the humor of Mark Twain. Translated into a character trait, the static aspect—the compulsion to make fun—becomes a built-in irreverence which is as deeply rooted as an instinct in the burlesque personality. It is what Mark Twain would come to refer to in *What Is Man?* as the *temperament*, that quality of emotion which dominates a particular personality. It is what makes him automatically choose the society of the Sinners; indeed they are the very embodiment and expression of the impulse. Thus as the guide ecstatically describes the bust of Columbus, the doctor asks soberly, "Christopher Columbo—pleasant name—is—is he dead?"[15] So self-persuaded are the boys by the devastating humor of this question that they ask it again and again. Looking at the grinning skull of a monk in the Capuchin Convent, Mark Twain wonders what extraordinary joke inspired the permanent expression: "At this moment I saw that the old instinct was strong upon the boys, and I said we had better hurry to St. Peters. They were trying to keep from asking, 'Is—is he dead?' "[16] This irreverence reduces all European guides to the single cognomen "Ferguson," and it insists on calling a Syrian village "Jonesborough." It manifests itself almost as if it were one of those uncontrollable impulses to make faces which possessed Kingsley Amis' Lucky Jim. Mark Twain liked to lament the power of its sway, and one of the chief duties of his self-appointed censors—Olivia Langdon and later William Dean Howells—was to "protect" him from this power in him-

[14] *Ibid.*, p. 93.   [15] *Ibid.*, p. 305.   [16] *Ibid.*, II, 5.

self. He informed Archibald Henderson that it was his wife's editing which saved him from the overpowering tendency to destroy the beautiful effects he had created.[17] The *locus classicus* of the compulsion—one might say, following Kenneth Burke, the *perfection* of the tendency —is the ending of *Huckleberry Finn*, which has seemed to so many readers a deplorable parody marring the beauty of the book.

The emergent aspect of the humorous personality—the repeated discovery or disillusionment—becomes in terms of character traits the somber mien of the narrator. When the living Mark Twain performed on the lecture platform for delighted audiences, it was of course the famous deadpan expression which, even as it produced the "humor," betrayed no recognition that anything was funny. In *The Innocents Abroad* the deadpan is implied by the endless "disappointments," the exquisite "sufferings," and the repeated "tortures" the narrator undergoes on his pilgrimage to the Holy Land. He suffers the agony of being shaved by the Parisian barbers, he undergoes the ordeal of hearing the same clichés, the same jokes, and the same guidebook descriptions. He hears about Michelangelo so many times that he finally is driven to exclaim, "I never felt so fervently thankful, so soothed, so tranquil,

[17] Archibald Henderson, *Mark Twain* (London, 1911), p. 183. According to Henderson, Mark Twain had this to say about the seriousness in his work: "I never wrote a serious word until after I married Mrs. Clemens. She is solely responsible—to her should go the credit—for any deeply serious or moral influence my subsequent work may exert. After my marriage, she edited everything I wrote. And what is more—she not only edited my works, she edited *me*! After I had written some side-splitting story, something beginning seriously and ending in preposterous anti-climax, she would say to me: 'You have a true lesson, a serious meaning to impart here. Don't give way to your invincible temptation to destroy the good effect of your story by some extravagantly comic absurdity. Be yourself! Speak out your real thoughts as humorously as you please, but—without farcical commentary. Don't destroy your purpose with an ill-timed joke.' I learned from her that the only right thing was to get in my serious meaning always, to treat my audience fairly, to let them really feel the underlying moral that gave body and essence to my jest."

so filled with a blessed peace, as I did yesterday when I learned that Michael Angelo was dead."[18] The torture of the pilgrimage reaches its height in the Holy Land as the pilgrims subject themselves to desert travel on horseback.

The irreverence and the sadness combine to form the face of innocence. For it is the role of Innocent that Mark Twain finally assumes, a role he played for the rest of his life. When, 35 years later, he came to wear his famous white suit, he moved into Stormfield and called it Innocence at Home. Considered in relation to *The Innocents Abroad*, the terms "innocent" and "innocence" are doubly appropriate, for the book records the journey of a relatively provincial pleasure party into a sophisticated European World rich in history and tradition. The Innocent in such a world of experience is the untutored, the unsophisticated, the culturally naïve. But the journey is also a pilgrimage whose goal is the Holy Land. Here the Innocent, in addition to being unsophisticated, becomes the unfallen, the not guilty, the free. It is with all these possibilities of "innocence" that Mark Twain plays. Yet the point constantly remains that he is playing with the attitudes of innocence; he is never trapped in them.

Sometimes the play takes the form of extravagant naïveté, as when Mark Twain recounts the difficulties he has with his horse Jericho:

> I wanted a horse that could shy, and this one fills the bill. I had an idea that shying indicated spirit. If I was correct, I have got the most spirited horse on earth. He shies at everything he comes across, with the utmost impartiality. He appears to have a mortal dread of telegraph-poles, especially; and it is fortunate that these are on both sides of the road, because as it is now, I never fall off twice in succession on the same side. If I fell on the same side always, it would get to be monotonous after a while.[19]

[18] *Writings*, I, 300-301.   [19] *Ibid.*, II, 160.

After describing the astonishing depletion of the horse—Jericho having lost his tail, "has to fight the flies with his heels"—Mark Twain ends by reflecting on how it would surprise the Arab who sold him the horse to know Jericho's true character:

> I think the owner of this prize had a wrong opinion about him. He had an idea that he was one of those fiery, untamed steeds, but he is not of that character. I know the Arab had this idea, because when he brought the horse out for inspection in Beirout, he kept jerking at the bridle and shouting in Arabic, "Whoa! will you? Do you want to run away, you ferocious beast, and break your neck?" When all the time the horse was not doing anything in the world, and only looked like he wanted to lean up against something and think. Whenever he is not shying at things, or reaching after a fly, he wants to do that yet. How it would surprise his owner to know this.[20]

At other times, Mark Twain's innocence leads him into taking figurative relations literally. Thus in the famous episode at Adam's tomb he is overcome by grief:

> The tomb of Adam! How touching it was, here in a land of strangers, far away from home, and friends, and all who cared for me, thus to discover the grave of a blood relation. The unerring instinct of nature thrilled its recognition. The fountain of my filial affection was stirred to its profoundest depths, and I gave way to tumultuous emotion. I leaned upon a pillar and burst into tears. I deem it no shame to have wept over the grave of my poor dead relative. Let him who would sneer at my emotion close this volume here, for he will find little to his taste in my journeyings through Holy Land. Noble old man—he did not live to see me—he did not live to see his child. And I—I—alas, I did not live to see *him*.[21]

[20] *Ibid.*, p. 161.   [21] *Ibid.*, p. 307.

The passage makes a series of exposures. First, Mark Twain parodies the tourist's emotional indulgences before the ruins of the past; second, he exposes the threadbare clichés in the language of personal grief; finally, when he says "Let him who would sneer at my emotion close this volume here . . . ," he exposes, by suddenly assuming, the self-righteous posture of reverence.

The nonexistent tomb of Adam is discovered in the Church of the Holy Sepulchre, that spot toward which the whole journey has tended. The transparent burlesque which Mark Twain there enacts is thus at the mythical center of the earth. He elaborately prepares for his "tumultuous emotion" by solemnly arguing that this is the center of the earth. Since no one can prove that it isn't the center, he insists it must therefore inexorably be the central spot; the fact that Adam was born here is further proof, because the Lord would have gone to no other place than the center of the earth for the dust to make man; moreover, the presence of Adam's tomb clinches the point, for again no proof exists that Adam's tomb is elsewhere.

Henry Nash Smith has pointed out that the burlesque at Adam's tomb was one of the most memorable moments in the book as far as contemporary reviewers were concerned.[22] Though it may seem overdone to a modern reader, it is nevertheless the burlesque revelation in the Church of the Holy Sepulchre, and in its way it *is* the center of Mark Twain's world, for in this transparent moment when Mark Twain exposes reverence by impersonating it, he reveals that impersonation is his chief art of exposure.

The extent of Mark Twain's commitment to impersonation carries *The Innocents Abroad* far beyond the bounds of a mere travel book or a mere burlesque. This does not mean that it goes on to become something else; instead,

[22] Henry Nash Smith, *Mark Twain: The Development of a Writer* (Cambridge, Mass., 1962), p. 35.

by realizing the possibilities of burlesque, Mark Twain vastly extended the range of the travel book. *The Innocents Abroad* is not a course in how to see Europe, though there have doubtless been Americans who acted on such a belief. It is rather an education in seeing—a training of the reader to see with his own eyes.

The education begins with the repeated discoveries and disillusions of the humorous narrator. The emergent Mark Twain is, as I have noted, constantly exposing his own illusions. His progress toward the Holy Land is at once an exposure of his fatuity and a comical self-discovery. It is not something awaited in suspense but a process repeated again and again. Nor is it an experience which teaches and reforms the narrator; instead he remains mechanized in a series of repeated acts of discovering the deceptions and illusions in which he has been locked. The only way he keeps going—and keeps extending his book to a fat 800 pages—is to keep supplying himself with more illusions by impersonating more and more styles. The commitment to this extensive impersonation finally begets its own deceptions. Any reader can see the farce of referring to the town of Mellalah as Baldwinsville; and he can see the hoax of the weeper by Adam's tomb. But what about the passage on the Pisan tear-jug?

It was found among the ruins of one of the oldest of the Etruscan cities. . . . It spoke to us in a language of its own; and with a pathos more tender than any words might bring; its mute eloquence swept down the long roll of the centuries with its tale of a vacant chair, a familiar footstep missed from the threshold, a pleasant voice gone from the chorus, a vanished form!—a tale which is always so new to us, so startling, so terrible, so benumbing to the senses, and behold how threadbare and old it is! No shrewdly worded history could have brought the myths and shadows of that old dreamy age before us clothed with human flesh and

> warmed with human sympathies so vividly as did
> this poor little unsentient vessel of pottery.[23]

Taken outside the total context of *The Innocents Abroad* such a passage seems like a competent example of a certain stylized mode of eloquence. And even within the context of the book the last sentence seems to clinch the seriousness of intent. Yet the reader who has been exposed to the repeated impersonations of style is likely to be more skeptical about the passage. The apostrophe is, after all, addressed to a Pisan tear-jug; moreover, the astonishing manner in which the passage seems upon inspection to dissolve into an easily mobilized sequence of clichés provides an additional reason for skepticism. The point is not whether the passage is genuine or spurious but that the reader is brought by virtue of the pervasive irreverence, burlesque, and mock innocence to suspect that every attitude of reverence may be an impersonation.

Indeed, the narrator has brought himself to the point where burlesque imitation and genuine emotion seem to dissolve into each other, and it can be argued that Mark Twain is trapped in his own impersonation. This is the ultimate danger of irony, burlesque, parody, and satire. Inevitably the genius of burlesque is drawn toward the razor's edge where impersonation becomes persona, and the ironist is gradually forced to yield his identity to a mask. Yet Mark Twain is not really trapped in the business of impersonation. The skepticism to which the alert reader is brought is surely one of the intentions of the narrative. Without going through the absurd ritual of proving whether Mark Twain consciously intended to have his readers educated to such skepticism—the Preface indicates that he apparently did—there is the intention of the form itself. The fulfillment of that intention involves extending the range of impersonation from vernacular illiteracy (the Oracle) through bourgeois respectability

[23] *Writings*, I, 258-59.

(the Pilgrims) to gentility (the unnamed, genuinely refined travelers who *did* appreciate the Old Masters). At
this stage of impersonation, dialect, leers, and other overt
signals drop away and the reader is left to determine for
himself what he sees. His determination is not, however,
some inchoate provocation toward thought; it is rather
a skeptical cast of eye which the book both bestows upon
and demands of him.

The reader who is brought to this attitude—and I take
it that anyone reading the book begins to take second
looks, even if for the purpose of proving that at such and
such an "eloquent" moment Mark Twain is "serious"—
enacts the experience of the journey. For *The Innocents
Abroad* is the record of a journey not to the New Jerusalem but the old one. The Innocent Mark Twain is no
American Adam going jauntily through the Garden; he is
instead an incredibly enlightened member of Adam's
posterity who weeps in simulated grief at his ancestor's
tomb. When he visits Damascus, he remarks of the legend
that it is the fabled site of the Garden of Eden, "It may
be so, but it is not paradise now, and one would be as
happy outside of it as he would be likely to be within."[24]
The Innocent, though he is the descendant of Adam,
is really the discoverer of the Old World—he quite appropriately queries whether Columbus really *is* dead—but his
discoveries are the repeated disillusions which he undergoes, as the dream of the past, instead of accumulating
in a grand process of recovery, drops from his eyes like
scales. Moving back up the stream of history toward the
source of the Christian myth, the irreverent Innocent
keeps taking up the burden of history only to cast it off
again. His discovery is constantly that the myth, though
not *certainly* worthless, well may be. And he feels that
impersonated grief is as appropriate a response in the
Church of the Holy Sepulchre as real grief, for the simple

[24] *Ibid.*, II, 178.

reason that the tourist cannot tell what *is* real in the context of the fraudulent excrescences upon the body of the myth.

That is the dilemma which confronts the pleasure-seeker. His discoveries are an unending series of disillusions—which means that they are not fulfillments but negations of expectations—and the ultimate questions are inevitably "What *is* the true self?" and "Where *is* the genuine emotion as opposed to the spurious?" The book comes to these questions in the apostrophe to the Sphinx which Mark Twain added in the process of revising the *Alta* letters. As the Innocent walks down to the Sphinx from the pyramid of Cheops, he finds himself unable to conjure up any "comparison that would convey to my mind a satisfactory comprehension of the magnitude of a pile of monstrous stones that covered thirteen acres of ground and stretched upward four hundred and eighty tiresome feet." Upon confronting the fabled monument, he bursts into a rapturous appreciation.

> After years of waiting, it was before me at last. The great face was so sad, so earnest, so longing, so patient. There was a dignity not of earth in its mien, and in its countenance a benignity such as never anything human wore. It was stone, but it seemed sentient. If ever image of stone thought, it was thinking. It was looking toward the verge of the landscape, yet looking *at* nothing—nothing but distance and vacancy. It was looking over and beyond everything of the present, and far into the past. It was gazing out over the ocean of Time—over lines of century-waves which, further and further receding, closed nearer and nearer together, and blended at last into one unbroken tide, away toward the horizon of remote antiquity. It was thinking of the wars of departed ages; of the empires it had seen created and destroyed; of the nations whose birth it had witnessed, whose progress it had watched, whose annihilation it had noted; of the joy and sorrow, the life and death, the grandeur

and decay, of five thousand slow revolving years. It was the type of an attribute of man—of a faculty of his heart and brain. It was Memory—Retrospection—wrought into visible, tangible form. All who know what pathos there is in memories of days that are accomplished and faces that have vanished—albeit only a trifling score of years gone by—will have some appreciation of the pathos that dwells in these grave eyes that look so steadfastly back upon the things they knew before History was born—before Tradition had being—things that were, and forms that moved, in a vague era which even Poetry and Romance scarce know of—and passed one by one away and left the stony dreamer solitary in the midst of a strange new age, and uncomprehended scenes.

The Sphinx is grand in its loneliness; it is impossible in its magnitude; it is impressive in the mystery that hangs over its story. And there is that in the overshadowing majesty of this eternal figure of stone with its accusing memory of the deeds of all ages, which reveals to one something of what he shall feel when he shall stand at last in the awful presence of God.[25]

This is Mark Twain's greatest impersonation of the genteel mode, his finest flight into the platform rhetoric of nostalgia. And it is of course possible to argue that Mark Twain is "serious" in this passage. The sustained command of eloquence inevitably teases even the most skeptical reader toward accepting the possibility that the passage is "genuine" emotion.

Actually, the passage enacts the last step on the journey, and after it, everything is perfunctorily dealt with in three mechanical closing chapters. But it is an appropriate last step. In answer to the question "What is burlesque and what is serious?" the passage describes in a remarkable impersonation of the most genteel travel rhetoric—the Sphinx. The riddling figure of the Sphinx

[25] *Ibid.*, pp. 382-83.

thus broods over the last moment of the journey—broods in language which assumes the cadences and sentiments of a serious book of travel, thus forcing the reader educated by the burlesque vision to doubt the "truth" of the emotion. The reader's doubt is the answer to the riddle of the Sphinx, for in *The Innocents Abroad* the ultimate truth turns out to be the burlesque spirit of negation impersonating "genuine" emotion. The reader is at last brought to ask the fatally absurd question of the humorist: *"Is—is he humorous?"* To ask that helpless and hopeless question is to be reduced to the transcendent stupidity the boys impersonated when they contemplated the bust of Columbus. Yet to be so reduced, so taken in, is not a loss but a gain of pleasure. It is the true initiation of the book—the complete experience of Mark Twain's innocence.

CHAPTER

III

THE MUSE OF
SAMUEL CLEMENS

EXTENDING impersonation to the very heart of seriousness
—this is the intention of Mark Twain's form and the intention of "Mark Twain" *as* form. Taking the reader in,
making him vaguely but pleasurably suspicious that he
has been "sold"—these are his effects. Not everyone, of
course, gets the last full measure of Mark Twain's humor.
The best and most common way to avoid "suffering" the
full pleasure is to insist that Mark Twain is serious![1] That
word "serious," so inevitable in the discussion of literature
and art, becomes fatal in the discussion of humor. For
how can a humorist be serious when he must be humorous? Seriousness is, after all, the very antithesis of humor,
and as a descriptive term it paradoxically denies the
identity of the object. The end of humor is surely not to
be serious—no matter how much critics, and even humorists, trick themselves into such a notion—but to invade
the very citadel of seriousness, transforming it into humor
with each encroachment.[2]

---

[1] This is, of course, the best way open for enthusiasts of Mark
Twain. There is always the possibility of avoiding humor altogether by placing it as a "low" form of expression precisely because it is not serious. Such a response, familiar enough in De-
partments of English, is a convenient way for neo-genteel souls to
keep Mark Twain "down."

[2] The whole problem of seriousness arises because the term is
the chief means of transmitting moral value to an experience

Making such encroachments was at once the identity and the act of Mark Twain; it was also a hazardous and delicate operation. For if he failed to encroach, he was confined to a very restricted field of vision, having in effect decided to "keep his place" as a humorist. Given such a move, he could only hope for the limited success of the mere entertainer; he could never hope to be taken seriously. Yet if he encroached too aggressively or grossly he would become too irreverent, offending the genteel audience by his lapse of taste; more important, he would lose his sense of humor and become a moralist or a satirist. Small wonder that Mark Twain meant to be taken seriously. Or was it that he meant to please the "serious" readers and critics who required the illusion that he was serious? The question inevitably brings us back to the skeptical edge of Mark Twain's identity as a humorist. This skepticism is no mere ambivalence, for it is predicated not upon whether Mark Twain is serious or humorous—we know he is preponderantly humorous—but upon whether he ever is or can be serious.

To entertain the doubt is to be afflicted with the growing certainty that Mark Twain is a complete humorist. It is also to begin to see the necessities of his art. For to be a complete humorist, he could never be serious. Yet if he were never serious or never seemed serious, he would

---

whose essence is directly pleasurable. By calling a work of art or an artist _serious_, one can, without making a single conceptual effort, shift completely from aesthetic to moral grounds. Given the full secularization of art after the seventeenth century, the term "serious" comes to serve as a neat replacement of the term "religious," and can be applied with the utmost complacency to tragedy, epic, and novel. But when' comedy, burlesque, and humor are under discussion, the value-giving term comes to be at odds with the identity of the object, and each effort at praise has the unfortunate consequence of denying the reality of the form. The problem is intensified by the fact that comic forms are considered to be "lower" in the genre hierarchy and therefore need transfusions of value if they are to be elevated into the realm of the more "serious" forms. Small wonder that book reviews, quarterlies, and academic journals abound with reflexive references to serious art, serious artists, and serious literature.

offend the serious minded and culturally ambitious readers who formed such a sizable and influential segment of his audience. Mark Twain met this requirement largely through the art of impersonation, which allowed him to seem serious without necessarily being so.

But being serious was not the only requirement of the complete humorist. He had to please—and to be really complete he had, theoretically, to please everyone, or at least as many as he possibly could. Such a task—impossible in the eyes of some, immoral in the eyes of others—was the challenge always before him; he met it by developing a strategy of pleasure equal in importance to his extended impersonation—the strategy of censorship. Intuitively determining the chief taboos of the society, conforming to them religiously and so appeasing the largest possible segment of his audience, he gained approval by assiduously and publicly assuring his readers that on certain crucial conventions he was as strict and pure as any of them. Chief among the conventions he publicly endorsed were those promoting the sexual taboos and respect for women. By holding up his hyper-conventionalism, he was able to gain the approval for whatever subversions his humor would enact. The entire process was central to his humor, a kind of bargaining and compensation worked out by an instinct so deep that it was part of his life as a humorist. Both the depth and the expression of Mark Twain's instinct for censorship can best be measured in his discovery, courtship, and lifelong need of Olivia Langdon Clemens.

If a wife's influence upon her husband's literary work is measured by the importance his imagination accords her presence, Olivia Langdon Clemens is one of the most influential wives in the nineteenth century—which amounts to saying that she is one of the most influential wives in any century. For it was in the nineteenth century that the wife came into her own, in the study as well as in the parlor. Not, to be sure, the dominant figure in that bearded century, she nevertheless hovered by the threshold of the imagination almost as much as by the hearthside in the manner of an attendant spirit approving rather than brooding over the creative process. The eighteenth-century man of letters had had his mistress; the Romantic artist had had his sister; the Victorian author had his wife.

Yet even in such a period—which produced an Elizabeth Barrett, an Emily Sellwood, a Virginia Clemm, a Sophia Hawthorne—Olivia Langdon was the object of extreme adoration. From the moment when, as Mark Twain remembered it, he saw the ivory miniature of her in her brother's stateroom on the *Quaker City*, she was, he confidently asserted, never out of his mind.[3] And throughout his 34 years of married life he did all in his power to make a legend of their happiness together. Sustained by his seemingly boundless devotion, she rose out of the semi-invalidism of her adolescence to become the mother of four children. Though never strong, she clearly enjoyed a degree of health and energy she had never known before her marriage. Though misfortune, disaster, and finally something akin to despair overtook Mark Twain, causing him to doubt the fabric of his own experience, there is no sure hint that he ceased to believe absolutely in Olivia Langdon. The arc of his career discloses that she was the one thing he did believe in even after he came to doubt all else—even himself.

Yet for all his proclaimed adoration, the literary immortality he bequeathed her was hardly flattering, for he insistently presented her as censor, not as muse. Much of his talk about her censorship was of course part of the humorous game he played with his intimate friends, particularly with William Dean Howells. But the conse-

[3] Paine, *A Biography*, I, 339. Describing the momentous first gaze at the portrait, Paine proclaims that Mark Twain "looked long and steadily at the miniature, resolving in his mind that someday he would meet the owner of that lovely face—a purpose at once in accord with that which the fates had arranged for him, in the day when all things were arranged, the day of the first beginning."

quence of his humorous accusations and his feigned stupidity in matters of literary taste was a shifting of the responsibility for his shortcomings and failures upon the shoulders of others, chief among them his wife. He did not intentionally make her the scapegoat for his self-advertised failure, but he made possible, no matter how unwittingly, the attacks which were to be made upon her. She came to be seen as the figure representing all the social and artistic values antithetical to Mark Twain's native genius. Even the extravagant praises which Mark Twain, and after him Albert Bigelow Paine, lavished upon her were interpreted by Van Wyck Brooks and others as shameless demonstrations of his acquiescence to an impotent respectability.

The chief reason she was singled out for attention and attack was her apparent activity in curtailing Mark Twain's "free" expression. For Mark Twain succeeded in conveying to posterity an image of himself as a writer suppressed by the society. Interestingly enough, his chief efforts in creating such an image were made after Olivia's death in 1904. Long before her death, however, Mark Twain had complained of the innumerable shackles which enslaved him and frustrated his creative instincts. In view of his concerted effort throughout his career to present himself as a victim of suppression it is hardly surprising that Brooks could develop a fairly substantial thesis that Samuel Clemens was a repressed artist. And given the myth of repression—few authors have tried harder to create the illusion that their unpublished work held The Great Secret—it was inevitable that Olivia Langdon Clemens would in time become the scapegoat in the drama. Mark Twain had himself invented her in the role of censor, an invention that dated all the way back to the autumn of 1868 when he began the written phase of his courtship with her. Even at that early time he assigned her a more important role in his creative life than any subsequent critic has been willing to grant her. By virtue of the power he himself invested in her, she was both his muse and censor, or, to put it more precisely, his muse *as* censor. The manner in which he invented her role during their courtship goes far toward defining the significance of her presence to his art.

The first and possibly the last fact to remember about Samuel Clemens' courtship with Olivia Langdon is that he fell in love with her image, or so he maintained, before he saw her in the flesh. And that image, which he said was never out of his mind, is really all that remains of Olivia. Considered apart from her husband, she seems no more than a portrait, having no personality, no essential individuality. Like Virginia Clemm, she lacks personality because her identity has been relocated in her husband's image of her. That is why both Virginia and Olivia seem more ideal than individual. It is why Olivia is seen—and cannot really be seen otherwise—as a kind of apotheosis of respectability.

Olivia was by nature apparently more representative than individual. Certainly her taste, wherever it declares itself before her marriage, seems the very epitome of respectability, as if conventionality were rooted in the core of her imagination. Her commonplace book, which she kept as a young girl—and which is now in the Mark Twain Papers in Berkeley, California—is so commonplace that it seems more like a transcript of standard passages chosen by the head matron of a female seminary than a private individual's favorite literary selections. In her neat and absolutely regular schoolgirlish hand are copied the most familiar and edifying passages from the approved writers. Portia's speech from *The Merchant of Venice* is there, along with innumerable platitudes culled from such worthies as Holmes, Ruskin, Horace Greeley, Theodore Parker, Thackeray (*The English Humorists!*), and her own Elmira pastor, Thomas K. Beecher. Beecher's more famous brother, Henry Ward, is amply represented by such sonorous profundities as "The past belongs to Gratitude and Regret; the present to Contentment and Work;

the future to Hope and Trust." As a matter of fact, the prose of Henry Ward Beecher seems to have represented to Olivia a pattern of moral and literary excellence quite as satisfactory as one could wish. When Samuel Clemens began the extensive correspondence with her which culminated in engagement and marriage, she sent him regularly as a kind of spiritual tonic the weekly sermons issuing from Beecher's Plymouth pulpit.

Her life and taste form a picture which even Brooks and De Voto, for all their war with each other, could agree to deplore. Brooks, in describing her taste, observed with confident assurance:

> Profane art, the mature expression of life, in short, was outside Mrs. Clemens's circle of ideas; she could not breathe in that atmosphere with any comfort; her instinctive notion of literature was of something that is read at the fireside, out loud, under the lamp, a family institution, vaguely associated with the Bible and a father tempering the wind of King James's English to the sensitive ears and blushing cheek of the youngest daughter. Her taste, in a word, was quite infantile.[4]

And De Voto, for all his passionate refutations of Brooks, saw her in equally pejorative terms. She was, he averred, "completely of her generation in the neurasthenia that afflicted her throughout her life, driving her into repeated 'collapses.'"[5]

Yet if her picture seems sterile and shallow to Brooks and De Voto, the point remains that, according to the myth Mark Twain made, he "recognized" Olivia from her image and wanted her before he saw her. He clearly did not submit to her wiles, but aggressively spent his energies in winning her. He was thirty-two when he met her, thirty-

[4] Van Wyck Brooks, *The Ordeal of Mark Twain* (New York, 1920), p. 120. Brooks's extensive account of the relationship between artist and wife (pp. 106-27), for all its dogmatic assurance, will always remain the point of departure for efforts to understand Mark Twain's marriage.

[5] Bernard De Voto, *Mark Twain's America* (Cambridge, Mass., 1932), pp. 207-208.

four when they were married, and for all his mock-innocence he was experienced in range and depth beyond any man she could have known. He was experienced enough to discover in the pose of innocence a power which no American before him, with the single exception of Franklin, had begun to realize. He was also experienced enough to know that he wanted her more than anything else he had ever wanted. Even so, he approached cautiously, not recklessly. He saw her in person for the first time in New York on December 27, 1867, six weeks after the *Quaker City* voyage had ended; and again during the week which followed, on one occasion going so far as to accompany her to a reading by Charles Dickens.[6] After that first week, however, there is only his word that she was never out of his mind. Obeying the conventions of nineteenth-century courtship, he so discreetly kept his distance that during the entire eight months he spent in revising his *Quaker City* travel letters into *The Innocents Abroad* he did not write to her or indicate his love to anyone.

But he did have an intimate correspondent during that period. She was Mary Mason Fairbanks of Cleveland, Ohio. Mrs. Fairbanks had been a reporter for the Cleveland *Herald*—her husband was one of the owners of the paper—and had accompanied the *Quaker City* party. During the excursion Mark Twain had formed a friendly attachment with her, calling her "Mother," and for the remainder of his twenty-year correspondence with her he continued to use the affectionate epithet. How much of a mother she actually was during the voyage is difficult to say because the relation is projected almost entirely through the magnifying lens of his imagination. His letters cast her in the role of the kind, straight-laced but indulgent mother whose desire was to reform her Prodigal Son. In the little drama he composed for them, she had cured him of bad habits, kept his clothes clean, sewed

[6] Dixon Wecter (ed.), *The Love Letters of Mark Twain* (New York, 1947), pp. 5-6.

on his buttons, fed him jam when he behaved, and lectured him when he had not. Her character, as it emerges in the course of his letters, points forward toward the figure of Aunt Polly. But it points backward in his career to the character of Samuel Clemens' mother which he had invented in the silver fields of Nevada. Mrs. Fairbanks seems both an elaboration and a reincarnation of that earlier figure who had been cast in the role of Keeper of Conventions to whom the remote Prodigal reported his astonishing and outrageous excursions.

Yet Mrs. Fairbanks was not simply a second "mother" for the bad boy; she was the "editor" for her "cub." She was, he insisted, his "mentor" and copyreader, who corrected his travel letters to the San Francisco *Alta California*. Her duties as mother and mentor were more than merely compatible tasks; they were mutually reinforcing aspects of the character Mark Twain was inventing for her. His letters to her are the record of a surprisingly fertile little game which both players played with energy and imagination. As invented by her "son," Mrs. Fairbanks is a kind, shrewd, fairly intelligent keeper of the conventions, who scolds her cub for his use of slang, takes upon herself the education of his taste, and instructs him in the proprieties of authorship. He in turn is her eager disciple, assuring her that her good work of the recent voyage has not been in vain, that her reforms are still in force, and that her literary tutelage has carried beyond the schoolroom of the *Quaker City* to become a permanent influence for good in all the work that he will do. Informing her that the early letters he had written to the *Alta California* had little to recommend them, he adds that he looks forward with hope to the later ones which she had edited. "I may think better of those you weeded of slang," he remarks in one letter, and goes on to say, "There will not be any slang in this book except it should occur in a mild form in dialogues."[7]

[7] Dixon Wecter (ed.), *Mark Twain to Mrs. Fairbanks* (San Marino, Calif., 1949), p. 22.

It would be—and has been—easy to deplore Mark Twain's acquiescence to what seems the sterile gentility represented by Mrs. Fairbanks. In light of his almost eager efforts to put himself in the hands of conventional power, it is not surprising that he is often seen as one who sacrificed his bold spirit for the protection of vested artistic interests. Yet for all Mark Twain's advertisement of his efforts to please Mrs. Fairbanks's tastes, he was careful to leave his strictures on the Old Masters in *The Innocents Abroad*. He even went out of his way to report that his best friends, whose taste was far better than his own, had begged him to omit his remarks about the revered masterpieces of art. But he went on to say that, try as he would to acquire the proper taste, he still could, in effect, "see no p'ints about the old masterpieces any better than any other pictures." To this day there are those who, even though they lament Mark Twain's easy capitulation to Eastern gentility, still wish that he had had the good taste not to make fun of the Old Masters. Or, even more likely, they find his remarks about Michelangelo in bad taste or simply not funny. Urbanely secularized, they relish his irreverence about the pious pilgrims; yet when he touches upon the sanctity of art, he reaches the limits of their humor, and they wish that he had had the judgment to laugh only at bad art. But of course if Mark Twain had done that he would have proved himself able to laugh only at the ridiculous, not at the revered, and would thus have betrayed his own irreverent character and at the same time kept his place among the minor humorists. Instead, he used the approval of Mrs. Fairbanks not as a shield to protect himself but as a base from which to launch one of the boldest strokes in his book.

More than providing a framework for playing with and against the conventions, his correspondence with Mrs. Fairbanks formed a preparation for the invasion of Elmira. For in addition to securing the advantage of a valuable ally—a "mother" whom he could consult and in whom he could confide—Samuel Clemens was polishing his skills as a letter writer. Though he did not write to Olivia and though he did not mention her to Mrs. Fairbanks until late in the summer of 1868, the concentration he devoted to the assault which began in September, 1868, makes it difficult for a skeptic to deny his contention that from the time he saw her image she was never out of his mind.

Upon finishing the manuscript of *The Innocents Abroad* and turning it over to Elisha Bliss, his publisher in Hartford, he secured an invitation to visit the Langdons, and accordingly made his pilgrimage to Elmira. Bringing matters directly to the point, he proposed—or at least made a reckless declaration—and was as immediately repulsed by his frail lady and her parents. He was not completely banished, however, being allowed to address her in letters as his "honored sister." From this initial defeat he literally wrote his way back into her favor. First he regained a position where he no longer had to call her "sister"; from there he moved close enough to declare his love; then to the point where he persuaded her to declare her own; on to engagement; and finally—on February 2, 1870, eighteen months after his early setback—to marriage. During the most crucial period of his courtship, he was on an extensive lecture tour, writing her from such towns as Lockport, New York; Titusville, Pennsylvania; Ravenna, Ohio; Tecumseh, Michigan; and Galena, Illinois. Despite the exhaustion of traveling, lecturing, and the inescapable social engagements which attended his performances, he wrote her as much as a hundred pages a week. This correspondence in the year and a half of their courtship and engagement—less than 20 per cent of which is in Wecter's edition of the *Love Letters*—comprises a manuscript as long as that of *The Innocents Abroad*.

Yet these letters seem at first glance a remarkably different manuscript. For if Mark Twain's journey to the

Holy Land is rooted in irreverence and skepticism, Samuel Clemens' "manuscript" to Olivia which grew during the months *The Innocents Abroad* was being prepared for publication, chronicled the pilgrimage of a reverent lover toward the object of his worship and belief. She was, he playfully contended, his Human Angel, and he drew upon all the chivalric, royal, and religious associations at his command to effect her elevation. Thus he spoke of her at one time as the "matchless little princess"[8] whom he wished to enthrone, and at another as "a little martyr."[9] The attitude throughout is one of complete reverence sustained by a continual offering of every style at the lover's command to the service and devotion of his love in an effort to claim for her a state of earthly perfection. Thus, while all the traditional styles in *The Innocents Abroad* had been subverted by the irreverent Mark Twain who impersonated them, styles in the love letters are the offerings which Samuel Clemens brings to the worship of his earthly goddess.

His courtship involved a game similar to the one he had played with Mrs. Fairbanks. Again he offered himself as the repentant prodigal begging to be reformed and asking to be schooled in the tender refinements which only Olivia could teach. And again he asked for criticism, appointing her his "darling little Mentor"[10] and telling her that she must read each thing he wrote, keep a scrapbook of the clippings he sent her, collect his fugitive newspaper articles, advise him in matters of style, censor him when he was incorrigibly "bad," and edit his works after his death. Such were the duties of his new editor and mentor. He assured her, as he had assured Mrs. Fairbanks, that her presence was having the most salutary

[8] Unpublished letter of December 9, 1868, in the Mark Twain Papers. This and other quotations from Mark Twain's unpublished letters are used by permission of the Trustees of the Mark Twain Estate. Copyright © 1962 by the Mark Twain Company. Hereafter cited as MTP.

[9] February 28, 1869, MTP.

[10] December 27, 1868, MTP.

effect upon his spiritual and imaginative life. He stopped drinking hard liquor and even offered to give up cigars if she required such a sacrifice.

Yet Olivia's role was considerably more complex and elevated than the one Mrs. Fairbanks had played. Whereas Mrs. Fairbanks had been invented as the Mother, Olivia was cast as the Human Angel. Thoroughly playful, the term indicated precisely the areas of the imagination which were at stake. Mrs. Fairbanks had been operative in matters of convention and taste; Olivia, in addition to handling these concerns, was delegated authority over regions of sex and faith. The game of love with her included not merely the task of reforming Samuel Clemens; she was to take up the burden of saving him from physical ruin and mental doubt. Constantly holding her up as the one object he could believe in and adore, he reminded her that the responsibility for his salvation lay inexorably in her hands. When she deprecated the crown he insistently offered her, contending that it was unchristian to be so worshipped, he blandly replied that perhaps his idolatry might lead him toward her God. He told her of the grave doubts which seized him despite his earnest efforts to believe, "confessing" to her upon occasion that there were hopeless periods when "religion seemed wellnigh unattainable, & when one feels grimly like jesting with holy things, & giving up in despair."[11] And at times he was filled with self-abasement and a sense of unworthiness in the face of her spiritual perfection. Apologizing for having caused her pain, he wrote, "I do despise myself to think that all your precious love & all your patient gentleness & your beautiful nature were not puissant enough to curb my little peevish spirit & bridle my irreverent tongue. I was not fit to stand in such a presence in such a mood."[12] In addition to succeeding Mother Fairbanks as his mentor, she was to be his partner in a relationship physically passionate but passionately pure.

[11] December 30, 1868, MTP.
[12] August 8, 1869, MTP.

Thus he closed an early letter with the following fragmentary outburst: "If I could take you in my arms *now*, & imprint upon your forehead the kiss of reverent Honor, & upon your lips the Kiss of Love, imperishable & undefiled!"[13]

Through all the reverence of his style, Olivia was quick to sense the heresy of his courtly love. She perceived it much more clearly than the Mark Twain apologists—who explain away his reverence as an unfortunate sentimentality which occasionally threatened his rough frontier masculinity—and more clearly than the critics who point to his chivalry as proof of just how conventional Mark Twain finally was. The heresy was plain enough to see. Early in the game he put the matter abruptly: "I have faith in you—a faith which is as simple & unquestioning as the faith of a devotee in the idol he worships."[14] Even a parishioner in the liberated Congregationalism of Elmira could see that such a profession was hardly Christian. Though he assured her that her love might redeem him, she rather helplessly encouraged him to believe in God rather than in her and sent him Beecher's sermons in an effort to give him spiritual instructions. He replied—not without a touch of savagery—that he was learning to "devour" religious literature. Olivia betrayed increasingly weakening resistance to his worship, for against the tide of reverence which flooded toward her from his pen, the easy religion of Henry Ward Beecher afforded little protection indeed. Her early fears proved prophetic. Less than two years after they were married, when he was on another great lecture tour, she wrote half-wistfully and half-playfully that she had fallen away from God, adding that if she could only feel toward God what she felt toward her husband, she would feel no anxiety whatever about religion.[15]

The whole course of the courtship raises the inevitable question of how "serious" Samuel Clemens was in his

[13] December 4, 1868, MTP.
[14] Wecter (ed.), *Love Letters*, p. 25.   [15] *Ibid.*, p. 168.

efforts to be "saved." Did he really wish to be converted, or was he simply acting a part? Like all questions concerning Mark Twain, this one comes down to style. The reverent style is finally difficult to distinguish from the irreverent. Here is a sample of Samuel Clemens's reverence; it could easily be duplicated a hundred times in the love letters. Responding to Olivia's troubled reactions to Anna Dickinson's radical expressions on women's rights, he exhorted her to accept her fate:

> Therefore be content. Do that which God has given you to do, & do not seek to improve upon his judgment. You cannot do Anna Dickinson's work, & I can freely stake my life upon it, she cannot do yours.—Livy you might as well reproach yourself for not being able to win bloody victories in battle like Joan of Arc. In your sphere you are as great, & as noble, & as efficient as any Joan of Arc that ever lived. Be content with the strength God has given you, & the station that He has given into your charge—& don't be discouraged & unsettled by Anna Dickinson's incendiary words.[16]

The entire passage has about it the air of being borrowed instead of created; thus the manner in which the language echoes the conventional rhetoric of piety takes precedence over the argument of the passage. Instead of creating a new style, Samuel Clemens is impersonating an old one. As his own Tom Sawyer would later love to do, he is "putting on" style as if it were a garment. That is why the whole structure of his rhetoric seems more ready-made than handwoven. It is also why Samuel Clemens seems to have become Mark Twain.

His very willingness to employ and play with styles was mirrored in the play world the letters were inventing for himself and Olivia. For it was a play world, and it would be a somber person who failed to see the play from which Mark Twain could never save himself. The list of diminutives he used to describe her is an index to the

16 January 22, 1869, MTP.

perspective he was inventing. He constantly referred to her as his little mentor, his little angel, his little martyr, his little princess, his little darling. But it would be a blind person, who, seeing that the activity *was* play, dismissed it because it wasn't "serious." The point is that it *was* play—an elaborate imaginative engagement in impersonation by means of which Mark Twain converted the conventional Olivia Langdon into a mock-solemn companion of his art. She was, to use his own favorite term for her, his "dear little gravity"—a kind of straight man who was to collaborate in the creation of his humor.

Her censorship and tutelage did not constitute an alien authority impinging upon Mark Twain's imagination; rather, as De Voto shrewdly recognized, Olivia was his self-appointed censor,[17] and her censorship was really his own. It was, like his image of her, part of his imagination. In being his editor she played a part for him in a comic dialectic of his own arrangement. The fact that, beginning with *The Innocents Abroad*, she was his literary advisor until her death serves to emphasize how inextricably she was involved in his whole creative enterprise. Her role of editor and censor was in fact merely a concrete manifestation of the power he invested in his image of her as Human Angel. For as his angel, she was nothing less than his self-created muse. She was the good angel whose presence was not merely a protection against demonic forces but an assurance of sanity itself—as necessary to his imagination as the past which lay behind him waiting to be reconstructed. Writing to her from Hartford shortly before *The Innocents Abroad* was published, he assured her with all the conviction the reverent style would carry: "Livy, you are so interwoven with the very fibre of my being that if I were to lose you it seems to me that to lose memory and reason at the same time would be a blessing to me."[18]

[17] Bernard De Voto, *Mark Twain at Work* (Cambridge, Mass., 1942), pp. 84-85.
[18] May 8, 1869, MTP.

The image of Olivia did make both memory and reason possible to him. The authoritative definition of her role in his imaginative undertaking is to be found in a letter which is unquestionably one of the most interesting and important he ever wrote. It was written on February 6, 1870—four days after his marriage—to Will Bowen, a boyhood friend. He had written to Bowen two years earlier, "I have been thinking of schooldays at Dawson's, & trying to recall the old faces of that ancient time—but I cannot place them very well—they have faded out from my treacherous memory."[19] All that he could remember was a single incident involving a louse which Will had purchased from one Arch Fuqua. Two years later, however, he could reply that Bowen's recent, and evidently nostalgic, letter had stirred him "to the bottom." "The fountains of my great deep are broken up" he sonorously began, "& I have rained reminiscences for four & twenty hours." Continuing in this vein of nostalgic oratory, he eloquently proclaimed:

> The old life has swept before me like a panorama; the old days have trooped by in their old glory again; the old faces have looked out of the mists of the past; old footsteps have sounded in my listening ears; old hands have clasped mine; old voices have greeted me, & the songs I loved ages & ages ago have come wailing down the centuries! Heavens what eternities have swung their hoary cycles about us since those days were new!—

Then, as easily as he had assumed the stately smoothflowing commercial style, he ceased impersonating its florid eloquence in order to detail a particular past:

> —Since we tore down Dick Hardy's stable; since you had the measles & I went to your house purposely to catch them; since Henry Beebe kept that envied slaughter-house, & Joe Craig sold him cats to kill in it; since old General Gaines used to say, "Whoop!

[19] *Mark Twain's Letters to Will Bowen*, ed. Theodore Hornberger (Austin, 1941), p. 17.

Bow your neck & spread!"; since Jimmy Finn was
town drunkard & we stole his dinner while he slept
in the vat & fed it to the hogs in order to keep them
still till we could mount them & have a ride; since
Clint Levering was drowned; since we taught that
one-legged nigger, Higgins, to offend Bill League's
dignity by hailing him in public with his exasper-
ating "Hello, League!"—since we used to undress &
play Robin Hood in our shirt-tails, with lath swords,
in the woods on Halliday's Hill on those long summer days; since we used to go in swimming above
the still-house branch—& at mighty intervals wandered on vagrant fishing excursions clear up to "the
Bay," & wondered what was curtained away in the
great world beyond that remote point; since I
jumped overboard from the ferry boat in the middle
of the river that stormy day to get my hat, & swam
two or three miles after it (& got it,) while all the
town collected on the wharf & for an hour or so
looked out across the angry waste of "white-caps"
toward where people said Sam. Clemens was last
seen before he went down; since we got up a rebellion against Miss Newcomb, under Ed Stevens' lead-
ership, (to force her to let us all go over to Miss
Torry's side of the schoolroom,) & gallantly "sassed"
Laura Hawkins when she came out the third time
to call us in, & then afterward marched in in threatening & bloodthirsty array,—& meekly yielded, &
took each his little thrashing, & resumed his old
seat entirely "reconstructed"; since we used to indulge in that very peculiar performance on that old
bench outside the school-house to drive good old
Bill Brown crazy while he was eating his dinner;
since we used to remain at school at noon & go
hungry, in order to persecute Bill Brown in all possible ways—poor old Bill, who could be driven to
such extremity of vindictiveness as to call us "You
infernal fools!" & chase us round & round the
school-house—& yet who never had the heart to hurt
us when he caught us, & who always loved us &
always took our part when the big boys wanted to

thrash us; since we used to lay in wait for Bill Pitts at the pump & whale him; (I saw him two or three years ago, & was awful polite to his six feet two, & mentioned no reminiscences); since we used to be in Dave Garth's class in Sunday school & on week-days stole his leaf tobacco to run our miniature tobacco presses with; since Owsley shot Smar; since Ben Hawkins shot off his finger; since we accidentally burned up that poor fellow in the calaboose; since we used to shoot spool cannons, & cannons made of keys, while that envied & hated Henry Beebe drowned out our poor little popguns with his booming brazen little artillery on wheels; since Laura Hawkins was my sweetheart—

The mention of Laura Hawkins served to *recall* Samuel Clemens from this series of memories covering the whole spectrum of experience which was later to constitute the adventures of Tom Sawyer and Huckleberry Finn.

Hold: *That* rouses me out of my dream, & brings me violently back into this day & this generation. For behold I have at this moment the only sweetheart I ever *loved*, & bless her old heart she is lying asleep upstairs in a bed that I sleep in every night, & for four whole days she has been *Mrs. Samuel L. Clemens*! . . . & she is the *best* girl, & the sweetest, & the gentlest, & the daintiest, & the most modest & unpretentious, & the wisest in all things she should be wise in & the most ignorant in all matters it would not grace her to know, & she is sensible & quick & loving & faithful, forgiving, full of charity— & her beautiful life is ordered by a religion that is all kindliness & unselfishness. Before the gentle majesty of her purity all evil things & evil ways & evil deeds stand abashed,—then surrender. Wherefore without effort, or struggle, or spoken exorcism, all the old vices & shameful habits that have possessed me these many years, are falling away, one by one, & departing into the darkness.[20]

[20] *Ibid.*, pp. 18-20.

This letter to Bowen forms a fitting end to any account of Samuel Clemens' courtship. The reverent description of Olivia is in effect a summary and distillation of all that he had said again and again in his love letters.

But the letter also marks the recovery of a past. For what is new four days after the marriage is the presence and particularity of a vast memory of boyhood, which like a generative matrix, releases a compelling sequence of memories. These memories, though invariably containing elements of violence, death, sadism, shame, and cowardice, miraculously take the shape of a much swifter narrative than the ponderous rhetoric of nostalgia. The irrepressible spirit of humor, which ironically plays upon the memories even as they emerge, is itself the stylistic counterpart of the "real" world of childhood—a world of innocence and play. Moreover, the letter makes clear how the presence of the princess upstairs is related to the stream of memories being recorded. It is not simply that the memory of Laura Hawkins reminds Samuel Clemens of Olivia; rather, under the protection of the reverent spirit of Olivia, the old vices and shameful habits of the intervening years are falling away, leaving the past free from evil and available to the memory. The remarkable feature of this "purification" is that it occurs without effort on his part. Olivia is thus more than a protector; she represents the presence of a grace which blesses the memory, opening a window upon the territory of boyhood.

Finally, the very structure of the letter reveals as no document can—for the letter is in its way a work of art—how Olivia was a censor, not merely in her role of proofreader but in the deepest psychic meaning of the term. For even the "innocent" memories in the letter were being written to his boyhood friend while she slept. The letter is, in the last analysis, a dramatic summary of Mark Twain's *act* of writing. His "dream" of the past is made possible not only by her grace but by her sleep. And it is not an exaggeration to say that all of his "dream" of the past which lay before him was to be made possible by her presence and her sleep. When he had completed his dream and she had awakened, he dutifully submitted his manuscript for her "approval." This last gesture in the drama of his invention marked the ritual which "exposed" her function and assured them both that nothing was amiss.

Thus in making Olivia his editor he was explicitly and "humorously" defining the much deeper role her image played in his creative memory. She was, by virtue of his imagination, part of his identity as a man and as a writer. His headlong determination to have her had been in its way an expression of himself. After their marriage he insisted, not without reason, that theirs was a true marriage in that each shared the other's identity, she being his other self. And when she was stricken with her last illness, Mark Twain measured her necessity to his genius in a letter to Frederick Duneka of Harpers. "My wife being ill," he wrote, "I have been—in literary matters—helpless all these weeks. I have no editor—no censor."[21]

In her approaching death, he felt a grave threat to himself as a writer. For with the exception of a single volume of early sketches distinguished only by "The Jumping Frog," his entire literary work had been subjected to her benign censorship. His humorous genius required such a resistance in order to achieve expression in the same way that Tom Sawyer required Aunt Polly's indulgent suppression in order to create the dream of freedom. Mark Twain's "humor" was itself the conversion of real tyranny and slavery into play and adventure; and Olivia had been at once his muse and censor, whom he had "converted" to serve himself instead of Beecher's God. In this figure who embodied and represented the forms of reverence and respectability, Samuel Clemens had possessed both the convention and the style which Mark Twain would endlessly impersonate. The censor-

---

[21] Unpublished letter in the Berg Collection, New York Public Library. Typescript in the Mark Twain Collection in University of California Library, Berkeley, California.

ship which he invited her to impose upon him, far from restricting his imagination, actually freed it to move toward the "approved" world of childhood, which was at once the past of Samuel Clemens and the future of Mark Twain.

CHAPTER

IV

AUTOBIOGRAPHY

SURVEYED from a point remote in time, the shape of a career seems so inevitable that the freedom of the writer's life may be forgotten. After completing the manuscript of *The Innocents Abroad*, Mark Twain faced a world of possibilities. There was, first of all, the chance to repeat his success as a traveler. He thought of going to England and, employing the techniques of *The Innocents Abroad*, reporting his discoveries. He even wrote to Bliss that he thought he could write a "telling book" about such a journey. The lure of travel always lay before Mark Twain like a rich temptation. In the midst of writing *Roughing It*, he was seized with the impulse to go to the Kimberly Diamond Mines and—in all probability—experience anew the emotional frenzy he had lived through in the flush times along the Comstock lode. He hit upon what seemed to him the happy plan of sending a reporter—one J. H. Riley whom he had come to know and admire during his months in Washington—to Africa. From Riley's reports, he intended to "work up" the mines. Riley did go to Africa, but contracted a fever and died shortly after returning to Philadelphia and so became the first of a long line of victims of Mark Twain's speculative imagination.

But there were other possibilities, all of which seemed to afford a lucrative future for Mark Twain's speculative genius. The strongest of these was the chance to turn lecturer and capitalize doubly on the voyage of the *Quaker City*, an opportunity Mark Twain did not fail to take. Launching himself upon the Redpath lecture circuit, he performed throughout the East and Midwest, intending to end the tour with a grand overland journey to California and San Francisco. Olivia, however, persuaded him to abandon such an exhausting finale.

Traveling and lecturing were aspects of Mark Twain's identity, and he inevitably found himself drawn toward the journey and the platform as he began thinking of his next book. His marriage to Olivia Langdon in 1870 involved him in the additional role of making his way in the business world. Olivia's father, Jervis Langdon, had made a fortune in coal; not to be outdone, Mark Twain set out to be a literary tycoon, setting himself up as editor and partner of the Buffalo *Express*. But in order to sustain his investment in the business of journalism, Mark Twain had increasingly to tax his creative impulses—had to involve himself in the *business* of writing. He accordingly closed a lucrative contract with the *Galaxy* magazine and was a regular (and harassed) contributor to that periodical for fourteen months. Yet all of this frenzied effort did not prevent him from failing as an editor and businessman. The fortunes of the Buffalo *Express* declined, and Mark Twain lost $10,000 when he sold his interest and moved to Hartford.[1]

He had nearly lost much more. His career as a writer was at stake as he contended with being a traveler, a lecturer, and a businessman. These occupational distractions were the prodigious expense of his humorous genius making its way toward *Roughing It*.

In *The Innocents Abroad*, Mark Twain had discovered his perspective; in *Roughing It* he began to discover his past. These two statements sum up what the books share and how they differ. They share the form and style of

[1] Paine, *A Biography*, I, 398-433. Also Ferguson, *Man and Legend*, p. 159.

Mark Twain. To be sure, in *Roughing It* he is describing a different world and recounting different experiences, but he still poses as the innocent confronted by a new and unknown environment. This continuity, which led Mark Twain to give the book the tentative title of *The Innocent at Home*, has led critics and literary historians to consider the two books as successive stages in the adventures of Mark Twain.

But the books are different, in form as well as in substance. *The Innocents Abroad* is the record of a journey into a tourist world embodying the historical and institutional past. Though Mark Twain parodies guidebooks and travel literature, in the very process of parody he writes his own book of travel built around an itinerary and devoted to giving the reader information the author has acquired and impressions he has received. *Roughing It* is quite different, for it is a chronicle of a journey into a world devoted not to the past but to the future and dedicated not to reverence but to speculation. And *Roughing It*, though often considered as a book of travel, can also be called an autobiography. To be perfectly accurate, it begins as autobiographical narrative and ends as travel book.

Its itinerary, instead of being a planned tour through space, is a wandering journey through personal history from the time the author left St. Joseph on the overland stage until he was ready to return East and begin the *Quaker City* cruise. The first half of the book is thus a history of his Western experiences, recording his adventures in Nevada and California as a miner and reporter, and concluding with his journey to the Sandwich Islands as a special correspondent. There is about this journey no dominant sense of direction. Instead, the trip dissolves into a series of adventures having so much individual autonomy that, becoming ends in themselves, they take precedence over the continuity of travel. Thus, even on the overland trip, only the sketchiest references are made to place names and landmarks. Nor is the journey seen in terms of crises and turning points; though there are crises, they do not create or govern conditions of the future. Nor does geography organize the trip. South Pass is not a point struggled toward through arduous chapters, but a place name passed in a single sentence. Let any reader try to keep track of the traveler's progress, and he will discover how little authority space and time have in the territory. They are there, to be sure, but they are subordinate, almost buried details in the illusion of experience.

The narrative structure is essentially episodic and anecdotal. The interpolated narratives, the casually arbitrary digressions, and the recollected anecdotes combine, like stagecoach stops on a journey, to break up the narrative. Thus, episodes on the jackass rabbit, the coyote, the pony rider, and the Mexican plug function as entertainments along the route and are left behind in the form of autonomous moments of the past. Though each of these episodes describes an experience of speed, the episodic structure, as if to imitate the movement of the memory, threads its way in leisurely ease through recollections of the frantic past. Despite the frenzy which the episodes recount, the narrative moves with apparently casual abandon. Mark Twain was quite accurate when he observed in his preface that the object of the work was "to help the resting reader while away an idle hour."

Yet the looseness of structure cannot hide a fundamental division in the book. Between beginning and ending, the form has made a radical shift beneath the disguise of the episodes. The Mark Twain telling of his ride on the overland stage is describing an experience which he once had; he is writing autobiography. But the Mark Twain visiting Hawaii is describing his impressions of a landscape; he is writing a book of travel. This shift is customarily seen in geographical rather than in formal terms, and for this reason the Hawaiian portion of the book is usually considered as nothing more than an addition by Mark Twain in an effort to meet the required length of a subscription book. Believing that the Hawaiian travels were not organically related to the Western episodes, a recent editor simply omitted the last eighteen chapters in his edition.[2]

But the shift actually occurs at the beginning of the second volume[3] when Mark Twain starts to tell of his having become a writer. The first volume had begun with a series of expectations and grand anticipations. Upon learning that he was going West with his brother, Mark Twain had "dreamed all night about Indians, deserts, and silver bars. . . ." But the second volume begins with a recollection of the past. Having failed to win a fortune, the narrator summarizes his past, listing one by one the vocations he has tried since he was thirteen years old:

> I had once been a grocery clerk, for one day, but had consumed so much sugar in that time that I was relieved from further duty by the proprietor . . . I had studied law an entire week, and then given it up because it was so prosy and tiresome. I had engaged briefly in the study of blacksmithing, but wasted so much time trying to fix the bellows so that it would blow itself, that the master turned me adrift in disgrace, and told me I would come to no good. I had been a bookseller's clerk . . . I had clerked in a drugstore . . . I had made of myself a tolerable printer, under the impression that I would be another Franklin some day, but somehow had missed the connection thus far. . . . I was a good average St. Louis and New Orleans pilot and by no means ashamed of my abilities in that line . . . I had been a private secretary, a silver-miner and a silver-mill operative, and amounted to less than nothing in each, and now—
> What to do next?

[2] Rodman Paul in the Holt, Rinehart and Winston paperback edition 1953.

[3] The book was originally published as one volume. In the original one-volume edition the break comes at page 292.

This is the moment between the Mark Twain of *experi-ence* and the Mark Twain of *literature*, between Mark Twain the character and Mark Twain the writer. The structure of this moment implicitly defines the structure of the entire book. First of all, there is the dilemma itself. The momentous question of what to do is asked. Instead of answering it, the narrator turns instinctively toward a comic rehearsal of a past which exists much earlier in time than the beginning of his Western journey. But he cannot turn back into that past. The list of vocations brings him inevitably back to the question of going forward. The past behind him is the territory of variety and lazy waywardness—the area of freedom in which he wandered from job to job before settling down to the business of being a salaried reporter. The salary itself is the mark of his new regularity.

The past of Mark Twain the reporter is extremely different from the past of Mark Twain the miner—and the difference is not difficult to define. The Mark Twain of volume one moves in a world of anticipation and expectation. The distinguishing feature of that past is that it has a future. But the past of volume two has no future, no real possibility of change, for Mark Twain has moved from the world of memory to the world of record. On his way to Nevada, the legend of Slade reached his ears before he reached Slade, and the notorious desperado loomed in the traveler's future as a fear to be confronted. But once he is a reporter, Mark Twain, no longer afraid that something will happen, becomes afraid that nothing will happen. On his first full day as a reporter, a murder in a saloon provides his first real story, causing him to express his gratitude to the murderer:

> Sir, you are a stranger to me, but you have done me
> a kindness this day which I can never forget. If
> whole years of gratitude can be to you any slight
> compensation, they shall be yours. I was in trouble
> and you have relieved me nobly and at a time when

all seemed dark and drear. Count me your friend
from this time forth, for I am not a man to forget
a favor.[4]

His only regret, which comes as he reports the event, is
that the murderer was not hanged so that he "could work
him up too." The humor here comes from the impersona
tion of the language of gratitude which converts the
murder into an act of charity.

The situation humorously discloses the plight of Mark
Twain the reporter. Told by his editor never to use such
phrases as "We learn," "It is reported," or "It is rumored,"
as a substitute for going straight to the facts themselves
Mark Twain has to hope for exciting facts. When there
is no "news," he makes it by letting his fancy have free
play with the facts which do exist. Only after extensive
work at reporting does he cease to "require the aid of
fancy to any large extent" and become capable of filling
his columns "without diverging noticeably from the do
main of fact."

The documentary form of the second volume discloses
Mark Twain's increasing reliance upon the domain of
fact. There is a degree of documentation in the first
volume, but nothing to compare with what appears in
the second volume. Chapter openings reflect the direction
of the change. Chapter VIII of the second volume begins
"An extract or two from the newspapers of the day will
furnish a photograph that can need no embellishment."
Here the key words—"extract," "photograph," and "embel
lishment"—disclose how the point of view has shifted
toward reportorial dimensions and away from the shape
of adventure and anticipation. Mark Twain does not, of
course, drop totally into "facts"; instead, he employs a
structure which alternates between fact and anecdote
After the facts of Chapter VIII, Chapter IX begins, "These
murder and jury statistics remind me of a certain very
extraordinary trial and execution of twenty years ago.
But before telling the story of how Captain Ned Blakely

4 *Writings,* VIII, 6.

neted out justice to bullies and offenders, Mark Twain offers a comic apology for the arbitrary structure he is employing. The story is, he reminds his reader, a digression, but then it is his nature to digress; he is simply being himself. By Chapter XI he begins, "Since I desire, in this chapter, to say an instructive word or two about the silver-mines, the reader may take this fair warning and skip, if he chooses." Here he has adopted the eighteenth-century strategy of presenting himself as an eccentric, offering the reader the right to be as capricious in his reading as the author in his writing.

The direction of his caprice becomes fully evident when, in the midst of his instructive word about silver mining, he takes an extract not simply from the newspapers of the time, but from his own writing in the Virginia City *Enterprise*. The past having now been reduced to his own former account of it, Mark Twain is at the threshold of the guidebook form; and in Chapter XIII, when he deals with the Chinese population in Virginia City, the form of *Roughing It* has become indistinguishable from that of *The Innocents Abroad*. Virginia City stands in relation to the narrator precisely as Fayal in the Azores, Paris, Rome, or Jerusalem stood to the travelbook writer of *The Innocents Abroad*. Again in this chapter he falls back on one of his own reports in the *Enterprise*, prefacing his gesture with this remark: "What the Chinese quarter of Virginia was like—or, indeed, what the Chinese quarter of any Pacific coast town was and is like—may be gathered from this item which I printed in the *Enterprise* while reporting for that paper."

By the time he reaches the Sandwich Islands, the past is further reduced to long sections from his diary of the time. Chapter XXIII begins: "In my diary of our third day in Honolulu, I find this. . . ." And at the outset of Chapter XXVI, he says "I still quote from my journal." The entire section of the book devoted to the Sandwich Islands is thus an outcropping of the form Mark Twain tumblingly pursues throughout the second volume. As he moves forward in time toward the moment of *The Inno-cents Abroad*, both he and his book inevitably assume the form which that book had taken—but with a crucial element missing. The sense of discovery which had pervaded the European journey is nowhere to be found. The reason is quite clear. When Mark Twain quotes from his writing prior to the time of *The Innocents Abroad*, he is relying upon a reportorial past prior to his full realization of himself. He is at best completing the history of himself but he is not inventing himself through his creative memory as he had done in the first volume. But of course he cannot—for he is dealing with a past not of memory but a past of record, a past which is history instead of myth

To understand what happens in the second part of *Roughing It* is to begin to understand what happens in the first part. For it was in the first part that Mark Twain discovered the myth of himself. The term "myth" has been used so often and in so many diverse contexts that there are many who have come to distrust the term altogether. Yet Mark Twain is the one writer whose work must finally be considered in terms of myth. He is not a writer who uses myths; he invents them. Lawrence, Yeats, Eliot, Joyce, and Mann have all used myths in the twentieth century, and their literature has served to raise the value of the term in critical discussions. All of these writers have deliberately chosen myth either against the background of the world they lived in or as a means of portraying it. But there is in the very strategy of such choice a genuine anti-mythic tendency, if we mean by myth the drama we instinctively believe rather than an imaginative heritage we choose to adopt. Myth, after all, is the narrative from which we cannot escape. It is what remains after our skepticism trims experience to the core. Yet if myth is consciously adopted, it becomes not the inescapable narrative of our lives but an experience we are trying to recover. It is the forgotten language, the buried life, the undiscovered mode of awareness which, having existed all the time, must be brought up from the depths of the memory or out from behind the appearance of the world. Whether such a myth lies outside or inside the self, its values are discovered through struggle, sacrifice, initiation, and recognition. Sometimes the hero may himself discover the myth, as Alyosha does in *The Brothers Karamazov*; sometimes the reader discovers it ironically by means of characters who never recognize the associative links between themselves and the myth in which they are involved. Sometimes the characters may appear as worthy of the myth behind them, as Adam Verver in *The Golden Bowl*; sometimes the two are startlingly contrasted as in *Ulysses*; sometimes they seem like hopeless degenerations of the myth, as in Eliot's Sweeney poems or in his *Wasteland*. But whether the myth is being rediscovered heroically or revealed ironically, it is being deliberately used.

But the myth of Mark Twain is entirely different. Like Franklin before him and Frost after him, Samuel Clemens engaged in the activity of inventing himself. It is not surprising that Mark Twain, in *Roughing It*, mentions his having wished at one time to be another Franklin. Both his imagination and his life were enough like Franklin's to draw him toward parodying his forerunner.[5] At seventeen, when he first went East as a printer, Samuel Clemens made his way to Philadelphia and visited Franklin landmarks. Sitting on a bench Franklin had once occupied, he wrote home that he had thought of whittling a sliver from it for a souvenir. In San Francisco he had written a sketch singling out for bemused ridicule Franklin's rhyme about early rising. Like Franklin, he too had been a printer's apprentice in his brother's shop. According to his own questionable version of his beginnings, the first piece he had ever written, published while Orion was out of town, had gotten the paper into difficulty. Then too, Mark Twain all his life wanted to be an inventor. One of

[5] The parallel was clearly perceived by Paine (*A Biography*, I, 99).

the chief points of interest in his first trip East had been the patent office, and he never ceased to believe that inventors were the true poets of the world. He worked at inventing scrapbooks, history games, innumerable gadgets, and ultimately put his whole fortune into a typesetting machine. Finally, he turned to the literary form Franklin had early mastered: the epigram. *Pudd'nhead Wilson's New Calendar* reads like an extended inversion of *Poor Richard's Almanac.*

But the literary form Franklin and Mark Twain most fully share is autobiography. Franklin's *Autobiography* is the account of his life reduced to the simplest, most straightforward terms. Franklin transformed himself into a myth, not by inflation, comparison, or association, but by a relentless reduction of experience to terms of self-control in the most literal sense. Freedom for Franklin equaled the master restraint of self-government which translates private life into public action. He almost totally assimilated the inner world of guilt, conscience, compulsion, and imagination into the *act* of rising through the repressive layers of society to a position of power and influence. He likewise drained all significance from the other world of religion, symbol, legend, myth, and history in the act of getting ahead. In his *Autobiography*, Franklin's matter-of-fact life simply displaces both inner and transcendent experience. Franklin himself made clear at the outset that his book was not a memoir,[6] but an action akin to reliving his life. Knowing that no man had the opportunity to repent and amend his life in the way that an author could correct a second edition—the comparison is Franklin's—he observed that "the next Thing most like living one's Life over again, seems to be a *Recollection* of that Life; and to make that Recollection as durable as possible, the putting it down in Writing."[7] The significance of Franklin's

[6] Yet "memoir" was ironically the only extant term Franklin could appropriately apply to his book, since his record clearly was not a confession and since the term "autobiography" did not even exist at the time.

[7] *The Autobiography of Benjamin Franklin*, eds. Leonard W.

act becomes more apparent when the dates of composition are considered. The first part or "installment" of the life is dated 1771, the second, 1784.[8] Thus, between the parts the American Revolution "occurred," but it is mentioned in the text only in passing. Franklin's own "history" displaces the Revolution and is in a sense the myth of the Revolution. In the process Franklin made himself the first American and made his book the first masterpiece of American literature.

Mark Twain is much like Franklin. His myth too is the invention of himself, and his strategy remarkably parallels Franklin's. The world is reduced to terms of the self; the personality becomes the world; personal experience displaces history. Thus the Civil War was in full sway when Mark Twain was in Nevada, but he does not allude to it in the first volume of *Roughing It*. Instead, his commitment is totally to his own experience. Like Franklin, he believes in himself not by an act of will but because there is really nothing else to believe in.

Yet Mark Twain's myth of himself is uniquely distinct. Franklin's *Autobiography* was of himself, but although Mark Twain's life is of "himself," Mark Twain is to a large extent unreal. Franklin's facts run toward the truth; his *Autobiography* is the "true" story of his life. It may omit matters, it may select rigorously, it may be unconsciously wrong about facts, but, as Wayne Shumaker has defined autobiography, it *professes* to tell the truth.[9] Mark Twain, however, is not wholly committed to the truth. Indeed, one of his favorite jokes concerns the difficulty he has in sticking to facts. Whereas Franklin is committed to actuality, Mark Twain's "humor" helplessly leads him away from it.

Labaree, Ralph L. Ketcham, Helen C. Boatfield, and Helene H. Fineman (New Haven, 1964), p. 44.

[8] Actually, Franklin wrote an extended section of the *Autobiography* in 1788 and a brief one in 1790, shortly before his death; but these sections are undated in the text of the book.

[9] Wayne Shumaker, *English Autobiography: Its Emergence, Materials, and Form* (Berkeley, 1954), p. 105.

The fundamental difference inevitably comes back to Mark Twain's pseudonymous identity. The autobiography of Mark Twain is by necessity a particular kind of autobiography; it cannot be straight fact, for Mark Twain himself is not a straight fact until after his signature appears. After February 2, 1863, he is a fact—at least he has a "real" history, a history which constitutes all the work written under his signature. But in the past prior to the appearance of the actual pen name, Mark Twain's life must be *invented*. That invention, which includes the first volume of *Roughing It* and all of "Old Times on the Mississippi" is the autobiography of a pseudonymous figure before the pseudonym became a fact.

These "facts" are the necessities which shape the myth of Mark Twain. Now, of course, Mark Twain's life is based on the life of Samuel Clemens—it is founded on fact, and it can never depart from the basis of Samuel Clemens' life. But the very nature of the humorous Mark Twain is that, while his "life" runs directly in the channel of Samuel Clemens' past, his perspective always involves a measure of divergence. The *truth* of Mark Twain's statements is precisely the skeptical edge to which the discrepancy of his memory forces us. The more the biographer knows about what "really" happened to Samuel Clemens in Nevada, the more he must acknowledge that it is Mark Twain's humor to diverge from fact. The first half of *Roughing It* is at once the invention of Mark Twain and just such a humorous stretcher.

The blind-lead episode at the end of the first volume is the culmination of this divergence. The episode describes how Mark Twain and Calvin Higbie struck a "blind lead"—a vein of ore which, as Mark Twain defines it, does not crop out above the surface and is therefore discovered only when sinking a shaft or driving a tunnel in pursuit of *another* vein. Laying claim to the blind lead, they bask in unparalleled dreams of luxury; but because they fail to validate their claim by working it within the specified period of ten days after discovery, the claim is relocated outside their possession. The reason for their failure, according to the book, is that while Mark Twain was called to help nurse his ailing friend, Captain John Nye, Higbie—usually the soul of reliability—went in pursuit of a legendary cement mine. Both returned moments too late to work their claim. The entire episode depicts the narrator's personal involvement and self-betrayal in the speculative enterprise and thus provides a fitting climax to the experience of mining.

Yet it is the biographer's fate to discover from all available evidence, that the episode has no foundation in fact. There was a Captain Nye, a Calvin Higbie, and a prospecting effort in Esmeralda. And Mark Twain did leave the claim to help attend the ailing Captain Nye. But all available evidence indicates that beyond this point the episode dissolves into fiction. In a letter to his brother Orion at precisely this time, Samuel Clemens speaks of his return to Esmeralda from attending Captain Nye and mentions Higbie, yet makes no reference to their ownership of any blind lead.[10] Apparently the blind lead was a discovery made as Mark Twain pursued the vein of Samuel Clemens' past.

Speculation about the "truth" of an incident would be absurd in the work of many writers. No one expects Charles Dickens to stick to the facts of his past when narrating the life of David Copperfield; the assumption on which the fiction is predicated is that the story of David Copperfield has its own truth which transcends the biography of Dickens. But Mark Twain's autobiography assumes no such thing; instead it insists on its actuality. At the conclusion of the episode, Mark Twain insists:

> It reads like a wild fancy sketch, but the evidence of many witnesses, and likewise that of the official records of the Esmeralda District, is easily obtainable in proof that it is a true history. I can always

[10] Unpublished letter in Mark Twain Papers. Paine published parts of the letter in *Mark Twain's Letters* (2 vols.; New York, 1917), I, 78-79.

have it to say that I was absolutely and unquestionably worth a million dollars, once, for ten days.[11]

It is possible to argue that the reader should take the
statement at face value, but the question immediately
arises, "Why then should the author swear to the truth of
the episode?" An oath, after all, presupposes a doubt, not
a trust. The reader is being given a set of signals which
dare him to investigate the truth of the statement. If he
does investigate, he discovers—or at least patient investi-
gators have discovered—that official records of the Esmeralda District do not verify the truth of the episode.

Failure to discover such verification does not, of course,
mean that the episode is false but only that it *might* be
false. The investigator can never be sure that it is false.
More important, Mark Twain has, by the time he reaches
the last episode in the volume, established enough authority that his closing "assurance" carries a weight which can
never be totally discounted. All that the investigator can
ever do is to intensify his suspicions about the truth of
the story.

The biographer's dilemma is in fact the bitter end of
Roughing It. It is not the inevitable or climactic end—the
relatively free episodic structure precludes such inevitability and climax—but it is certainly the logical and wonderfully probable end for the first volume and may be termed
the absolute tall tale into which the autobiography
evolves. *The Innocents Abroad* pursued the act of impersonation until, at the conclusion of the journey, it evoked
humorous skepticism in relation to expressed attitude.
Roughing It pursues the possibilities of the tall tale, evoking humorous skepticism in relation to event.

The skepticism is the essential act of form in *Roughing
It.* Mark Twain's tall tale at the end of the first volume is
not simply a lie but a way of discovering the truth behind
the lie. For Mark Twain is not, after all, a liar, since his
"humor" is to exaggerate. He ends his preface by observing:

[11] *Writings*, VII, 287.

> Yes, take it all around, there is quite a good deal of information in the book. I regret this very much, but really it could not be helped: information appears to stew out of me naturally, like the precious ottar of roses out of the otter. Sometimes it has seemed to me that I would give worlds if I could retain my facts; but it cannot be. The more I calk up the sources, and the tighter I get, the more I leak wisdom. Therefore, I can only claim indulgence at the hands of the reader, not justification.[12]

The entire narrative of *Roughing It* is actually the exaggeration, the tall tale of Mark Twain. The "information" which leaks out comes both despite and because of the nature of his character.

To see that the ultimate form of *Roughing It* is the tall tale is to begin to see the use Mark Twain was able to make of the tall tale which he appropriated from Southwest humor. The smallest structural manifestation of the tall-tale form is the simple device of comic exaggeration, which seems almost to characterize the humor of the book. Take, for example, the first dream of anticipation which appears in Mark Twain's rapt imagining of what his brother was going to see in the West:

> He was going to travel! I never had been away from home, and that word "travel" had a seductive charm for me. Pretty soon he would be hundreds and hundreds of miles away on the great plains and deserts, and among the mountains of the Far West, and would see buffaloes and Indians, and prairie-dogs, and antelopes, and have all kinds of adventures, and maybe get hanged or scalped, and have ever such a fine time, and write home and tell us all about it, and be a hero.[13]

The entire passage is an exaggeration, but it is narratively plausible until it graduates into the absurdity of the hero's writing home to tell of getting hanged or scalped.

[12] *Ibid.*, p. ix.   [13] *Ibid.*, pp. 1-2.

This passage at the very outset of the book reveals the narrator who is neither innocent and naïve, nor uninitiated. Yet he is never really initiated. Like the author of *The Innocents Abroad*, he is the humorous narrator who keeps experiencing the same disillusion again and again and yet can never change his character. He has no crisis of recognition, no initiation ritual which marks the moment when he becomes a member of the group. The progression in the narrative is not through evolution in the narrator; his comic aspect is precisely his inability to learn, or, rather, his having to learn the same thing again and again. The line of development in the book follows the pattern of this opening passage—from plausibility to absurdity. The development is thus not in the character but in his *telling* of the tale. And he tells the tall tale in this paragraph to entertain the reader.

The entertainment afforded by the tall tale is not simple but complex. The tale emerges in a country without a history and in its rudimentary form is a kind of romance evolved by natives to gull the innocent traveler. The Slade legend is a good example. Hearing the "history" of Slade at the threshold of this land without a history, the narrator not only believes it but greedily devours every word he can about Slade until the very sound of the name possesses a magic for him. Though the actual Slade turns out to be, as far as the narrator can see from the surface of things, a rather ordinary figure, he prefers the romantic version:

> Here was romance, and I sitting face to face with it!—looking upon it—touching it—hobnobbing with it, as it were! Here, right by my side, was the actual ogre who, in fights and brawls and various ways, *had taken the lives of twenty-six human beings*, or all men lied about him! I suppose I was the proudest stripling that ever traveled to see strange lands and wonderful people.[14]

[14] *Ibid.*, p. 70.

The Slade legend is the history the traveler wants to believe in order to make life romantic and exciting. Believing is, after all, a way of making life interesting in a country so barren of entertainment the traveler must hear the same insufferable anecdote about Horace Greeley so many times that he finally threatens to kill a man about to embark upon it. The threat works: "We were saved. But not so the invalid. In trying to retain the anecdote in his system he strained himself and died in our arms."[15]

But the tall tale, in addition to satisfying the universal longing for a "story," also satisfies the longing to deceive the listener and trick him into belief. Thus it contains at its center the humor of the practical joke. It is told to a stranger or scapegoat so that his gullibility affords amusement for the "group," that party of insiders in the community who are privy to the game. The Buncombe trial is a case in point. Buncombe is the officious newcomer who is persuaded to take the case of one Hyde. Hyde's farm, it seems, has been covered by an avalanche which has moved his neighbor Morgan's farm on top of his, and now Morgan is claiming the property where his farm rests! The whole trial is a joke, fixed and formulated by the older citizens as a means of "breaking in" the new lawyer who thinks he knows his law. Of course, the joke is a way of pulling down Buncombe's vanity, but surely it does not enhance the moral status of the Westerners who perpetrate it any more than the coyote's deceiving the town-bred dog enhances the stature of the coyote.

Henry Nash Smith seems to think that value accrues to the coyote and to the community as a result of the lesson they teach.[16] Although their action manages to show that pride amounts to gullibility, the narrator moves on a plane considerably above the mere taking of sides; his humor therefore exposes—though it does not condemn—the essential cruelty at the heart of the practical joke.

[15] *Ibid.*, p. 142.
[16] Smith, *The Development of a Writer*, pp. 55-56, 60.

If *Roughing It* were simply setting the West against the East or the vernacular community against the official culture, Mark Twain's art would have been considerably less humorous and more satiric than it is.

The real triumph of *Roughing It*, particularly in the first volume, is that it realizes the form of the tall tale by converting it into an act of *art*. The episode in the book which best defines the art *and* the tall tale is—or should be—the episode which discloses a man telling a tall tale. That episode, which comes early in the book (Chapter VII), is Bemis' story about the buffalo hunt, an incident important to Mark Twain. He thought so well of it that he proposed to include it in the prospectus Elisha Bliss was preparing to send to his subscription agents.[17]

Everything about the episode is significant. The party has crossed the Platte, that "melancholy stream straggling through the center of the enormous flat plain, and only saved from being impossible to find with the naked eye by its sentinel rank of scattering trees standing on either bank."[18] Having barely managed to escape sinking in its quicksands, the stagecoach—or "mudwagon," as the narrator has come to call it—rushes westward, only to break down 550 miles from St. Joseph. To pass the time, the travelers join a party going for a buffalo hunt:

> It was a noble sport galloping over the plain in the dewy freshness of the morning, but our part of the hunt ended in disaster and disgrace, for a wounded buffalo bull chased the passenger Bemis nearly two miles, and then he forsook his horse and took to a lone tree. He was very sullen about the matter for some twenty-four hours, but at last he began to soften little by little . . .[19]

This introduction discloses the double way in which the tall tale substitutes for something else. Implicitly, Bemis' narrative is an ironic inversion of the "noble sport" of

[17] Hamlin Hill, *Mark Twain and Elisha Bliss* (Columbia, Missouri, 1964), p. 59.
[18] *Writings*, VII, 43.   [19] *Ibid.*, p. 44.

chasing buffaloes. Instead of giving a conventional account of "galloping over the plain in the dewy freshness
of the morning," the narrator substitutes Bemis' tall tale
of being chased by a buffalo. Explicitly on the same
psychological level, the tall tale is, for Bemis, a substitute for anger—it is, in fact, the process by which
Bemis softens up.

The tale itself moves through a series of increasingly absurd improbabilities. Angered because the spectators
had laughed at his predicament, Bemis says he would
have shot a particularly malicious offender had his Allen
revolver not been so "comprehensive" that six or seven
other people would have been crippled. He goes on to
describe his disastrous experience of finding himself pursued by the buffalo. The buffalo, says Bemis, uttered a
bellow "that seemed to literally prostrate my horse's
reason, and make a raving distracted maniac of him, and
I wish I may die if he didn't stand on his head for a
quarter of a minute and shed tears. He was absolutely out
of his mind—he was, as sure as truth itself, and he really
didn't know what he was doing."[20] Once the horse gets
straightened out, however, his speed is terrific:

> First we left the dogs behind; then we passed a
> jack-ass rabbit; then we overtook a coyote, and were
> gaining on an antelope when the rotten girths let go
> and threw me about thirty yards off to the left, and
> as the saddle went down over the horse's rump he
> gave it a lift with his heels that sent it more than
> four hundred yards up in the air, I wish I may die
> in a minute if he didn't.[21]

Falling near the only tree in "nine counties adjacent,"
Bemis struggles up out of reach. He is safe for the time
being, but there is one thing he dreads beyond all others:
that the buffalo bull will climb the tree. To save himself,
Bemis unwinds his lariat (his saddle has miraculously
landed in the tree); when the buffalo *does* climb the tree,

[20] *Ibid.*, p. 45.   [21] *Ibid.*, p. 48.

he slips the noose over the beast's head, and at the same moment fires the revolver at point-blank range:

> When the smoke cleared away, there he was, dangling in the air, twenty foot from the ground, and going out of one convulsion into another faster than you could count! I didn't stop to count, any-how—I shinned down the tree and shot for home.[22]

Long before this point, the listeners have begun to question Bemis' veracity, and when he completes his account he is subjected to a final cross-examination:

> "Bemis, is all that true, just as you have stated it?"
> "I wish I may rot in my tracks and die the death of a dog if it isn't."
> "Well, we can't refuse to believe it, and we don't. But if there were some proofs—"
> "Proofs! Did I bring back my lariat?"
> "No."
> "Did I bring back my horse?"
> "No."
> "Did you ever see the bull again?"
> "No."
> "Well, then, what more do you want? I never saw anybody as particular as you are about a little thing like that."
> I made up my mind that if this man was not a liar he only missed it by the skin of his teeth.[23]

The point is that Bemis is not telling the story to deceive but to entertain his listeners. Moreover, they do not question him in order to catch him in a lie but to encourage him to elaborate more daring departures from probability. He is not telling the tale to take revenge for the laughter at his expense but to keep from taking it; at the end of his account he has nothing but the *absence* of evidence to prove his truth. His only revenge is an entertainment which in a broadly comic yet highly sophisticated way

[22] *Ibid.*   [23] *Ibid.*, pp. 48-49.

sums up the entire action of *Roughing It*, and forecasts its end. For when the bystanders ask Bemis for proof in the face of his insistent assurances and oaths about his truth, they are performing in comic ritual what the reader will privately enact at the conclusion of volume one. Bemis' audacious insistence that the absence of any evidence against him is proof of his veracity would surely be Mark Twain's last response to questions about the truth of the blind-lead episode.

Roughing It enacts in its own terms the "humor" of *The Innocents Abroad*. Bemis' tall tale, like the boys' query about Christopher Columbus, is the broad exposure of the radical skepticism to which Mark Twain's humor ultimately brings the reader. It is the tall tale within the larger tall tale which, like the play within the play in *Hamlet*, at once dramatizes and defines the motive of the form. That motive is the narrator's conversion of his humiliation, failure, and anger into a tall tale which will both move and rouse the listener—move him to laughter and rouse him to skepticism. The tale is not a lie which conceals, but a lie which *exposes* the truth. In a world of lies, the tall tale is the only true lie because it does not mask as the truth but moves the listener to ask what the truth is. Thus the "morality" of the tale does not lie in the substance of the tale or in the community which produces the tale or even in the language of the tale—if we mean by language vernacular as opposed to refined language. All these elements are subordinated to the act of narration and the perspective of the narrator—to the motives which bring forth his lie in a world of lies. Bemis' tall tale and Mark Twain's tall tale which contains it are lies told not to deceive the listener but to make him see that the only truth which can be told is a lie which reveals rather than conceals the fact that it is a lie. The truth is not a series of facts, nor is it a transcendental "reality" hidden behind a world of dreams and shadows. It is rather the skeptical state of mind which the tall tale evokes in the listener, forcing him to maintain a questioning alertness in the face of experience. In fine, the truth is the humorous narrator Mark Twain whose tall tale converts himself, his past, and the American West into the entertainment of *Roughing It*. That entertainment, making us indulgently suspect its departure from veracity, is nonetheless the truth we helplessly enjoy. It is the myth of Mark Twain.

CHAPTER

V

ROMANCE

With "Old Times on the Mississippi," the seven sketches which appeared in the *Atlantic* from January to August, 1875, Mark Twain completed his "autobiography." Though he turned back to autobiography at many times in his career and ended his life submerged in the chaos of his *Autobiography*, his real autobiography, which is to say the *myth* of Mark Twain, ended with "Old Times on the Mississippi." For after inventing Mark Twain as a cub pilot on the Mississippi, never again was Samuel Clemens able to convert his experience into a tall tale which an entire nation would come to believe. The closest he came to such an achievement was in "The Private History of a Campaign that Failed," which dealt with his life as a soldier; but it, like all the autobiographical sketches he was to write, was an interesting performance *by* rather than a discovery *of* Mark Twain. "Old Times," however, was a genuine discovery—one which ended the tall tale of Mark Twain.

The humor of *Roughing It* provides an excellent point of departure for the *Atlantic* sketches. They are, after all, an extension of the "autobiography" of Mark Twain, and the structure of the experience they describe follows much the same pattern of the earlier work. The humor again pivots upon the innocent's confrontation of "experience"; again the expectation of romance constantly dissolves into the disillusion of experience; again there are the strategies of exaggeration, deception, and discovery. Beyond these necessities there is the very material of the past. The tall tale of Mark Twain's life carried Samuel Clemens inevitably backward in time beyond the beginning of *Roughing It* and across the abyss of Civil War to reconstruct the "free" experience of piloting on the great river. Here was a past which, never having been touched by the pen of Mark Twain, lay before Samuel Clemens like a rich, neglected claim.

There is evidence that he had long planned to write a book about the Mississippi. He had alluded to such a project in a letter to his mother in 1866, and again in 1871—just after completing *Roughing It*—he had written to his wife, ". . . when I come to write the Mississippi book, *then* look out! I will spend 2 months on the river & take notes, & I bet you I will make a standard work."[1] But not until William Dean Howells asked him for a contribution to the *Atlantic* did the project become an actuality. At first he wrote Howells that he couldn't think of anything, but wrote again two hours later: ". . . I take back the remark that I can't write for the Jan. number. For Twichell & I have had a long walk in the woods & I got to telling him about old Mississippi days of steamboating glory & grandeur as I saw them (during 5 years) *from the pilot house*. He said 'What a virgin subject to hurl into a magazine!' I hadn't thought of that before. Would you like a series of papers to run through 3 months or 6 or 9?—or about 4 months say?"[2]

The experience which Clemens reconstructed was different in form and substance from *Roughing It*. First of all, it was autobiography completely freed from the conventions of the travel book. *Roughing It*, though autobiographical, was nevertheless the history of a Western journey and even in the first volume of that work there were many instances—as in the excerpts from books upon

[1] *Love Letters*, p. 166.
[2] *The Mark Twain-Howells Letters*, eds. Henry Nash Smith and William Gibson (2 vols.; Cambridge, Mass., 1960), I, 35.

the outlaw Slade—of travel-book conventions employed by the Mark Twain of *The Innocents Abroad*. But in "Old Times" the traveler Mark Twain yields utterly to the apprentice Mark Twain.

For "Old Times on the Mississippi" is the experience of an apprenticeship, not the memory of a journey. It is therefore much more like a humorous initiation than any sequence in *Roughing It*. The apprentice Mark Twain is, after all, learning a discipline—the art of piloting. And since the book is the history of an apprenticeship, the humor focuses on the relationship between master and pupil in a completely realized way that does not exist in *Roughing It*. Although Mark Twain in the West does play the dupe before the society of insiders in a manner forecasting the cub pilot's performance before the society of pilots, he never really assumes the character of the tenderfoot. But the Mark Twain of "Old Times" is the apprentice, and the whole process of learning the river is a long series of defeats and depressions to which the cub's complacent dreams of glory expose him. From the moment when, on the *Paul Jones*, he naïvely offers to bring the mate a capstan bar and blushes under the mate's astonishment and subsequent sarcasm, the apprentice is subjected to a series of embarrassments and humiliations. These are the "lessons" which accompany his factual instruction; they are the price he pays for his romantic expectations in the face of an exacting art.

The greatest humiliation comes when Bixby, the master pilot, exposes the cub's ignorance and cowardice before an assembled audience in the pilot house. This ultimate failure constitutes the successful completion of Bixby's arduous river lesson. In terms of the structure of "Old Times," the episode corresponds almost exactly to the blind-lead incident of *Roughing It*. The blind lead is the final disillusion in the quest for fortune; the public humiliation is the last embarrassment in gaining entrance to the fraternity of pilots—the last exposure of the apprentice. Moreover, the humiliation scene marks the real end of "Old Times" in the same way that the blind-lead episode completed the imaginative structure of *Roughing It*. The first five sketches are built around the experience of the apprenticeship. But the last two sketches—comprising Chapters XIV through XVII of *Life on the Mississippi*—detail a history of the pilot's monopoly and racing days on the Mississippi. Interlarded with anecdote and conscious memories, these closing sketches assume the dimensions of the second volume of *Roughing It*. Quite clearly, Mark Twain had exhausted his narrative structure and was driven toward an historical form, in which the past was being recorded more than remembered. The central motive having run its course, the narrative impulse was exhausted; only the subject of piloting remained. And Mark Twain, who in the exuberance of the early sketches had written Howells that he could write a hundred papers on piloting, found himself incapable of continuing, despite Howells' unfailing encouragement and requests for more. Interestingly enough, Mark Twain felt that the sixth sketch—detailing the rank and dignity of piloting as well as the rise and fall of the pilot's monopoly—was the logical conclusion to the sketches. Writing to Howells about the matter he said:

> But No. 6 closes the series first-rate with the death of piloting, & needs no postscript. Therefore I would suggest that you leave out this No. 7 entirely & let the articles end with the June No. On the whole I should think that would be the neatest thing to do. I retire with dignity, then, instead of awkwardly.
>
> There is a world of river stuff to write about, but I find it won't cut up into chapters, worth a cent. It needs to run right along, with no breaks but imaginary ones.[3]

The structural hiatus which asserts itself in each of these autobiographical works is evidence of the necessity under which Mark Twain labored. The problem lies in the nature of the humorous character who cannot really

[3] *Ibid.*, p. 85.

change. In *Roughing It*, the crisis had involved the transformation from miner to writer. Unable to change his "character," which is to say his characteristic perspective, Mark Twain broke the structure of the book into two pasts—the past of experience, which could be invented; and the past of the career, the recorded past.

But in "Old Times," all the past is in its way "experience," yet the same structural difficulty appears. Even so, the problem is essentially the same. The narrator has moved to that point in experience where, occupation having superseded initiation, he will have to tell about his successes as a pilot instead of his failures as an apprentice. His whole identity as a character, however, arises from the failure of his experience to conform to his dreams. That failure is the substance of Mark Twain's humor. As pilot he could no longer be the fool to a Bixby; he would have had to invent a fool for himself, or describe the inner change by which he became a pilot, either of which would have been outside the realm of his humor. His determination to end the series reflects his instinctive awareness of the impasse he had reached. Had he broken off the series with the sixth sketch, the structural lesion would not have been evident; but with the addition of the seventh sketch enough weight was added beyond the break in structure to make the lesion visible. Indeed, the sixth sketch forms a fairly lucid and logical conclusion to the experience by providing an historical perspective on the power and greatness of the river pilots' organization; certainly the episodic structure of the narrative allowed for such a concluding movement. Yet the luxury of a perorative ending was largely alien to Mark Twain's humorous forms, depending as they did on anticlimax, interrupted departures, and abrupt foreclosures rather than grand finale and fulfillment. Moreover, Howells was begging for more sketches. With the addition of the seventh sketch, however, the summary effect of the sixth sketch was lost and Mark Twain simply had to break off his narrative as best he could. Fortunately, he could simply stop. Had he been meeting the demands of a subscription contract he would have had to continue the process of merely adding materials to meet the required length. But the relation he had with Howells and the *Atlantic* enabled him to escape the issue more successfully than he had been able to do in *Roughing It*. Not only could he stop when he wished, but the relative independence of the sketches coupled with their serial publication almost completely camouflaged the structural crisis. Most important, he had the happy inspiration of concluding the final sketch with an account of a pilot, one Stephen, who in the traditional position of the unfortunate debtor, succeeded in so haunting his creditor with prolonged accounts of his intentions to pay that the creditor fled at sight of his tormentor. The elaborately humorous inversion stands as a fitting end to a series of episodes devoted to the apprenticeship of a cub whose success lay always in abject failure.

To see *Roughing It* as a tall tale is to see how Mark Twain modified the form when he came to write "Old Times on the Mississippi." Though the character in both books is "Mark Twain," and though the structural problem of *Roughing It* reappears in "Old Times," a new dimension of Mark Twain appears in this second stage of the autobiography. Here Mark Twain learns a trade in a long series of humorous trials. The essence of this act of learning is usually located in a particular passage—the most familiar passage in "Old Times on the Mississippi" and one of the most frequently quoted in all of Mark Twain—which mourns the loss of romance involved in the recognition of reality. The passage, which concludes the third sketch, is revealing in so many ways that it deserves quoting at length. Having learned the place names of all river landmarks, having assimilated the shape of the river, and having pondered the face of the water, the cub asks his mentor Bixby how to tell a wind reef from a bluff reef when the two crucially different phenomena look exactly alike. Bixby replies, "I can't tell you. It is an instinct. By and by you will just naturally *know* one from another, but you will never be able to explain why or how you know them apart." Thus, beyond the absolutely essential knowledge and memory of the river, the pilot finally must have instinct—a deeply implicit and discriminating sensitivity to the face of the water. At this point, Mark Twain drops into the passage in question:

It turned out to be true. The face of the water, in time, became a wonderful book—a book that was a dead language to the uneducated passenger, but which told its mind to me without reserve, delivering its most cherished secrets as clearly as if it uttered them with a voice. And it was not a book to be read once and thrown aside, for it had a new story to tell every day. . . . The passenger who could not read it was charmed with a peculiar sort of faint dimple on its surface . . . but to the pilot that was an *italicized* passage . . . for it meant that a wreck or a rock was buried there that could tear the life out of the strongest vessel that ever floated. . . . In truth, the passenger who could not read this book saw nothing but all manner of pretty pictures in it, painted by the sun and shaded by the clouds, whereas to the trained eye these were not pictures at all, but the grimmest and most dead-earnest of reading matter.

Now when I had mastered the language of this water, and had come to know every trifling feature that bordered the great river as familiarly as I knew the letters of the alphabet, I had made a valuable acquisition. But I had lost something, too. . . . All the grace, the beauty, the poetry, had gone out of the majestic river! I still kept in mind a certain wonderful sunset which I witnessed when steamboating was new to me. A broad expanse of the river was turned to blood; in the middle distance the red hue brightened into gold, through which a solitary log came floating, black and conspicuous; in one place a long, slanting mark lay sparkling upon the water; in another the surface was broken

by boiling, tumbling rings, that were as many-tinted
as an opal; where the ruddy flush was faintest, was
a smooth spot that was covered with graceful circles
and radiating lines, ever so delicately traced; the
shore on our left was densely wooded, and the
somber shadow that fell from this forest was broken
in one place by a long, ruffled trail that shone like
silver; and high above the forest wall a clean-
stemmed dead tree waved a single leafy bough that
glowed like a flame in the unobstructed splendor
that was flowing from the sun. There were graceful curves, reflected images, woody heights, soft
distances; and over the whole scene, far and near,
the dissolving lights drifted steadily, enriching it
every passing moment with new marvels of color-
ing.

I stood like one bewitched. I drank it in, in a
speechless rapture. . . . But as I have said, a day
came when I began to cease from noting the glories
and the charms which the moon and the sun and
the twilight wrought upon the river's face; another
day came when I ceased altogether to note them. . . .
No, the romance and beauty were all gone from the
river. All the value any feature of it had for me
now was the amount of usefulness it could furnish
toward compassing the safe piloting of a steamboat.
Since those days, I have pitied doctors from my
heart. What does the lovely flush in a beauty's cheek
mean to a doctor but a "break" that ripples above
some deadly disease? . . . And doesn't he sometimes
wonder whether he has gained most or lost most
by learning his trade?[4]

It is not difficult to see why this passage is so often
quoted. It is a passage about art, and the scarcity of

[4] *Mark Twain: Representative Selections*, ed. Fred Lewis Pattee
(New York, 1935), pp. 266-69. I cite this text because there is
unfortunately no separate edition of "Old Times on the Mississippi." Mark Twain incorporated the sketches intact, with very
minor changes, into *Life on the Mississippi*, published eight years
later. The sketches form Chapters IV-XVII of the later book, each
sketch comprising two chapters. Pattee's text follows the original
Atlantic text.

such extended passages in Mark Twain's writing trebles the value of those which do appear. Moreover, the attitude expressed seems to provide a key to Mark Twain's position relative to romance and realism, those key terms in the literary history of the period. Yet the content of the passage has often prevented readers from seeing its elaborately mannered style, mounted like a gem for the reader to pocket as an assurance that Mark Twain is at heart a "serious" writer.[5] The entire passage with its conventionalized pretentiousness hovers along the borderline of two or three grandiose clichés. The extended metaphor of the river as book is fairly convincing but hardly fresh or bold. And the entire image of the sunset is quite clearly a verbalized approximation of a chromo. When the writer speaks of being "bewitched" and held in "speechless rapture," his language is recapitulating the standard pattern of genteel "appreciation." Finally, in the peroration, with the rhetorical question involving the plight of the doctor surveying the "lovely flush in a beauty's cheek," the Mark Twain of the *Atlantic* is impersonating the language of stylized genteel disillusion instead of inventing the humorous disillusion which characterizes the apprenticeship. It is but one more example of Mark Twain's vaunted seriousness which threatens, under scrutiny, to dissolve into burlesque. The passage seems more serious than anything in *The Innocents Abroad* because the sketches depend for their humor upon character and situation, rather than upon impersonation. Lacking the countervailing presence of burlesque, Mark Twain's identity is almost submerged by the genteel rhetoric.

The threadbare conclusion of the passage discloses the sterile nature of the elaborate literary analogy on which the rhetorical flight began. The whole passage is a sentiment masquerading as a thought, and all that can be really said of it is that the sentiment is relevant to the action of "Old Times on the Mississippi"—relevant but not

[5] Henry Nash Smith shrewdly perceived the genteel quality of the passage (*Development of a Writer*, pp. 78-80).

revelatory. For the narrator is, after all, describing his aesthetic "apprenticeship"; the "beauty" which he is verbally recreating is precisely the whole sentimental tradition of art which he must slough off if he is to learn the *art* of piloting. The sentimental, romantic view is itself the danger which blinds him to the reality of the river. This sloughing off the "romance" of the river is the cost of learning to be an artist on and of the river—which is what a pilot really is. Yet being a pilot is a much grander achievement than merely sloughing off sentimentality in favor of grim realism.

For "Old Times on the Mississippi" is not hard-boiled in its attitude. It is itself "romantic"; in fact, the entire act of "Old Times" is the humorous romance which Samuel Clemens puts in place of the sentimental romance he discards. The passage in question merely states what has to be done before genuine vision can take place. The vision itself is best exemplified at the beginning of the first sketch:

> When I was a boy, there was but one permanent ambition among my comrades in our village on the west bank of the Mississippi River. That was, to be a steamboatman. We had transient ambitions of other sorts, but they were only transient. When a circus came and went, it left us all burning to become clowns; the first negro minstrel show that came to our section left us all suffering to try that kind of life; now and then we had a hope that, if we lived and were good, God would permit us to be pirates. These ambitions faded out, each in its turn; but the ambition to be a steamboatman always remained.
>
> Once a day a cheap, gaudy packet arrived upward from St. Louis, and another downward from Keokuk. Before these events had transpired, the day was glorious with expectancy; after they had transpired, the day was a dead and empty thing. Not only the boys, but the whole village, felt this. After all these years I can picture that old time to my-

self now, just as it was then: the white town drows-
ing in the sunshine of a summer's morning; the
streets empty, or pretty nearly so; one or two clerks
sitting in front of the Water Street stores, with their
splint-bottomed chairs tilted back against the wall,
chins on breasts, hats slouched over their faces,
asleep—with shingle-shavings enough around to
show what broke them down; a sow and a litter of
pigs loafing along the sidewalk, doing a good business in water-melon rinds and seeds; two or three
lonely little freight piles scattered about the "levee";
a pile of "skids" on a slope of the stone-paved wharf,
and the fragrant town drunkard asleep in the shadow of them; two or three wood flats at the head
of the wharf, but nobody to listen to the peaceful
lapping of the wavelets against them; the great
Mississippi, the majestic, the magnificent Mississippi, rolling its mile-wide tide along, shining in
the sun; the dense forest away on the other side;
the "point" above the town, and the "point" below, bounding the river-glimpse and turning it into
a sort of sea, and withal a very still and brilliant
and lonely one. Presently a film of dark smoke
appears above one of those remote "points"; in-
stantly a negro drayman, famous for his quick eye
and prodigious voice, lifts up the cry, "S-t-e-a-m-boat
a-comin'!" and the scene changes! The town drunkard stirs, and clerks wake up, a furious clatter of
drays follows, every house and store pours out a
human contribution, and all in a twinkling the dead
town is alive and moving. Drays, carts, men, boys,
all go hurrying from many quarters to a common
center, the wharf. Assembled there, the people
fasten their eyes upon the coming boat as upon a
wonder they are seeing for the first time. And the
boat *is* a rather handsome sight, too. She is long and
sharp and trim and pretty; she has two tall, fancy-
topped chimneys, with a gilded device of some kind
swung between them; a fanciful pilot-house, all
glass and "gingerbread," perched on top of the
"texas" deck behind them; the paddle-boxes are

gorgeous with a picture or with gilded rays above
the boat's name; the boiler-deck, the hurricane deck,
and the texas deck are fenced and ornamented with
clean white railings; there is a flag gallantly flying
from the jack-staff; the furnace doors are open and
the fires glaring bravely; the upper decks are black
with passengers; the captain stands by the big
bell, calm, imposing, the envy of all; great volumes
of the blackest smoke are rolling and tumbling out
of the chimneys—a husbanded grandeur created
with a bit of pitchpine just before arriving at a
town; the crew are grouped on the forecastle; the
broad stage is run far out over the port bow, and
an envied deck-hand stands picturesquely on the
end of it with a coil of rope in his hand; the pent
steam is screaming through the gauge-cocks; the
captain lifts his hand, a bell rings, the wheels stop;
then they turn back, churning the water to foam,
and the steamer is at rest. Then such a scramble
as there is to get aboard, and to get ashore, and to
take in freight and to discharge freight, all at one
and the same time; and such a yelling and cursing
as the mates facilitate it all with! Ten minutes later
the steamer is under way again, with no flag on
the jack-staff and no black smoke issuing from the
chimneys. After ten more minutes the town is dead
again, and the town drunkard asleep by the skids
once more.[6]

In reaching backward in time for the substance of this
passage, Mark Twain made a great step forward in the
act of inventing himself. Quite clearly this is the "romance" which displaces the sentimental "appreciation"
he discarded. Yet it is not a romance which avoids "reality" or fails to detect the fundamental sham which is so
integral a part of the picture. The town itself is no lovely
pastoral—the hogs are moving among the watermelon
rinds, the accumulated freight and piles of skids are not
"beautiful" subjects; and the steamboat is not really

[6] *Mark Twain: Representative Selections*, pp. 236-38.

grand, but a "cheap, gaudy packet" with gilding, gingerbread, and an element of sham present in her entire appearance. Even the smoke which issues from her chimneys is part of the "husbanded grandeur" of the occasion.
She has precisely the glamor which charms the apathy
of the village.

Yet the adjective "realistic," as it is ordinarily understood, fails to characterize the vision. Though the details
are part of the scene, and though they stand in ironic relation to the wonder which the scene recovers, the emphasis on the wonder is dominant. The governing action
of the passage is the recovery of the wonder, the memory
of anticipation; its tenor is really more romantic than
realistic—if these overworked terms have any actual
meaning—but the memory preserves as well as notes the
discrepancies at the center of the romance. Mark Twain's
nostalgia is rarely if ever a simple longing for or cele-
bration of the past. Irony is, even in so "happy" a recollection as this one, such a clear and present undertone
as to be considered an integral part of the memory which
strives to make the past into the present tense.

It is possible to object that the initial passage of "Old
Times" is not really typical. As a matter of fact, it is not
typical—the particular quality of its prose tone is never
repeated in the seven sketches. The passage is actually
an overture, an introduction which holds in lyric suspension the various aspects of the narrative which follows. It is an embodying projection of the memory out
of which the narrative is to flow. As such an expression,
it reveals much—reveals the apathy of the village, the
splendor the steamboats had in the eyes of the provincial
villagers, the cheap gaudiness characterizing the gorgeous
style put on by the steamboatmen, and the longing desire of youth to participate in such a glory. The steamboat itself is a floating palace to the villagers; it is a
flamboyant stage exploiting and mimicking the clichés
of traditional fantasy. The "romance" it represents is at
once genuine and sham in the eye of the reconstructing

memory—genuine to the villagers who have no standard of comparison, a sham to the mature memory which notes the discrepancies of its imitation and veneer.

This combination of anticipation and irony is only a part of Mark Twain's romantic vision. The added element in his scene is the river itself, the "great Mississippi, the majestic, the magnificent Mississippi rolling its mile-wide tide along, shining in the sun; the dense forest away on the other side; the 'point' above the town, and the 'point' below, bounding the river glimpse and turning it into a sort of sea, and withal a very still and brilliant and lonely one." The river and the forest are the great stage against which the gorgeous steamboats and their crews perform. The river is, throughout the course of the sketches, the larger scene defining the actions which take place upon it. It is the central fact of the sketches; and the entire action of the apprenticeship is a discovery of its reality. Mark Twain, who set out to explore the Amazon, turns out to discover the river which is literally at his feet. And the river is the element within the scene itself giving perspective to all the values which emerge. In the face of its genuine majesty and magnificence, the imitation grandeur and childish fantasies of the life upon it are revealed.

"Old Times on the Mississippi" is Mark Twain's return to the river on which Samuel Clemens had once been a pilot. For Samuel Clemens, mastering the river had no doubt been the fiercely complex act of becoming a pilot. For Mark Twain the river was the avenue into a world where his humorous genius would achieve its full realization. As the image of reality and power for him, the river constituted the central stage property of the drama he was to project; and in discovering it as a writer, he was literally beginning to translate the power which he had absorbed from it as a boy and young man.

The fullness of this translation can best be seen by looking at a typical passage of the notebook Samuel Clemens kept as a pilot on the Mississippi. The notebook was

nothing more or less than the pilot's guide to "run" the
river, and the young pilot Samuel Clemens had carefully
filled it with obscure shorthand and directions involving
place names, landmarks, and shifting danger signs. For
Wolf Island Bend he instructed himself as follows:

> Get far enough bel upper bch to get S *against* it,
> then pull a little above old warehouse ¼ m below
> Gray's—it is ½ m above Jones'. U.S.—st fm any
> where above Jones Say [Beptaizths] W house & wear
> slow out to pt of bar, up opp W house & over.
> D.S.—h on Jones till clear of upper bar, then pull
> *almost* plum on Way's. Later—S on Jones, h on pt
> of bar shap l. h. bar (Chalk Bnks—S on little dwell
> house, 800 bel Grays, h lying against the bch aft—
> shap r. h. bar, 300 fm it. (These are pt. S. marks.)
> no bottom. 3 bchs (& 1 [on ext.] pt.) (hol. f. pt
> Dougherty's Ldg, 2d little field above pt—(double
> white house). Gray's Ldg. big white house under,
> pt. head of Bend. Allen's on extreme pt below Wolf—
> Beckwith—Jones—Farris—Dougherty—Ayres on Pt.[7]

[7] This passage appears on pp. 3-4 in Samuel Clemens first
piloting notebook (pp. 13-14 in the typescript of Notebook #1 in
the Mark Twain Papers). Mr. Allan Bates, who is preparing an
edition of *Life on the Mississippi*, offers the following tentative
"translation":

> Get far enough below upper beech to get Stern *against* it, then
> pull a little above old warehouse ¼ mile below Gray's—it is ½
> mile above Jones's. Upstream—start from anywhere above Jones,
> say Beckwith's warehouse, and bear slow out to point of sand
> bar, up opposite warehouse and over. Downstream—head on
> Jones [that is, a staff on the bow of the boat must be lined up
> with Jones's house] till clear of upper bar, then pull almost
> plumb on Gray's. Later—Stern on Jones [looking to the stern, a
> staff on the boat must be lined up toward Jones's house], head
> on point of bar, shape left hand bar [follow along the sand bar].
> (Chalk Banks [these banks were prominent landmarks which
> would identify a position on the river, but they probably were too
> large to steer by].) Stern on little dwelling house, 800 feet be-
> low Gray's, head lying against the beech aft [the upstream beech
> tree]—shape right hand bar, 300 feet from it. (These are point
> stern marks.) [He probably means that he is to judge the dis-
> tance from the stern of the steamboat.] Water depth is good:
> the leaded line did not reach the bottom of the river. Three

Mark Twain in all probability did not have access to this private and technical language of Samuel Clemens, for the notebook which contained the directions lay stored in Charles Webster's attic in Fredonia, New York, and Mark Twain did not come across it until December, 1880, more than five years after he had written the sketches.[8]

But the translation occurred all the same, for in those sketches Mark Twain did what he had been doing throughout his "autobiography." The past, which had been devoted to an act of learning the particular details of a vocation, he reconstructed and enlarged into the mastering of an art. He had in 1874 and 1875 reached back to that whole domain from which the very name of his genius had been taken and had defined himself in the act of learning to be an artist. In remembering Samuel Clemens' apprenticeship in 1857 before the Civil War, Mark Twain was in 1875 actually reaching the end of his autobiography. The past which he was reconstructing involved learning to be a pilot; the act of reconstruction involved learning to be a full-fledged artist. Thus, though the life of the pilot carried Mark Twain backward in time from the life of a miner, the reconstruction of the memory carried him forward in the career of art.

And "Old Times on the Mississippi" does represent a great step forward. In sheer performance, Mark Twain had never succeeded so well in moving through a complex experience with such economy of space. The economy was a direct result of a genuine dramatic structure. The essential difference between the sketches and *Roughing It* is to be measured by the development and importance of the master pilot Bixby. He occupies a place of

---

beeches (and one on [word illegible] point) hold for point. Dougherty's Landing is the second little field above the point—(double white house). Gray's Landing is the big white house under the point at the head [upstream end] of the Bend. Allen's is on the extreme point below Wolf Island—In order downstream are Beckwith—Jones—Farris—[a second] Dougherty—Ayres is on the point.

[8] I am indebted to Frederick Anderson for this information.

command in the short space of the sketches that no character ever manages to acquire in the entire two volumes
of *Roughing It*. Whereas the progress of *Roughing It* was
built around the adventures of the traveler encountering
the varied experiences on the road and in the territory,
"Old Times" is much more like a succession of performances by a vaudeville company featuring the team of
Bixby and his cub pilot. Such a structure both made possible and required a synthesis between information and
humor which the genre of *Roughing It* tended to pro-
hibit.[9] Thus, in the exchanges between Bixby and his cub,
an incredible amount of "information" about piloting is
transmitted not in addition to the humor but as part of
it. Bixby and his cub, though reminiscent of the primitive
Mr. Brown-Mr. Twain axis, actually represent a great
advance. For Bixby and the cub, dramatizing much more
than alternate styles and attitudes, create between them
a dialectic which converts the pain of learning and the
shame of failure into an act of entertainment.

The episodes are really the series of "acts" featuring
the two characters miming master and apprentice—Bixby
outraged and consternated at the cub's ignorance, the cub
incredulous at the master's skill and knowledge. Thus,
at Jones's Plantation, the cub cannot believe that anything
but an accident could have enabled Bixby to discover a
particular end of the plantation on a pitch dark night.
At another time, in a performance demonstrating that

[9] The form of the humorous travel book required both entertainment and information, a demand which Mark Train met by
alternating humorous episodes and serious, informative chapters.
He pursued the same arrangement in his lectures. Writing to Livy
in 1871 after a lecture in Bennington, Vermont, he observed:
"Any lecture of mine ought to be a running narrative-plank with
square holes in it, six inches apart, all the length of it, & then
in my mental shop I ought to have plugs (half marked 'serious'
& the other marked 'humorous') to select from & jam into these
holes according to the temper of the audience." In describing
literature and literary creation, Mark Twain was very likely to
employ analogies from trade and technology which "lowered" the
subject. Thus, he spoke of inspiration as his "inspiration tank,"
which he had to let fill up when it ran low.

Bixby is no ordinary pilot impressing a novice, Bixby pilots his steamboat through the precarious Hat Island Crossing before an admiring audience, which includes the cub and the whole society of pilots. The presence of the inside audience emphasizes that the episodes are as much acts as action. The two characters are not so much historical or "real" personages as they are actors engaged in performances. Their essentially theatrical identity makes possible a perspective of pleasurable indulgence upon the recollected action, converting the humiliation of the past into genuinely pleasurable performances.

For "Old Times on the Mississippi" enacts just such a conversion. Thus, although the book is about an apprenticeship, the cub never really learns. At least he is never seen learning. Instead, he continually fails to learn, while Bixby administers harsher and harsher lessons of humiliation, the last of which constitutes the climax of the sketches. Significantly enough, this last lesson, coming at the end of the fifth sketch, takes the form of a public humiliation. In the third sketch, Bixby, pretending to go below, had hidden in the pilot house to watch his pupil's mounting fright at what seemed to be a dangerous bluff reef but was actually a harmless wind reef. Remaining concealed until Mark Twain in desperation almost rammed the bank in an effort to escape the reef, he had stepped forth calmly, rescued the steamboat from imminent disaster, and inquired with mock-innocent sarcasm why his protégé had attempted a landing.

But this had been a "private" lesson. The public humiliation comes after the cub has become a good steersman and has once more given way to his irrespressible vanity. Leaving his conceited apprentice alone at the wheel in apparently safe water, Bixby asks a parting question designed to disconcert him. This is only the beginning. The master has instructed the leadsman to give false reports of the river depth and has also told officers to come into the pilot house to watch the proceedings.

Already ruffled by Bixby's taunting question about the

safety of the river, the cub experiences mounting apprehension as the onlookers begin to assemble. When the leadsman's cries break the stillness, he is seized with panic:

> Then came the leadsman's sepulchral cry:
> "D-e-e-p four!"
> Deep four in a bottomless crossing! the terror of it took my breath away.
> "M-a-r-k three! M-a-r-k three! Quarter-less three! Half twain!"
> This was frightful. I seized the bell-ropes and stopped the engines.
> "Quarter twain! Quarter twain! *Mark* twain."
> I was helpless. I did not know what in the world to do. I was quaking from head to foot, and I could have hung my hat on my eyes, they stuck out so far.
> "Quarter-less-twain! Nine-and-a-half!"
> We were drawing nine! My hands were in a nerveless flutter. I could not ring a bell intelligibly with them. I flew to the speaking-tube and shouted to the engineer:
> "Oh, Ben, if you love me, *back* her! Quick, Ben! Oh, back the immortal soul out of her!"
> I heard the door close gently. I looked around, and there stood Mr. Bixby, smiling a bland, sweet smile. Then the audience on the hurricane deck sent up a thunder gust of humiliating laughter. I saw it all, now, and I felt meaner than the meanest man in human history.[10]

This last humiliation to which the cub is exposed marks the end of the apprenticeship, the last torture of the initiation. It is no accident that the term "Mark Twain" appears in the center of the episode. Having discovered the pseudonym in Nevada, Samuel Clemens had in 1875 at last moved backward in time to recover the context from which the name had been transported. This was the second time in the series of sketches when he had actually used the term; the other had been in the second sketch

[10] *Mark Twain: Representative Selections*, pp. 293-94.

when Bixby ran the Hat Island crossing. In that episode the term had appeared at a moment when an heroic act was in the making—an act which evoked an aesthetic ecstasy in the audience. "It was done beautiful—beautiful!" exclaims one of the onlookers of Bixby's consummate mastery of the steamboat. And in each episode the term "Mark Twain" is a signal for danger, not for safe water, which shows how inadequate the conventional understanding of the term actually is.

The entire episode goes far toward defining Mark Twain. First of all, it is professedly from his own experience; second, it deals with the context from which his name was taken; third, it sounds his name in its original context; finally, the episode casts Mark Twain as the shamed dupe of a practical joke, the object of humiliating scorn and laughter. It is a situation which in one form or another appears again and again in the works of Samuel Clemens, and here as elsewhere, the narrator is the victim. It is impossible to say what deep humiliation lay at the core of Samuel Clemens' consciousness, causing him to dramatize it again and again in what may have been an endless effort to exorcise the memory. But it is quite possible to define the episode in relation to the Mark Twain of "Old Times on the Mississippi."

The humiliation is the searing memory of public shame which the humorous artist, in the very act of recounting as a joke on himself, is able to convert into pure and overt pleasure without taking vengeance on anyone else. The whole process, for all the apparent ease with which it is accomplished, requires all the art of a pilot on the Mississippi. The two acts—the skill of piloting and the art of humor—are triumphantly united in this series of sketches. Thus, Mark Twain in the very act of defining himself— in naming his number, as it were—creates in Bixby the supreme pilot of the great Mississippi.

The best example of Bixby's instruction is in his effort to teach the hopeless cub the shape of the river. Upon asking whether he has to know the million variations of shape along the river banks, the cub is informed that he has to know them better than he knows the halls of his own home. Bixby goes on to say:

> "You see, this has got to be learned; there isn't any getting around it. A clear starlight night throws such heavy shadows that, if you didn't know the shape of a shore perfectly, you would claw away from every bunch of timber, because you would take the black shadow of it for a solid cape; and you see you would be getting scared to death every fifteen minutes by the watch. You would be fifty yards from shore all the time when you ought to be within twenty feet of it. You can't see a snag in one of those shadows, but you know exactly where it is, and the shape of the river tells you when you are coming to it. Then there's your pitch dark night; the river is a very different shape on a pitch dark night from what it is on a starlight night. All shores seem to be straight lines, then, and mighty dim ones, too; and you'd *run* them for straight lines, only you know better. You boldly drive your boat into what seems to be a solid, straight wall (you knowing very well that in reality there is a curve there), and that wall falls back and makes way for you. Then there's your gray mist. You take a night when there's one of these grisly, drizzly, gray mists, and then there isn't *any* particular shape to a shore. A gray mist would tangle the head of the oldest man that ever lived. Well, then, different kinds of *moonlight* change the shape of the river in different ways. You see—"
>
> "Oh, don't say any more, please! Have I got to learn the shape of the river according to all these five hundred thousand different ways? If I tried to carry all that cargo in my head it would make me stoop-shouldered."
>
> "No! you only learn *the* shape of the river; and you learn it with such absolute certainty that you can always steer by the shape that's *in your head*, and never mind the one that's before your eyes."[11]

[11] *Ibid.*, 258-59.

Whereas in *Roughing It* the dialectic between tall tale and straight fact produced the effect of leading to doubt of all facts, the exchange between Bixby and his cub creates the absolute fact of the mysterious river. Bixby's flamboyant exaggerations, instead of casting doubt upon his veracity, serve instead to emphasize the reality and power of the Mississippi. The reality of the West had been its unreality; the ever-shifting appearance of the Mississippi is the assurance of its reality. It had been the pilot's art in 1857 to discover and retain the shape of the river which lay beneath the myriad variations of its banks. The humorist's art in 1875 lay in reconstructing through the creative memory the apprenticeship which would at once recover and translate the lost river of experience. Having traveled first to the storied East and then to the fabled West only to discover that the truth of Eastern time and Western space lay in the radical skepticism of the humor which confronted them, Mark Twain had discovered in the river of his youth the reality which would sustain him in his reconstruction of the past. Yet the river he would celebrate was not the river of his past so much as it was the river "in his head"—the timeless shape which would become the natural heart of the childhood world he was about to invent. That invention was to be the form of fiction.

Roughing It and "Old Times on the Mississippi" had carried the autobiography of Mark Twain backward in time by successive stages to the threshold of Samuel Clemens' boyhood. With *The Adventures of Tom Sawyer*, Mark Twain crossed into the enchanted territory of childhood, where he was to make his greatest discoveries as a writer. It is possible to argue that he had crossed the threshold before completing "Old Times," for *Tom Sawyer* was actually begun before the first *Atlantic* sketch was written. In a real sense, the beginning of *Tom Sawyer* may have made possible "Old Times" itself, for in terms of chronology of composition, "Old Times" comes between the beginning and end of *Tom Sawyer*. Certainly the two books illuminate each other. For although the opening passage of "Old Times" is an overture to the sketches, its tone and substance are much more characteristic of the *matter* of *Tom Sawyer*. The cub Mark Twain has more in common with the boy Tom Sawyer than he probably had with the young Sam Clemens who became a pilot in 1857. The boy and the cub are so much alike that at times their experience almost seems to merge. Indeed, the scene in "Old Times" in which a certain "Tom" steals the cub's girl by virtue of a lucky escape could easily double as an adventure of Tom Sawyer. Though Samuel Clemens was twenty-two when he became a pilot, the cub Mark Twain seems scarcely older than Tom Sawyer; he is a pre-adolescent, interested in nothing but puppy love, and his fantasies are essentially the same as Tom's.

Short though the step is from the cub pilot to the dreaming boy, it involves a passage from one world to another. For in crossing the frontier dividing apprenticeship from boyhood, Mark Twain made the great transition from tall tale to fiction. The necessity which defined Mark Twain's life had been the experience of Samuel Clemens. Although Mark Twain might enlarge and be an enlargement upon that experience, he was nonetheless held in bondage to it by the ligature of actuality. The fictive element in the reconstruction of the past was actually an aspect of the humorous personality—it was, after all, Mark Twain's *humor* to exaggerate. As long as "Mark Twain" remained in the foreground of the action, there could be no fiction, but only more tall tale. To achieve true fiction, Mark Twain had to invent a character to take his place and discover a plot which would free him from history.

The Adventures of Tom Sawyer, as its title discloses, is that discovery. The road there had been long and involved. Mark Twain had first to discover, exploit, and exhaust the myth of himself—which he had done in the course of *The Innocents Abroad, Roughing It*, and "Old Times on the Mississippi"—so that he would need to develop another claim. Yet even as he proceeded with the tall tale of himself, he was laying tentative and casual claims in the territory of fiction, some of which presaged *Tom Sawyer*. There is, for example, "The Story of the Bad Little Boy Who Did Not Come to Grief," a burlesque of the sentimental moral fables about good and bad little boys, which appeared in 1866. As burlesque, it depends much more upon inverting the parent form than inventing a new plot. Yet even in the idea of The Bad Boy, Mark Twain is pointing toward the figure of Tom Sawyer. Then there is the fragmentary "A Boy's Manuscript," probably written in 1870, which is actually a kind of scenario of

Tom Sawyer. Written in dramatic form, this fragment contains the rudimentary character and situations of the novel. Yet the very facts that it is a fragment and is in the form of a drama suggest not how close Mark Twain was to the form of the novel, but how far he had to go to reach it.

The book which both defined that distance and helped span it was *The Gilded Age*, Mark Twain's first extended effort in fiction. Significantly enough, the book is a collaboration, in which Mark Twain contributed the character and Charles Dudley Warner furnished the plot. Much later, Mark Twain said that Colonel Sellers, the one memorable character in *The Gilded Age*, was his only real property in the book. Though he is not to be freed completely from the responsibility of the flimsy plot detailing the fortunes of Philip Sterling, there is no question that Sellers is Mark Twain's property and the plot is Warner's. The point is not whether Mark Twain is better than Warner, but that Mark Twain's invention lay primarily in character, not in plot—that, in fact, he needed someone else to provide the plot.

The whole process should not be surprising, for his invention of "Mark Twain" had been to impose a character upon a form. Thus, in *The Innocents Abroad*, he gave the world not so much a new travel book as a new traveler—a new perspective, a new point of view. In *The Gilded Age*, he left the narrative design to Warner and contented himself with inventing a character who would, and did, steal the show. Yet for all Sellers' grandiose imagination, for all his instant appeal, he cannot accomplish the "fiction" of the book; he exists as a creature unto himself rather than a character involved in the action. What the two writers fully share is the satiric-burlesque perspective. Yet here again, the point is that they share it. Each was only half a satirist by himself, but together they were able to write the satiric novel of their age which gave the age its name.

In the character of Tom Sawyer, however, Mark Twain fully entered the realm of fiction. The preface to the novel makes clear the different order of conception between fiction and the tall tale:

> Most of the adventures recorded in this book really occurred; one or two were experiences of my own, the rest those of boys who were schoolmates of mine. Huck Finn is drawn from life; Tom Sawyer also, but not from an individual—he is a combination of the characteristics of three boys whom I knew, and therefore belongs to the composite order of architecture.
>
> The odd superstitions touched upon were all prevalent among children and slaves in the West at the period of this story—that is to say, thirty or forty years ago.
>
> Although my book is intended mainly for the entertainment of boys and girls, I hope it will not be shunned by men and women on that account, for part of my plan has been to try to pleasantly remind adults of what they once were themselves, and of how they felt and thought and talked, and what queer enterprises they sometimes engaged in.[1]

To be sure, Tom Sawyer is said to be based on real people, but he is a composite character freed from the "experience" in which he had his origins. He is not bound by the laws of biography but by the laws of fiction, which is to say plot and character. It does not finally matter whether "most of the adventures recorded . . . really occurred," and by insisting they did, Mark Twain was doing no more than echoing a convention familiar to the novelist from the earliest emergence of the novel form.

The entire preface discloses how much Mark Twain relied upon the conventions of narrative structure and fictive reality. What Mark Twain discovered was the character of Tom himself—a boy in action. That is why Tom's presence has remained in the national memory while the

[1] *Writings*, XII, vii.

organization of the narrative has been forgotten. For the reality of the adventures lies not so much in their order as in their relation to Tom. They are *his* adventures, and remain in the reader's memory as extensions of his character. Having come to accept Tom's freedom from the context in which he appeared, readers forget that it was the book itself which set him free.

There are four essential elements which make up the world of Tom Sawyer. First there is, of course, the figure of Tom himself, standing at the center of the stage. Second, there is the stage, the summer world of St. Petersburg. Third, there is the audience—the society of St. Petersburg, composed of adults as well as children, all of whom function at one time or another as Tom's audience inside the action. Finally, there is the narrator, who acts as an indulgent audience himself. Though he exercises as much power over his characters as Thackeray does in *Vanity Fair*, the narrator creates the illusion of being a spectator who draws the curtain at his performance rather than a puppet master pulling the strings. Although the perspective upon the characters is equally remote in both novels, Thackeray exercises control in terms of plot and history, Mark Twain in terms of age and time. Thackeray's genius, following mock-heroic strategies, reduces adult rituals and momentous events to the status of acts upon a dwarfed stage. Tom Sawyer and his gang, on the other hand, are children at play— their world is a play world in which adult rituals of love, death, war, and justice are reenacted in essentially harmless patterns. To be sure there is violence in the play world of Tom Sawyer, and Bernard De Voto was in a certain way right to observe that the idyl of Hannibal is surrounded by dread. Yet the boy's world is charmed; it is safe simply because the narrator's perspective enchants whatever terror and violence exist inside the world. Like the "once upon a time" of the fairy tale, this perspective reduces the size of the action by keeping it at a distance from the reader.

The distance is maintained in two ways—through the perspective of burlesque and the perspective of indulgence. Franklin Rogers, in his study of Mark Twain's burlesque patterns, observes that the seminal "Boy's Manuscript" was in all probability a burlesque aimed at *David Copperfield*. He goes on to show how the first part of *Tom Sawyer* burlesques the good-boy cliché by showing how a bad boy prospers.[2] The soundness of Rogers' observations is evident throughout *Tom Sawyer*, from the blustering fight in the first chapter to the discovery of the treasure in the last. The relationship between Tom and Becky burlesques romantic conventions; the conversions of Tom and Huck, after the graveyard murder, parody religious conversions; lamentations of the village over Tom's apparent death mock funeral rituals and conventional language of grief. In brief, the entire action of the boys' world burlesques adult rituals.

And yet *Tom Sawyer* is neither burlesque nor primarily satiric novel. The reason is that the narrator's impulse toward burlesque and satire is largely assimilated in his indulgent posture. The burlesque personality of Mark Twain has undergone a genuine transformation. No longer the traveler or autobiographer, he is the observer of an action which, though intimate, is so remote in time that he patronizes the behavior of the actors at almost every point. The second chapter begins:

> Saturday morning was come, and all the summer world was bright and fresh, and brimming with life. There was a song in every heart; and if the heart was young the music issued at the lips. There was cheer in every face and a spring in every step. The locust trees were in bloom and the fragrance of the blossoms filled the air. Cardiff Hill, beyond the village and above it, was green with vegetation, and it lay just far enough away to seem a Delectable Land, dreamy, reposeful, and inviting.[3]

[2] Rogers, *Burlesque Patterns*, pp. 102-104.
[3] *Writings*, XII, 12.

Thus the scene is set, the idyl defined. In this scene the whitewashing episode takes place. The opening sentence of Chapter IV, "The sun rose upon a tranquil world, and beamed down upon the peaceful village like a benediction,"[4] provides an unobtrusive but nevertheless clearly evident "screen" for the Sunday school recitations. In Chapter XIV, Tom awakens on Jackson's Island:

> It was the cool gray dawn, and there was a delicious sense of repose and peace in the deep pervading calm and silence of the woods. Not a leaf stirred; not a sound obtruded upon great Nature's meditation. Beaded dewdrops stood upon the leaves and grasses. A white layer of ashes covered the fire, and a thin blue breath of smoke rose straight into the air. Joe and Huck still slept.
>
> Now, far away in the woods a bird called; another answered; presently the hammering of a woodpecker was heard. Gradually the cool dim gray of the morning whitened, and as gradually sounds multiplied and life manifested itself. The marvel of Nature shaking off sleep and going to work unfolded itself to the musing boy.[5]

Each of these passages at once qualifies and generalizes the scene—qualifies it by screening out the impact of unpleasurable impulses; generalizes it by stabilizing and stylizing action into the form of tableau. Though there is murder in the world, its impact does not reach the reader but is used up in the explosion it has upon the boys who move at a great distance from the reader. And though there is "realism" in the book, if one means by realism an antitype of romance, there is neither uniqueness of character nor particularity of incident. Instead of individuals, the book generates types. Thus there is not even a minute description of Tom Sawyer; it is impossible to tell what he looks like—how tall, how heavy, how handsome or ugly he is. He emerges as the figure, the *char-*

[4] *Ibid.*, p. 29. [5] *Ibid.*, p. 121.

acter, of the Boy. Yet he is not allegorical, simply because he is a *character* and not a personification.[6]

The indulgent and burlesque perspectives do not exist in isolation; they are combined to form the particular humor of the invisible narrator. A fairly typical example of this humor occurs at the beginning of Chapter VIII, in which Tom, stung by Becky's angry rejection at discovering his earlier affection for Amy Lawrence, rushes away to solitude:

> Tom dodged hither and thither through lanes until he was well out of the track of returning scholars, and then fell into a moody jog. He crossed a small "branch" two or three times, because of a prevailing juvenile superstition that to cross water baffled pursuit. Half an hour later he was disappearing behind the Douglas mansion on the summit of Cardiff Hill, and the schoolhouse was hardly distinguishable away off in the valley behind him. He entered a dense wood, picked his pathless way to the center of it, and sat down on a mossy spot under a spreading oak. There was not even a zephyr stirring; the dead noonday heat had even stilled the songs of the birds; nature lay in a trance that was broken by no sound but the occasional far-off hammering of a woodpecker, and this seemed to render the pervading silence and sense of loneliness the more profound. The boy's soul was steeped in melancholy; his feelings were in happy accord with his surroundings.

[6] Mark Twain's characterization of Tom Sawyer is similar in method to Chaucer's in the *Canterbury Tales*. Two assumptions lie at the base of such characterization: (1) that people are not unique but ultimately similar in motive and behavior; (2) that social and psychological reality are wedded rather than divorced. Thus neither Chaucer nor Mark Twain develops characters with singular personalities; rather, they emphasize the traits, motives, and behavior which are easily recognizable by being individually manifest yet socially held in common. Thus, also, they have the capacity to typify characters (as knight, miller, friar, or boy) without in any way seeming to threaten their individuality. Indeed, both Chaucer and Mark Twain achieve the effect of reinforcing individuality by emphasizing typifying aspects of character.

He sat long with his elbows on his knees and his
chin in his hands, meditating. It seemed to him that
life was but a trouble, at best, and he more than
half envied Jimmy Hodges, so lately released; it
must be very peaceful, he thought, to lie and slum-
ber and dream forever and ever, with the wind
whispering through the trees and caressing the
grass and the flowers over the grave, and nothing
to bother and grieve about, ever any more. If he
only had a clean Sunday-school record he could be
willing to go, and be done with it all. Now as to this
girl. What had he done? Nothing. He had meant the
best in the world, and been treated like a dog—like
a very dog. She would be sorry some day—maybe
when it was too late. Ah, if he could only die *temporarily*!

But the elastic heart of youth cannot be com-
pressed into one constrained shape long at a time.
Tom presently began to drift insensibly back into
the concerns of this life again.[7]

The indulgent and burlesque impulses are inextricably
joined throughout the passage to create an essential condescension to the scene, making the narrator a tolerant
adult observer fondling yet patronizing the world he
evokes. Tom's retreat to the woodland, the solitude of the
scene, and his brooding meditations are impersonations
of conventionalized romantic melancholy; the whole
scene and action lead up to Tom's boyish death wish. The
entire passage is utterly characteristic of the narrator's
attitude toward his subject. The humor of the burlesque
personality of *The Innocents Abroad* was characterized by
irreverence; that of the autobiographer was the tall tale,
the lie. The humor of the narrator of *Tom Sawyer* is a
gently indulgent irony, a tender yet urbanely superior attitude toward the subject of his affection, which defines
his focus upon the boy he creates.

This perspective is not some mere device for seeing
Tom; it contributes immeasurably to the illusion Tom

[7] *Writings*, XII, 73.

sustains—the illusion of Tom as performer. The fact that the society of St. Petersburg, both old and young, is involved in watching Tom's play from the inside world of the novel while the narrator is engaged in watching it indulgently from the outside goes far toward creating Tom's role of chief actor in a drama which the juvenile reader can believe and the adult reader can indulge with a mixture of nostalgia and gentle irony. The narrator, an almost invisible agent with whom the adult reader unwittingly identifies, provides the perspective through which Mark Twain meant to reach an adult audience.[8] What Mark Twain did was to treat his fiction as a performance rather than a story. If, in the preface, he alluded to the adult audience he was creating, he defined the nature of his characters in the conclusion. "Most of the characters that perform in this book still live," he said, "and are prosperous and happy." He continued, "Some day it may seem worth while to take up the story of the younger ones again and see what sort of men and women they turned out to be; therefore it will be wisest not to reveal any part of their lives at present."[9] Here in the midst of the conventional Victorian epilogue is the disclosure that Mark Twain visualizes his characters in performance rather than in action, on stage rather than in the world.

Though the sense of a double audience contributes greatly to the illusion of a performance, there is still the performer—the actor and his "act." Tom Sawyer fully collaborates with the audience watching him; he puts on a

---

[8] After initially recommending that Mark Twain take Tom Sawyer on into manhood, Howells, upon seeing the manuscript, wrote: "It will be an immense success. But I think you ought to treat it explicitly *as* a boy's story. Grown-ups will enjoy it just as much if you do; and if you should put it forth as a study of a boy character from the grown-up point of view, you'd give the wrong key to it" (*Mark Twain-Howells Letters*, I, 110-11). In seeing it as a boy's story, Howells was evidently advising Mark Twain to avoid the narrow *Atlantic* audience in favor of the mass audience, advice Mark Twain was eager enough to have.

[9] *Writings*, XII, 292.

show throughout the novel, one of the chief aspects of his character being his desire to be stage center. He is a performer in almost everything he does, whether he is showing off for Becky, parading with Joe and Huck into the arena of his own funeral, becoming the central figure in the trial of Muff Potter, or proudly producing the bags of gold before the startled eyes of St. Petersburgers. In a word, he is the show-off, and though he is not simply that, he cannot resist the temptation to perform to an audience. Thirty years after the writing of *Tom Sawyer*, Mark Twain observed that Theodore Roosevelt was a political incarnation of Tom Sawyer. "Just like Tom Sawyer," he remarked of Roosevelt's eagerness to keep the public eye; "always showing off."[10] This sense of showmanship defines Tom's desire to be a hero, for it is the spectacle of heroism as much as its achievement which fascinates Tom. The narrator gives us the image: "Tom was a glittering hero once more,"[11] he observes after Tom's performance at the trial, and the adjective tells the story. Tom simply has to shine if he can, and he utilizes every resource at his command to do so. In this respect he is a forerunner of Hank Morgan, whose chief character trait is his inveterate love of the effect. Morgan, like Tom, can never resist the temptation to be the central attraction, and both characters rely on electrifying their audiences. They nourish the tactics of the grand entrance, the great surprise, the splendid disclosure.

But Tom is a boy. His age, his size, and the security of his world—accentuated by the adult perspective upon it—place severe limits on the range of effects he can achieve. There are two areas of heroic achievement open to him in this enchanted world. The one is to be a hero on the St. Petersburg stage—in Becky's eye, the school's, the church's, the court's, or the town's. The other is to be victorious in the world of make-believe, in the world of play.

[10] *Mark Twain in Eruption*, ed. Bernard De Voto (New York, 1940), p. 49.
[11] *Writings*, XII, 198.

Tom's genius lies in his ability to realize the possibilities of make-believe in the life of the village, combining both possibilities of achievement into a single act. Thus he succeeds in playing out his fantasies for the entertainment and salvation of the town.

The best example is the mock funeral, the motive or seed of which appears in the long passage in which Tom wants to die temporarily. At this early moment of the book, it is no more than a desire, an almost ineffectual and childish death wish which the narrator can patronize. But in the course of the narrative not only does Tom's wish become a reality—if that were all, the book would be no more than a juvenile success story—but the entire village is made to play the dupe in the performance. And not simply made to play the dupe but made to like the role.

The boy's resurrection, occurring precisely at the center of the book, is the central episode. By central, I mean characteristic or characterizing, for it dramatizes the full union between narration and action. First, the narrator sets the scene. In contrast to the joyous plans of the fugitives on Jackson's Island, he describes the village grief:

> But there was no hilarity in the little town that same tranquil Saturday afternoon. The Harpers, and Aunt Polly's family, were being put into mourning, with great grief and many tears. An unusual quiet possessed the village, although it was ordinarily quiet enough, in all conscience. The villagers conducted their concerns with an absent air, and talked little; but they sighed often. The Saturday holiday seemed a burden to the children. They had no heart in their sports, and gradually gave them up.[12]

The two adjectives in the initial sentence define the narrator's visual and auditory perspective on the action. He discloses to the reader a scene so remote in distance that the village is a *little* town hung in a tranquil air. This distance is not something physical or definite in time and

[12] *Ibid.*, p. 149.

space—the narrator never says that the action happened so many miles away or so many years ago—but an objectification of a mental state. Thus the action and scene which the narrator unfolds in his first paragraph do not have the status of actuality; they are themselves an image, an idyl, which reflects in turn the narrator's role of complacent and superior observer.

His superiority is not simply one of size and actuality; it is superiority of knowledge which he shares with the reader. For the villagers do not know what the narrator and his readers are only too aware of—that Tom is not dead. Thus their grief, though real to them, is ultimately unreal because it has a false object and the narrator is free to ridicule it at will. He accomplishes his burlesque by exposing the clichés of conventional grief. The entire episode is handled remarkably, for the target of the burlesque —the threadbare clichés of conventional grief—is perfectly paralleled by the nature of the villagers' grief, which like their platitudes, is *sincere*, but nevertheless essentially unreal.

Tom's resurrection before the stunned townspeople who have ceremoniously gathered to lament his death is the surprise performance which he has prepared for the purpose of electrifying his audience. For Tom it is the act by which he gains the center of the stage; he has carefully made the resurrection his drama in which Huck and Joe will be supporting actors. Tom, completely unaware of the burlesque, remains imprisoned in his ego. While the choir bursts into song, "Tom Sawyer the Pirate looked around upon the envying juveniles about him and confessed in his heart that this was the proudest moment of his life."[13]

In the world of *Pudd'nhead Wilson*, such a practical joke would have provided the source of unrelenting hostility and hatred, but here in the idyl, where burlesque commingles with indulgence, the townspeople are tolerant of Tom's boyish pranks and forgive him, as does his Aunt

[13] *Ibid.*, p. 153.

Polly, for making them ridiculous. They expect him to be bad and, like Aunt Polly, they love him for it—not because Mark Twain's world is "realistic" but because they are his audience and collaborate with Tom in creating the illusion that the world is ultimately given over to play. Thus what was to have been a funeral is transmogrified by Tom into an entertainment, enhancing rather than undermining the burlesque element. For Tom's joke, his play funeral, provides the ultimate definition of what the "sincere" funeral was to have been for the town in the first place—an entertainment! A tearful, lugubrious, and hackneyed production in which each of the participants was fully working up his part—but an entertainment nonetheless.

Tom's resurrection offers in fairly clear outline the essential realization of his character. He is of course the bad boy, but not simply the bad boy, though he breaks rules and plays practical jokes. Thomas Bailey Aldrich's Tom Bailey in *The Story of a Bad Boy* broke rules, and Peck's Bad Boy existed by means of an endless succession of practical jokes on his Pa. Neither is it Tom's subtler psychology nor his more realistic character which set him apart. Nor is it his celebrated independence and pluck, nor his essentially good heart. Tom is really no freer than Sid and clearly has no better heart. Though the indulgent Mark Twain felt a deep invitation to sentimentalize Tom in this way and thus affirm that he was for all his badness really a good good boy, the burlesque perspective afforded protection against such sentimentality. As it had been for Mark Twain in the beginning and as it was throughout his career, burlesque functioned as a reality principle—a reliable anchor in a storm of dreams.

Tom's play *defines the world as play*, and his reality lies in his commitment to play, not in the involuntary tendencies which are often attributed to him. Actually Tom is in revolt against nothing. To be sure, he feels the pinch of school and the discipline of Aunt Polly, but he has no sustained desire to escape and no program of rebellion. What he does have is a perennial dream of himself as the hero and a commitment to the dream which makes it come true not once, but as many times as he can reorganize the village around his dream. The truth the dream invariably comes to is *play*—a play which converts all serious projects in the town to pleasure and at the same time subverts all the adult rituals by revealing that actually they are nothing but dull play to begin with.

Thus in the famous whitewashing episode, the ritual of the chore is converted into pleasure by Tom's stratagem. And not simply converted, but shrewdly exploited by Tom. To be sure, the episode discloses that Tom is an embryo businessman and that he has a bright future in the society of commerce and advertising, but such a criticism of Tom's character ignores the essential criticism the episode itself makes of the original chore. The chore was, after all, a kind of dull-witted stratagem for getting work done at low pay in the name of duty. Tom discovers—and surely it is a discovery worth making—that the task can be done four times as thick and as well in the name of pleasure. Though Tom shows off his handiwork, he does no more than Aunt Polly meant to do with him and the fence.

The adults throughout the book are engaged in showing off as much as are the children. If Tom apes the authorities of romance, Mr. Walters, the Sunday school superintendent, has his own authorities which he likewise strives to emulate:

> This superintendent was a slim creature of thirty-five, with a sandy goatee and short sandy hair; he wore a stiff standing-collar whose upper edge almost reached his ears and whose sharp points curved forward abreast the corners of his mouth—a fence that compelled a straight lookout ahead, and a turning of the whole body when a side view was required; his chin was propped on a spreading cravat which was as broad and as long as a bank-note,

and had fringed ends; his boot-toes were turned sharply up, in the fashion of the day, like sleigh-runners—an effect patiently and laboriously produced by the young men by sitting with their toes pressed against a wall for hours together. Mr. Walters was very earnest of mien, and very sincere and honest at heart; and he held sacred things and places in such reverence, and so separated them from worldly matters, that unconsciously to himself his Sunday-school voice had acquired a peculiar intonation which was wholly absent on week-days.[14]

Mr. Walters, like Tom, puts on style. Indeed, the whole village, adults as well as children, puts on style of various sorts on various occasions—all for the purpose of showing off. On the opening page of the book, Aunt Polly has to look for Tom over the top of her spectacles because "they were her state pair, the pride of her heart, and were built for 'style,' not service—she could have seen through a pair of stove-lids just as well." The style of *Tom Sawyer* is the vision which at once looks over and exposes the old dead styles which are impersonated and gently burlesqued as the boy stages his action.

If Tom must stage his shows, he is doing no more than the adults who are busily engaged in staging their own performances, casting the children as characters. At the end of the Sunday school episode, for example, as the Thatchers make their impressive entrance, Tom occupies himself by showing off for Becky and the rest of the society shows off for the impressive Judge Thatcher.

Mr. Walters fell to "showing off," with all sorts of official bustlings and activities, giving orders, delivering judgments, discharging directions here, there, everywhere that he could find a target. The librarian "showed off"—running hither and thither with his arms full of books and making a deal of the splutter and fuss that insect authority delights in. The

[14] *Ibid.*, pp. 35-36.

young lady teachers "showed off"—bending sweetly
over pupils that were lately being boxed, lifting
pretty warning fingers at bad little boys and patting
good ones lovingly. The young gentlemen teachers
"showed off" with small scoldings and other little
displays of authority and fine attention to discipline. . . . The little girls "showed off" in various
ways and the little boys "showed off" with such
diligence that the air was thick with paper wads
and the murmur of scufflings. And above it all the
great man sat and beamed a majestic judicial smile
upon all the house, and warmed himself in the sun
of his own grandeur—for he was "showing off," too.[15]

The satiric direction of this passage points to the activity
which unites the entire community, from the revered
Judge down to the youngest child. The entire Sunday
school is a show in which everyone is showing off. No
sooner are the Thatchers seated than Mr. Walters proceeds to the next act of his performance—the delivery of
the Bible prize to the student who had earned the most
tickets for memorizing Bible verses. This little act gives
him a chance—the language of the book unfailingly discloses the terms of the action—to "exhibit a prodigy." Tom,
however, steals the scene. Having traded spoils taken at
the whitewashing exploit for tickets awarded to Bible
quoters, he emerges with the largest number of tickets,
to the amazement and envy of the little showmen he
has outmaneuvered. His performance elevates him to the
height of Judge Thatcher. "It was the most stunning
surprise of the decade, and so profound was the sensation that it lifted the new hero up to the judicial one's
altitude, and the school had two marvels to gaze upon
in place of one."[16]

The Sunday school is merely one of the shows in St.
Petersburg. The sermon which follows is another. While
the minister drearily enacts his performance, Tom, again
cast into the background, becomes interested only upon

[15] *Ibid.*, p. 38.   [16] *Ibid.*, p. 39.

hearing the minister say that at the millennium when the lion and lamb should lie down together a little child should lead the world's hosts. This is the minister's verbal effort to produce a great scene. "But the pathos, the lesson, the moral of the great spectacle were lost upon the boy; he only thought of the conspicuousness of the principal character before the onlooking nations; his face lit with the thought, and he said to himself that he wished he could be that child, if it was a tame lion."[17] Unable to effect such a miracle, Tom does the next best thing, which is to set up a competing act. Releasing a pinch bug, he succeeds in diverting attention from the minister and—when a dog chances to sit upon the beetle—breaking up the minister's performance completely.

Like church, school is also a dull show over which the schoolmaster Mr. Dobbins presides. Almost the only way Tom is able to gain attention from the audience, and particularly Becky Thatcher, is to secure a thrashing at the hands of the teacher. Interestingly enough, the two times Tom receives whippings at school are results of his having sought out the punishment in order to show off. First, when Becky enters school, he blatantly announces to Mr. Dobbins his tardiness is a result of talking to Huckleberry Finn, and is thus flogged before his lady love. Much later, he sacrificially offers himself to Mr. Dobbins' wrath to keep Becky from receiving the whipping due her for tearing Mr. Dobbins' anatomy book. When Tom is not consciously engaged in securing attention, he unconsciously secures it by entertaining himself to the point of forgetting Mr. Dobbins and the schoolroom until the entire audience fixes its attention on his self-absorption. At one moment he is so engaged in teaching Becky to draw that he does not realize Mr. Dobbins is at hand observing the instruction; at another, he and Joe Harper are so deeply engrossed in entertaining themselves with a tick as to be unaware of becoming the center of attention:

[17] *Ibid.*, p. 47.

> A tremendous whack came down on Tom's shoulders, and its duplicate on Joe's; and for the space of two minutes the dust continued to fly from the two jackets and the whole school to enjoy it. The boys had been too absorbed to notice the hush that had stolen upon the school awhile before when the master came tiptoeing down the room and stood over them. He had contemplated a good part of the performance before he contributed his bit of variety to it.[18]

The language here discloses the essential psychology of the schoolroom. The whipping does not hurt Tom; it does not humiliate him. The other children do not shiver under Mr. Dobbins' tyranny, nor do they suffer for Tom. Though such responses would be possible and even necessary in the world of *David Copperfield*, they do not exist in the world of St. Petersburg. Instead of carrying in the roots of his memory the scars of Mr. Dobbins' blows, Tom never reflects upon the flogging he has received. And Mr. Dobbins' fall comes not in the form of a series of disasters or crimes which bring him low enough to ask mercy from the boys he has tormented; rather, it comes in the form of a trick played upon him during the commencement exercises, when he is at the height of his annual effort to show off. After the long series of dreary exercises which make up the tedious performance, the monotony is broken when the boys lower a cat from the garret to lift the master's wig, exposing a bald pate elegantly gilded by the sign painter's boy.

This episode, with all its slapstick elements, is directly appropriate to the form of the book. For once again the boys have defined to the community the essential boredom of the adult theatricals. The source of that boredom, as the narrator's burlesque perspective discloses, is the utter lack of spontaneity in the exercises. Like little machines, the children go through the motions of performing without in any way expressing themselves. Their

18 *Ibid.*, p. 67.

gestures and their expressions are as manufactured as the occasion itself; and their selections are characterized by a dead language. The appearance of the cat in this program is the surprise which redeems the deadly performance, converting it into genuine entertainment for the adults who have gathered to suffer through it.

What every episode of *Tom Sawyer* enacts is the conversion of all "serious" community activity—all duty, pain, grief, and work—into pleasure and play. Tom Sawyer himself is the agent of this conversion. His imaginative force, his *reality*, lies precisely in his capacity to make his dreams and fantasies come "true" in the form of "acts" which entertain the villagers. Nowhere is David Riesman's fine observation, that glamor in an actor measures the apathy in the audience, better borne out than in the world of *Tom Sawyer*.[19] For Tom's glittering power, his heroism, invariably defines at the same time it feeds upon the boredom of the villagers.

In discovering Tom, Mark Twain had actually gained a new perspective on himself as entertainer, for he had managed to objectify in a new character the possibilities of the pleasure principle. The method of objectification was the burlesque-indulgent perspective upon the world of boyhood. Such a perspective enabled Mark Twain to see, in a way no writer had seen before him, an entire area of action where entertainment dissolved into play. In seeing it he recognized possibilities of both entertainment and play which he himself could have but dimly imagined prior to the emergence of Tom Sawyer.

For the real audacity of *Tom Sawyer* is its commitment to the pleasure principle. Though the book participates in parody, burlesque, and satire, it clearly cannot be characterized by any of these terms. It is, after all, a tale—an *adventure*—and its commitment is not to exposing sham, as in the case of satire; nor is it to mocking a prior art form as in the case of parody and burlesque. Instead,

[19] David Riesman, *The Lonely Crowd* (New Haven, 1950), p. 313.

the positive force—the force to which the world of St. Petersburg succumbs—is play itself.

Play is the reality principle in the book. What makes Tom Sawyer seem more real than the adults who submit to his power is his capacity to take his pleasure openly in the form of make-believe while they take theirs covertly under the guise of seriousness. Tom's virtue lies not in his good heart, his independence, or his pluck—none of which he really has—but in his truth to the pleasure principle which is the ultimate reality of the enchanted idyl. The very enchantment results from the indulgent perspective the author assumes toward the action. The narrator's indulgence is none other than the pleasure he takes in disclosing the play world.

The coupling of the outer pleasure with the inner world of play causes Tom's make-believe to seem true, whereas the adult "reality" and "duty" appear false and pretentious. This conversion, not so much process as point of view, is at once the humor and truth of the book. By inventing Tom Sawyer, Mark Twain had actually succeeded in dramatizing in a fictional narrative the possibilities of entertainment. He had projected through Tom Sawyer's imagination a world of boyhood in which play was the central reality, the defining value. The money Tom discovers in the cave in the final episode is a reward not for his courage or heroism—the indulgent perspective discloses his cowardice and essential self-love—but for his capacity to have dreamed it into reality with his make-believe imagination. And Tom quite characteristically appears before the townspeople to show off his treasure in one last exhibitionistic fling before the final curtain. The world of boyhood as it emerges in the pages of *Tom Sawyer* is a world where play, make-believe, and adventure are the living realities defining the false pieties and platitudes which constitute the dull pleasure of the adult world.

Mark Twain's invention of Tom Sawyer and his invention of the novel are thus one and the same thing. The reality principle of this first independent fiction is, as we have seen, play. The approach to fiction through the boy-character of a master player is an index to Mark Twain's inability to "believe" in conventional fiction. The exaggerated contempt in which he held fiction was his characteristic "humor" embodying his true perception. Mark Twain had no real use for conventional fiction because his entire genius—the "Mark Twain" in Samuel Clemens—had his being in the tall tale, a form which presented the truth as a lie, whereas the fiction he condemned presented the lie as the truth. That is why Mark Twain could say to Howells that he would not take Tom Sawyer into manhood because he "would just be like all the other one horse men in literature." Though he had promised in his conclusion to trace his figures into adult life, he never did; he could only call the changeless Tom Sawyer back on stage for more—and poorer—"acts."

In moving to the form of fiction, Mark Twain subverted the conventions of the form, not only by means of the burlesque and indulgent perspectives, but also through the character of Tom himself, whose "adventure" or plot is projected in terms of play and make-believe. The enchantment, the idyl, and the boy—the chief components of the book—create fiction as play instead of as truth. The book is no testimonial to the child's unfettered imagination transcending the materialism of the adult world. Instead, it creates existence under the name of pleasure, and portrays all human actions, no matter how "serious," as forms of play. Thus the imagination is shorn of the religious, romantic, and transcendental meanings with which Coleridge invested it; in Mark Twain's world of boyhood, the imagination represents the capacity for mimicry, impersonation, make-believe, and play. That is why the boy of Mark Twain's idyl is so different from the child of Wordsworth's vision. The child of the romantic poet has a direct relationship to God and Nature. Mark Twain's boy has a direct relationship to pleasure. The romantic child *is*, has being; Mark Twain's boy plays, has pleasure.

The achievement of *Tom Sawyer* becomes more distinct when viewed against the failure of *The Prince and the Pauper*. Though that failure is universally acknowledged, explanations for it are diverse and often conflicting. One of the most common accounts of the book's deficiency is that Mark Twain, off his home ground, did not really know English life as he knew life on the Mississippi. Unable to assimilate the texture of the alien history into his book, he surrendered the marvelous realism of Tom Sawyer to the strained sentiment of *The Prince and the Pauper*.[20] Another argument is that Mark Twain attempted simply to meet the juvenile audience and thus produced nothing more than a conventional juvenile book.[21] There is also the explanation that Mark Twain, surrendering to the canons of genteel taste, wrote for his wife's approval, which is to say that he consciously pursued the saccharine sentimentality on which she presumably battened.[22]

All of these explanations are partially true. Not only do they shed light on the book; they can all be corroborated by evidence from the life and letters of Mark Twain. Certainly Mark Twain did not have the easy aplomb in the English scene he determined to portray that he had along the Mississippi of his memory. For in moving from St. Petersburg to sixteenth-century London, he was moving from his personal past to the *literary* past.

[20] De Voto, pointing to the weaknesses of the book, observes that "the court of Edward VI was not the happiest occupation for a man who, more than any other novelist, had experienced the breadth and depth of American life" (*Mark Twain's America*, p. 272).

[21] The juvenile aspect of the book is best treated by Albert E. Stone, Jr., *The Innocent Eye: Childhood in Mark Twain's Imagination* (New Haven, 1961), pp. 91-125.

[22] For an excellent account of the genteel dimension of the book and of the pressures which produced it, see Kenneth R. Andrews, *Nook Farm: Mark Twain's Hartford Circle* (Cambridge, Mass., 1950), pp. 190-98.

In the one fiction he was reconstructing experience; in the other he was fabricating a tale. And certainly he was writing consciously for the juvenile audience. The dedication of the book "To those good-mannered and agreeable children, Susy and Clara Clemens" has an irony, which whether it is intentional or unintentional, measures him and gives credence to the argument that he was writing for approval.

Yet *The Prince and the Pauper* is clearly addressed to an adult audience as much as or more than *Tom Sawyer* was. It is ostensibly more satirical than its predecessor. Certainly for anyone interested in Mark Twain's thought or social criticism, *The Prince and the Pauper* is a far more valuable repository than *Tom Sawyer*. His democratic impulses and broadly liberal humanitarianism are evident here in a way they had never been in his earlier work. Still the book fails—and fails decisively. It is actually an extremely weak performance, interesting only in the light it can throw upon the success which preceded it and the masterpiece soon to follow.

His failure lay, in part, in his attempt to repeat the triumph of *Tom Sawyer*, an almost inevitable impulse after the success of the earlier book. Mark Twain was in much the same position he had occupied after his first travel book. He had carved out a great success for himself and the invitation to keep at the same line was strong. His career after *Tom Sawyer* shows much the same confused groping and futility so prominent after *The Innocents Abroad*. First, he began *Huckleberry Finn*, wrote for a time with a good deal of intensity, but, unable to push the book beyond its sustained opening movement, he gave up, shelving what was to be his greatest discovery in order to try possibilities he had already realized. After collaborating with Bret Harte on the drama *Ah, Sin*, he involved himself in a drama of his own in which the "garrulous, good natured old Simon Wheeler" would be forced back into service in the role of detective. When that project proved a disaster, he began work on *The*

Prince and the Pauper. He had intended to write a drama—the dramatic element in *Tom Sawyer* apparently was playing itself out in these groping theatrical efforts—but wrote a story instead. Before he was to complete *The Prince and the Pauper,* he involved himself in the Whittier birthday fiasco; took a two-year European travel jaunt; returned to America, where in November, 1879, he accomplished the marvelous success of the Grant speech which he felt atoned in part for the galling Whittier birthday failure; and finally completed *A Tramp Abroad,* surely the dreariest of all his travel books. During his difficulties with *A Tramp Abroad,* he again resumed work on *The Prince and the Pauper* and completed it at Quarry Farm during the summer of 1880, while he was also back at work on *Huckleberry Finn*—if Walter Blair is right in his excellent surmises on the subject.[23]

Yet the failure of *The Prince and the Pauper* is as much a result of Mark Twain's attempt to surpass *Tom Sawyer* as to repeat his old success. Quite clearly he meant to show himself not simply a humorous and commercial artist. He wrote to Howells that he did not care whether it sold or not, so much had he enjoyed inventing it—implying that the book was to be an elegant show piece more for art than money.[24] Above all, it was not to be merely funny.

Here was the heart of its failure. It lacked humor. It is tiresome because it strives to be serious rather than humorous. Now, of course, this begs the question of the nature of humor, but the discussion of *Tom Sawyer* goes far toward answering that question. In that book, Mark Twain's humor had lain precisely in the discovery of a character who could create the world as play. In this book, however, he sacrifices his character to a plot de-

[23] Walter Blair, "When Was Huckleberry Finn Written," *American Literature,* XXX (March, 1958), 1-25. This article is only in part incorporated into Blair's book *Mark Twain and Huck Finn* (Berkeley, 1960), the most detailed account yet written of Mark Twain's reading and writing during the years 1874-84.

[24] *Mark Twain-Howells Letters,* I, 290.

signed to illustrate the injustices of monarchy. To be sure, the book is in certain ways an interesting democratic fable, turning on a plot device which elevates a commoner to a king and reduces a king to a commoner. But the characters are sacrificed to the device of the plot; the book is a fable more than a fiction, which is to say that it subordinates action to a set of assumed values. Though the values may be admirable, the result is essentially static and impotent. For the more Samuel Clemens attempts to be "serious" the more he betrays his genius, Mark Twain. Rather than being repressed by Mark Twain, as Brooks has it, Clemens was suppressing Mark Twain. It was this "seriousness" which Howells ceremoniously approved in his unsigned review in the New York *Tribune* (25 October 1881). "The fascination of the narrative and the strength of the implied moral are felt at once," observed Howells, "and increase together to the end in a degree which will surprise those who have found nothing but drollery in Mark Twain's books, and have not perceived the artistic sense and the strain of deep earnestness underlying his humor."[25]

Howells' remarks offer a way into the heart of the "problem" of Mark Twain. The modern reader, possessing a perspective on the Gilded Age, would classify the remarks as simply one more example of the genteel aesthetic. But to patronize Howells' taste on such a basis usually eventuates in covertly substituting a new genteel tradition for the old. Thus people who freely condemn Howells' judgment on *The Prince and the Pauper* believe no more than he in Mark Twain's humor. They too, it often develops, want Mark Twain to be serious; the only

[25] Quoted in *Mark Twain-Howells Letters*, I, 378. In his letter recording his response to the manuscript, Howells made the point with equal emphasis. "I think the book will be a great success unless some marauding ass, who does not snuff his wonted pasturage there should prevail on all the other asses to turn up their noses in pure ignorance. It is such a book as I would expect from you, knowing what a bottom of fury there is to your fun; but the public at large ought to be led to expect it, and must be" (*Mark-Twain-Howells Letters*, I, 339).

difference is that their focus upon Mark Twain has the inevitable advantage which a perspective of eighty years provides. Their taste is no better than Howells', really, and their aesthetic is practically the same. Thus their reasons for not liking *The Prince and the Pauper* do not revolve around the fact that it lacks humor, but that it is not realistic; or that it is a commercial exploit; or that Mark Twain's knowledge of history was cursory; or that his theory of history and his idea of progress were inadequate; or that Mark Twain "sold out" to the genteel and juvenile markets. There is evidence to support all these contentions, but none is definitive. All remain partial answers.

Their very partiality brings us back to the central failure of the book—its apparent commitment to humor, yet its failure to be humorous. Not that Samuel Clemens had to write humorous works; he did not have to, but Mark Twain did, and in this book Samuel Clemens clearly could not surrender to the idea of being a humorist. He wished to exploit his humorous genius without fully committing himself to humor. That is why he considered concealing his authorship, but at the last moment, after Howells expressed delight in the book, he decided to go on intrepidly and reveal himself. His indecision—it could have been mock-indecision—is an index to his uncertainty about his own identity in the book. This uncertainty manifests itself within the book as a failure to believe in humor. Thus, "Mark Twain," the genius of Samuel Clemens' humor, is betrayed in the name of piety and "noble" sentiment.

The sign of the betrayal lies in the way in which the characters are subordinated to the plot. The plot, which hinges on the device of mistaken identity, rides the action, seeming always to be imposed from without. It presents coincidence in the guise of trick, not of fate; and its logic, instead of evoking that sense of inevitability which relates character to event, is a mechanism which processes the characters and times the action. In many ways, the plot—with its devices, tricks, and surface exposure—is a comic plot, and it would be wrong to deplore its lack of tragic doom. But the plot is not finally humorous, for it is designed to point a moral. More than being a juvenile romance, an adventure story, or a comedy, the book is a fable—a democratic fable. That fable, which few critics of Mark Twain have elucidated,[26] discloses through the device of mistaken identities, how the "divine right" of monarchy comes from the capacity of the commoner to *remember* the action in his remote past by means of which the king transferred the power to him. Seen as a democratic fable, the book is remarkably worked out, the plot acting as an analogue of the "moral" or "truth" toward which the action points. Thus the prince and the pauper, once the trick of their change is effected, cannot prove who they are. King and commoner are finally one; they are divided only to serve the purposes of "fiction," something which, as Mark Twain observed in his preface, *could* have happened. Only through Tom Canty's memory is the true king proved to be king instead of pretender.

Yet the book remains a fable and not a humorous narrative of boyhood adventure. This in itself is not bad; there are worse things than fables. But—and here the difficulty comes in—the book is Mark Twain too. In a sense he was right to sign his name, for there is enough of his characteristic style present to establish his identity beyond doubt. But it is Mark Twain betrayed. For insofar as Mark Twain *is* present, the impulse necessarily is toward humor—which is to say the impulse is to discover the world as entertainment. But since Mark Twain's humor is imprisoned in the plot, it is subverted; in effect, it is being used for a "serious purpose." This is why the book seems so sentimental. Lacking the courage of its deepest impulse, it betrays that impulse and forces humor

[26] John Macy, in his fine discussion of Mark Twain in *The Spirit of American Literature* (New York, 1925), pp. 262-63, defined the work as a democratic parable, but did not really work out the parable other than to point to the mistaken identity as an illustration that all men are equal.

to serve a noble purpose instead of forcing all noble purposes to serve humor.

The Prince and the Pauper was not Mark Twain's first
failure; in many of the early sketches he had done no
more than exercise clichés or indulge in reflexive repeti-
tions of successful "acts." And after *The Innocents
Abroad*, there had been a long moment in which he had
done no more than prostitute his talent in a series of
futile gestures, as if he were a literary entrepreneur who
could buy experience by hiring reporters to have his experiences for him. But all these failures represented baldly
commercial ventures—attempts to capitalize his humor.
The Prince and the Pauper, however, was a failure of an
entirely different order. Instead of trying to "sell" his
genius, Samuel Clemens was betraying it. He was submitting to the other invitation which lures the humorist—
the invitation to be "serious"; it would be an invitation
which would come again and again, and it was perhaps
more subtle and dangerous than the commercialism
which was equally difficult to resist. For if in commercial-
izing himself, Samuel Clemens was wasting his genius,
in trying to be serious he was failing to believe in it.

CHAPTER

VII

SOUTHWESTERN

VERNACULAR

Huckleberry Finn is the book in which Mark Twain discovered the fullest possibilities of his humor. Later in his career he was to try what he thought were more ambitious projects, but never again was his humor to embody so rich a range of experience, never again was it able to hold so many contradictions in suspension. That is why *Huckleberry Finn* stands not only chronologically but critically at the center of Mark Twain's career, and why any study of Mark Twain is irrevocably anchored to it. Without it, Mark Twain would be in the position of Nathaniel Hawthorne without *The Scarlet Letter*, Herman Melville without *Moby Dick*, or Henry Thoreau without *Walden*. From the time it was published, sensitive critics were able to see its power. Andrew Lang, for example, recognized it as the masterpiece which Americans were overlooking in their lofty search for the Great American Novel.[1] To be sure, the book *was* overlooked, but not to the extent that one can indulge in sentimental regret about the wrong done to its author. The commercial suc-

[1] Lang's brief article on the book—published in *Illustrated News of the World* (February 14, 1891), p. 222—is masterly in critical sensibility and perception. It is reprinted in *Mark Twain: Selected Criticism*, ed. Arthur L. Scott (Dallas, 1955), pp. 36-40. For an account of the reception of *Huckleberry Finn*, see Arthur L. Vogelback, "The Publication and Reception of *Huckleberry Finn* in America," *American Literature*, XI (November, 1939), 260-72.

cess it had in its own time, coupled with the intelligent response fairly lavished on it in our own, more than compensate for any neglect it may have suffered. In the face of its almost universal acceptance, a defense of *Huckleberry Finn* can be little more than a sentimental posture. The attitudes of acceptance fall essentially into two categories: those which try to discover meaning in the book and those which insist that it is a humorous book. Critics who pursue the meaning, the myth, the sociology, or even the structure of the book, usually fail to explore its humor. Their typical reaction is likely to be, "Of course the book is humorous, but behind the humor there is a serious world," and they proceed to search for this seriousness. Critics who insist upon the humor fare even worse, for they seem never to say anything *about* the humor. Instead, they strike negative postures, resisting meaning by proclaiming that the book is simply and marvelously a humorous narrative of a boy's adventure. The humor to which they proudly point is left untouched, presumably on the grounds that it is too delicate to touch. Their standard locution becomes "Despite the pompous attempts to read grand interpretations into *Huckleberry Finn*, the book remains indefinable in its simplicity and beauty," or some equivalent evasion.

Both attitudes describe part of the reality of the book; neither begins to define it. For quite clearly the book does powerfully touch upon "serious" themes, yet just as clearly it remains a humorous narrative. Its being humorous does not mean that it has no sad moments or violent actions, but rather that all the sadness and killing and morality are contained within a humorous point of view. Thus, although *Huckleberry Finn* contains much more serious matter than *Tom Sawyer*, it is just as certainly the much more humorous book. The critic's task is to define the form of that humor, to approach its sources and its power, and to recognize its possibilities and necessities. Such an approach should accomplish, or at least begin to accomplish, three things. It should give us a better understanding of *Huckleberry Finn*—both in relation to its creator and its narrator—than we have hitherto had; it should throw genuine light on the problem of the ending of the novel; and, most important, it should bring us closer to a recognition of Mark Twain's humor.

The first—and, one wants to say, the most important—fact about *Huckleberry Finn* is that Mark Twain began it the summer after he completed *Tom Sawyer* and considered it a continuation of the earlier book, which in many ways it is. He had thought of elaborating Huck's experiences at the Widow Douglas' in the last chapter of *Tom Sawyer*, but—as he wrote to Howells—something told him that he had reached the end of the story, and he restrained his impulse to extend himself.[2] When he did begin the book in the summer of 1876, he wrote four hundred manuscript pages of it. He told Howells that he did, and there is no reason to believe that he did not. According to De Voto and Walter Blair, both of whom have struggled manfully to establish a chronology of composition, Mark Twain's first impulse took him to the point in the novel where the raft is overrun by the steamboat.

Then almost as quickly as he had begun the book, he stopped, saying in his well-known letter to Howells that he liked it only tolerably well and might pigeonhole or burn the manuscript. According to De Voto, who studied the manuscript and typescripts, Mark Twain did not return to *Huckleberry Finn* for seven long years, until, upon returning from his Mississippi trip in 1883, he mounted the buoyant stream of composition which carried the book to completion. But Walter Blair, beginning from Paine's statement in the *Biography* that Mark Twain worked alternately on *The Prince and the Pauper* and *Huckleberry Finn* during the summer of 1880, has painstakingly gathered evidence showing that Mark Twain *did* work on the book during those seven years.[3]

[2] *Mark-Twain-Howells Letters*, I, 113.
[3] Blair's argument ("When Was *Huckleberry Finn* Written,"

If Blair is right, and there are excellent reasons for believing that he is, then *Huckleberry Finn* is not only "our" book of all those years; it was Mark Twain's book too. It was the defining act for him, and of all his novels it took him longest to complete. If he went out of his way to leave the impression that his relation to his masterpiece was perfunctory rather than profound, leaving such an impression was precisely the necessity of the humorist. He could not project himself as the seriously laboring craftsman any more than he could write a long preface to *Huckleberry Finn* in the manner of Henry James. This does not mean that Mark Twain worked long and laboriously plotting and planning his masterpiece. In all probability he did not; but it is absurd to lecture Mark Twain, as many critics have done, for failing to take his genius seriously—as if he could![4] What becomes evident to anyone considering the years *Huckleberry Finn* was in the process of being born is that it emerged slowly and at great cost.

The cost is to be measured in all the literary failures which lay between the beginning and ending of *Huckleberry Finn*. There were three book-length efforts—*A Tramp Abroad*, *The Prince and the Pauper*, and *Life on the Mississippi*—not to mention the countless short stories, sketches and literary projects which have value only for whatever obscure light they throw on Mark Twain's masterpiece. In every instance, the failure is for one of two reasons—either Mark Twain wrote reflexively, which is to say he simply exercised his art, or he took himself seriously. He either sold himself or betrayed himself, or— and this was the usual case—did both. When he sold himself, he became merely Mark Twain acting his role,

---

American Literature, xxx [March, 1958], 1-25) is a lucid account and gives a fine summary of De Voto's contentions.

[4] Van Wyck Brooks beautifully set the style for those who assume a readiness to lecture Mark Twain. It is as if Mark Twain in typical bad-boy fashion had played truant to his art and put himself in line to be disciplined by a generation of serious critics.

doing what was expected of him. When he betrayed himself, as in *The Prince and the Pauper*, he betrayed his genius by trying to be serious—which is to say that he put truth, virtue, and morality before pleasure.

The two modes of failure are not contradictory but complementary, one begetting the other. For the more Mark Twain dropped back into his act, the more he needed to do something noble, to show somehow that he was a serious writer. The burlesque routine is fairly clear, for it is no more than a repetition of the perspective which was discovered in *The Innocents Abroad*. But the "serious" Mark Twain, who emerges in *The Prince and the Pauper* plays two roles. On the one hand he is satiric, disclosing a growing indignation at the world's injustice. This is the bitter Mark Twain who ultimately came to make sad jokes about the damned human race. On the other hand, he becomes respectable and literary—the genteel Mark Twain. Instead of being contradictory, these two roles reinforce each other. The satiric Mark Twain who flays the world's abuses is actually the respectable Mark Twain trying to please members of a cultured audience who approved the right causes.

This serious and satiric Mark Twain is increasingly evident in *A Tramp Abroad*, *The Prince and the Pauper*, and *Life on the Mississippi*. In all three books, beyond the growing tendency to criticize, there is a marked emergence of outrage at monarchy, class, caste, and slavery—an outrage related to all the "serious" issues in *Huckleberry Finn*. But the language of *Huckleberry Finn* was the form of humor which contained the serious issues Mark Twain saw between 1878 and 1884. Yet this language was more than a way of containing such issues—it was a way of seeing them. To recognize this is to be reminded how much Mark Twain, who seems such a writer of experience, was a writer of style. Just as his pseudonym had both required humor and made it possible, the language of *Huckleberry Finn* both caused and required experience. The experience that the language made Mark Twain need was precisely that which would arouse the emotions of indignation, pathos, and guilt—which the language of Huck Finn would in turn control and convert into humor.

Probably the best way to see this necessity at work is to examine *Life on the Mississippi*, the record of Mark Twain's return to the river in 1882, twenty-two years after he left it to join the Confederate Army. To make up this travel book, Mark Twain simply used "Old Times on the Mississippi" as the first part of the book—the part devoted to an account of the flush times of the river's great steamboating epoch. He then laboriously expounded his own record of his return trip, which constitutes the last two-thirds of the book. It is finally impossible to tell how much the emergent *Huckleberry Finn* affected the vision and substance of the travel book, and how much the travel book provided the raw material of *Huckleberry Finn*.

Certainly much material of *Life on the Mississippi* is either directly or subtly woven into *Huckleberry Finn*. There is Mark Twain's memory of the two Englishmen who came to Hannibal, "got themselves up in royal finery," and did *Richard III*, *Othello*, and *Hamlet* to a group of gawking villagers. Then there are the two drummers who sell oleomargarine and synthetic cottonseed oil respectively; there is the burglar Williams, who writes the fraudulent conversion letter as a means of exploiting the charity of a hundred gullible congregations; there is the undertaker who considers himself to be a member of the "dead surest business in Christendom"; there is Mr. Manchester, the false spiritualist. All of these confidence men bear striking resemblance to the King and Duke. Then, too, there is the chapter on ornate funeral preparations which is quite obviously assimilated into the Peter Wilks episode. There is also the fine description of the House Beautiful which reads like a conventionalized version of Huck's description of the Grangerford home.

Finally, there is Mark Twain's obsession with Sir Walter Scott's influence on Southern Culture which finds its way into several of Huck's observations of manners and morals of the "quality," and is also tallied in the name of the steamboat Huck and Jim board in order to have an adventure. Obviously the content of *Life on the Mississippi*, written during the late summer and fall of 1882, has much to do with the magnificent writing drive which carried Mark Twain through the latter stages of *Huckleberry Finn* during the summer of 1883.

But there are aspects of Mark Twain's trip down the river which reveal that he may have been instinctively *acting out* the novel which lay half-finished and waiting behind him. For example, Mark Twain's attempt to travel down the river incognito recalls Huck's voyage—a voyage begun six years before Mark Twain, in company with Major Pond, boarded the packet *Ajax* for a rather breezy trip to New Orleans. Most revealing, however, is the character of Brown, the pilot of the *Pennsylvania* who sarcastically lashes the cub pilot. Clearly modeled upon Pap, Brown resembles that derelict even more than does John Canty, the other representation of the evil father.

The dominating figure of Brown actually constitutes the transition between "Old Times on the Mississippi" and *Life on the Mississippi*. Since the last *Atlantic* sketch stopped abruptly with no hint of what became of the fledgling initiate, it was necessary for Mark Twain to invent a concluding episode in order to incorporate "Old Times" with *Life on the Mississippi*. The tyrant pilot Brown, who speaks in the tone if not the very accents of Pap, is the chief figure of that episode. Brown had appeared in "Old Times," but there he played the role of the victim of total recall, something like the figure in "My Grandfather's Ram" who could not forget anything. In the new episode, however, he becomes a ruthless brute who takes pleasure in humiliating his cub.

After a siege of Brown's sarcasm, the cub rebels. The incident rousing him to action is Brown's physical assault upon his younger brother, Henry, also on the *Pennsylvania*. Springing to the defense of his brother, the cub Mark Twain commits the crime of crimes—he attacks, and thrashes, the pilot with a handy stool. The Captain, being apprised of the situation, instead of hanging the mutinous cub, secretly congratulates him for his pluck. And when Brown demands that the insubordinate cub be taken off the boat, the Captain blithely says that if anyone goes it will be Brown himself. Mark Twain describes his elation: "During the brief remainder of the trip I knew how an emancipated slave feels, for I was an emancipated slave myself."[5] But the incident culminates in tragedy. Unable to work with Brown, Mark Twain transfers to the *A. T. Lacey*, just before the *Pennsylvania* leaves New Orleans for St. Louis. He arrives at Memphis on his new vessel in time to see his beloved brother die—a victim of an explosion on the *Pennsylvania*. Thus the episode of Mark Twain's piloting which had been executed as a masterpiece of humor in the *Atlantic* sketches ends in *Life on the Mississippi* on a note of the utmost pathos.

If Brown is no longer the old Brown, the cub in this new episode is no longer the apprentice Mark Twain of "Old Times on the Mississippi." Far from being the mock-ignorant apprentice, he is the Boy of Pluck bravely fighting the tyrant and applauded for his derring-do by the Benevolent Protector himself. The death of Henry Clemens constitutes the theatrically sad ending of the little melodrama. In this essentially Victorian theatrical, Bixby the mock tyrant is replaced by Brown the villain; and Mark Twain, the mock innocent cub, becomes the sensitive, injured boy bearing the blows which Brown mercilessly inflicts.

This story not only marks the transition from "Old Times on the Mississippi" to the travel book *Life on the Mississippi*; it defines the change from the essential humor of the earlier work to the essential pathos of *Life*

[5] *Writings*, IX, 176.

on the Mississippi. In this new structure, "Old Times on the Mississippi" becomes merely one of the stages in the irrecoverable past of the great river. And the "present" trip of 1883, from St. Louis to New Orleans, becomes a chronicle of the changes which have all but blotted out the landscape of Mark Twain's remote past. In his downward journey to New Orleans, Mark Twain, the apostle of progress, sees the false pasts which the society has erected to defend itself from the ruins of time; at the same moment, he laments the lost glory of the steamboating epoch. From the irony of recognizing the false pasts and the nostalgia for the lost past which characterize the down-river journey, Mark Twain moves back up-river toward his Hannibal home, recalling along the way episodes from his childhood. These memories which Mark Twain indulges are, like the story of Henry, essentially guilt fantasies cast in the form of nostalgic recollections and boyhood adventures. Although there is an element of play in Mark Twain even at his most nostalgic, there is a strong presence of the sensitive author recounting the guilt, injury, and fear of his bygone youth as he tells of burning the jail house and killing the prisoner, of diving into the river and touching the hand of his drowned companion, and of lying in terror while the thunder storms raged in the night.

All of these experiences are essentially false in a way that the tall tales of Mark Twain are not false. The tall tale, as told in *Roughing It*, is true in that it is the only lie in a world of lies which reveals itself to be a lie. But these experiences are not tall tales of Mark Twain; they are the fantasy life of Samuel Clemens which remained to be converted into the *fiction* of *Huckleberry Finn*. Although interesting as biography, they are essentially conventional.

The most genuine truth in *Life on the Mississippi* is to be found, characteristically, in the one authentic tall tale in the volume—the tale of the birth of "Mark Twain," which Mark Twain tells for the first time. That tale, as it is told, identifies "Mark Twain" as having emerged from an essentially guilty act. Samuel Clemens had gratuitously parodied old Captain Isaiah Sellers and had adopted the old gentleman's pseudonym of "Mark Twain" years later—half-humorously in order to carry on the tradition of Sellers' incredible memory, half-guiltily to pay off the debt incurred by the wound the parody had inflicted. Here is the tall tale told in the grand manner, for it exposes Mark Twain as the figure who, like old Captain Sellers, has a memory which invariably *enlarges* upon fact. Mark Twain concludes his account by emphasizing how the old man had been hurt by the burlesque, and how he had tried to make up for the wound he had dealt.

> Captain Sellers did me the honor to profoundly detest me from that day forth. When I say he did me the honor, I am not using empty words. It was a very real honor to be in the thoughts of so great a man as Captain Sellers, and I had wit enough to appreciate it and be proud of it. It was a distinction to be loved by such a man; but it was a much greater distinction to be hated by him, because he loved scores of people; but he didn't sit up nights to hate anybody but me.
>
> He never printed another paragraph while he lived, and he never signed "Mark Twain" to anything. At the time the telegraph brought me the news of his death, I was on the Pacific coast. I was a fresh, new journalist, and needed a *nom de guerre*; so I confiscated the ancient mariner's discarded one, and have done my best to make it remain what it was in his hands—a sign and symbol and warrant that whatever is found in its company may be gambled on as being the petrified truth. How I've succeeded, it would not be modest in me to say.[6]

Here is an exquisite bit of self-definition. The tale, so far as the most serious Mark Twain scholars have been able

6 *Ibid.*, pp. 402-403.

to discover, cannot be corroborated from the life of Samuel Clemens. But then why should it be? For Mark Twain, even as he insists upon his extreme veracity, actually arouses comic doubt about the entire episode. All this, of course, is the ancient strategy of Mark Twain's tall tale. What is new for Mark Twain is the substance of the tale. As he defines himself almost on the eve of making the great endeavor which was to complete *Huckleberry Finn*, "Mark Twain" is at once a name and an act. As a name it has to do with the most ancient memory of the great Mississippi—a memory containing an ancient yet personal past in which possibilities existed on a grander scale than in the dwarfed present. As an act, the name is an attempt to make reparation for a personal injury inflicted as a result of a literary burlesque. The act is a *making up* in both senses of the phrase. It is an invention or tall tale; at the same time, it is an effort to make amends for the humiliation suffered by the old Captain.

In "Old Times on the Mississippi," Mark Twain had converted his own humiliations into humor. The climactic scene of the sketches came when Mark Twain humorously reconstructed the public humiliation to which Bixby had exposed him. But in *Life on the Mississippi*, Mark Twain identifies himself as having been born not out of humiliation inflicted upon him, but out of humiliation he had inflicted upon another. In other words, to the sense of shame, Mark Twain had added, or was adding, a sense of guilt. Whereas he had converted the shame into the series of humorous humiliations of "Old Times on the Mississippi," the guilt, which he had gone almost out of his way to experience from 1876 until 1883, had been indulged rather than converted. It had manifested itself either in the form of indignation—as in *The Prince and the Pauper* and portions of *A Tramp Abroad*—or in the emergence of the nostalgia and sentimental guilt fantasies of *Life on the Mississippi*.[7] The book which was

[7] Kenneth Lynn (*Mark Twain and Southwestern Humor*, p. 203) perceptively observes that the coming revolt against the

assimilating, and finally converting into humor the guilt, indignation, and nostalgia—those aspects we want to call the darker side of Mark Twain's genius—was *Huckleberry Finn*. Growing through the years between *Tom Sawyer* and *Life on the Mississippi*, it was the book which was extending Mark Twain's humor into all that "serious" territory both discovered and required by the style of *Huckleberry Finn*.

To say that in *Huckleberry Finn* Mark Twain extended his humor into serious territory is not to say that his humor became serious, but that larger areas of seriousness came under the dominion of his humor. If the turning of serious issues into the form of humor was the substantial inversion of the book, the formal inversion lay in transforming dialect into vernacular, which is to say making it the vehicle of vision. In terms of literary history, *Huckleberry Finn* marks the full emergence of an American language, and although Mark Twain did not accomplish the process alone, he *realized* the tradition which he inherited. The "Southwest" humorists—Hooper, Longstreet, Harris, and Thorpe; the comic journalists—Artemus Ward, Petroleum V. Nasby, Josh Billings, and John Phoenix; and the local colorists—Harriet Beecher Stowe, Bret Harte, Mary E. Wilkins Freeman, and Sarah Orne Jewett—had all used dialect. Yet in the humor of the old Southwest and in the literary achievements of the local colorists, the dialect was framed by a literary language which invariably condescended to it. The comic journal-

---

conservative opinions of his friends could be heard in the humor of "The Facts Concerning the Recent Carnival of Crime in Connecticut," a sketch Mark Twain read to the Monday Evening Club of Hartford on January 24, 1876. This sketch, interestingly enough, depicted Mark Twain killing his conscience after being haunted and taunted by it beyond endurance. Having accomplished the murder, he has a carnival of crime. Though the sketch does disclose possible revolt, its strong fantasy element provides ample protection and forecasts the relatively safe exercises into fantasy Mark Twain was to make much later in his career.

ists, though they dropped the literary frame to appear as "characters," reduced dialect to a comic image. If the Southwest humorists tended to brutalize dialect characters and local colorists to sentimentalize them, the comic journalists, by reducing themselves to dialect, sought to give pungency and quaintness to conventional thought.

But something altogether different happens in *Huckleberry Finn*. The language is neither imprisoned in a frame nor distorted into a caricature; rather, it becomes a way of casting character and experience at the same time. This combination is the fine economy of Huckleberry Finn's style. Thus when Huck declares at the outset that he, not Mark Twain, will write this book, the language at one and the same time defines character and action.

> You don't know about me without you have read a book by the name *The Adventures of Tom Sawyer*; but that ain't no matter. That book was made by Mr. Mark Twain, and he told the truth, mainly. There was things which he stretched, but mainly he told the truth. That is nothing. I never see anybody but lied one time or another, without it was Aunt Polly, or the Widow, or maybe Mary. Aunt Polly—Tom's Aunt Polly, she is—and Mary, and the Widow Douglas is all told about in that book, which is mostly a true book, with some stretchers, as I said before.[8]

Nothing more seems to be going on here than in previous uses of dialect. But by allowing Huck's vernacular merely to *imply* the literary form, Mark Twain was reorganizing the entire value system of language, for all values had to be transmitted directly or indirectly through Huck's vernacular. In turning the narration over to Huck, Mark Twain abandoned the explicit norms and risked making his vernacular force the reader to supply the implied norms. The vernacular he developed created the means of control within the reader's mind, chiefly in

---

[8] *Writings*, XIII, 1.

three ways. First of all, Huck's incorrect language implied standard, correct, literary English. Second, Huck's status as a child invited an indulgence from the reader. Finally, Huck's action in time and place—freeing a slave in the Old South before the Civil War—insured moral approval from the reader. Though he is being a bad boy in his own time, he is being a good boy in the reader's imagination.

All these controls, which are really *conventions*, exist outside the novel. They are just what the style of the novel is *not*; for the style is the inversion which implies the conventions yet remains their opposite. And this style is Mark Twain's revolution in language, his rebellion in form; and it marks the emergence of the American language to which both Hemingway and Faulkner allude when they say that Mark Twain was the first American writer, the writer from whom they descend.[9]

The freeing of the vernacular from the conventions is the larger historical fact of form which provides an index to the action of the novel. For this vernacular language, which implies respectable language, is not only the form of the book; it is at one and the same time the character of Huckleberry Finn. To talk about the revolt of the one should be to talk about the revolt of the other. I say *should*, because Huck's revolt seems on the face of things a genuinely tame performance. He is involved in a subversive project which has the reader's complete approval—the freeing of a slave in the Old South, a world which, by virtue of the Civil War, has been declared morally reprehensible because of the slavery it condoned. Huck's rebellion is therefore being negotiated in a society which the reader's conscience indicts as morally wrong and which history has declared legally wrong. Moreover,

---

[9] Hemingway's words were: "All modern American literature comes from one book by Mark Twain called *Huckleberry Finn* . . . it's the best book we've had. All American writing comes from that. There was nothing before. There has been nothing as good since" (*Green Hills of Africa* [New York, 1935], p. 22).

Huck is a boy, a relatively harmless figure who drifts helplessly into his rebellion, making his subversion not only an act which the reader can approve but can indulge. His badness is inverted into goodness.

All this seems obvious, yet many readers never cease to celebrate the pluck of Huck's rebellion, when if this were all there was to it we would have nothing but the blandest sentimental action. What, after all, was courageous about writing in Hartford twenty years after the Civil War—or what is courageous about reading in a post-Civil War world—a book about a boy who was helping a slave to freedom? Such an act would be roughly equivalent to writing a novel in our time about a boy in Hitler's Germany helping a Jew to the border. Not that a great novel could not emerge from either of these subjects. In the case of *Huckleberry Finn* one did. Yet the boldness of the book—its exploration and discovery—does not reside in so tame a representation, but in the utilization of the action to gain the reader's assent to make the voyage downstream.

This built-in approval, stemming from Huck's initial "moral" advantage and from his being a boy—and thus evocative of the indulgent nostalgia Mark Twain had learned to exploit in *Tom Sawyer*—is what I take to be the "moral sentiment" of the book. But this moral sentiment is not the action of the book any more than the implicit conventional language is the style of the book. Rather, Huck's action is the inversion of the sentiment.

The humor of the book rides upon and at the same time requires this crucial inversion. For the more Huck berates himself for doing "bad" things, the more the reader approves him for doing "good" ones. Thus what for Huck is his worst action—refusing to turn Jim in to Miss Watson—is for the reader his best. When Huck says "All right, then, I'll *go* to hell," the reader is sure he is going to heaven. If this ironic relationship should ever break down, Huck's whole stature would be threatened. If Huck ever begins to think he is doing a good thing by helping Jim, he will become a good boy like Sid—one knowingly engaged in virtuous action; or a bad boy like Tom—one who can seem to go against society because he really knows that he is doing right. Clear though all this should be, the moral sentiment implied by the style inexorably arouses a wish that Huck have some recognition of his achievement.

It is just this wish which the ending of the novel frustrates; and since the wish is so pervasively exploited by the action of the novel, it is no wonder that the ending has been not a small problem. Of course, defenses of the ending can be made and have been made, but the point remains that they are defenses. No matter how adroit the critic, he begins from a position of special pleading, as if he were trying to convince himself that in an acknowledged masterpiece there could not really be such a wanton collapse. Even the most sympathetic critics of Mark Twain find the wiser path is to regret the closing ten chapters. Thus, Ernest Hemingway, after observing that modern American literature stemmed from *Huckleberry Finn*, went on to say, "If you read it you must stop where the Nigger Jim is stolen from the boys. That is the real end. The rest is just cheating."[10] Philip Young, following Hemingway, has gone so far as to declare that the beginning as well as the end could well be omitted without substantially taking away from the book.[11] So passionate an admirer of the book as Bernard De Voto acknowledged that Mark Twain lost his purpose at the end and drifted into "inharmonious burlesque":

> A few pages earlier he had written the scene in which many readers have found his highest reach.
> . . . And now, without any awareness that he was muddying the waters of great fiction, he plunges into a trivial extravaganza on a theme he had exhausted years before. In the whole history of the

[10] *Ibid.*
[11] Philip Young, *Ernest Hemingway* (New York, 1952), p. 196.

English novel there is no more abrupt or more chilling descent.[12]

Probably the most formidable attack ever made on the
ending of the book is found in Leo Marx's extremely interesting essay, "Mr. Eliot, Mr. Trilling, and Huckleberry
Finn." Exposing Trilling's and Eliot's rather perfunctory
and evasive approvals of the ending, Marx presents a
rigorous analysis of Mark Twain's failure in the closing
chapters of his masterpiece. Mark Twain failed, Marx
believes, because he refused the responsibilities which
went with the vision of the journey. For the journey was,
according to Marx, the Quest—the great voyage toward
freedom which Huck and Jim had so precariously made.
But in the last ten chapters, Marx feels that Mark Twain
simply turns the book over to the high jinks of Tom Sawyer, while Huck shrinkingly assumes the stature of a
little straight man, observing the burlesque antics of his
companion, but apparently unmoved by them. The cause
of this slump on Mark Twain's part, Marx concludes, is
simply that the journey, the Quest, *cannot* succeed. The
drifting river has taken Huck and Jim ever deeper into
slavery, and Mark Twain, unable to resolve the paradox
of this reality which defeats his wish, simply evades the
entire issue by shifting to burlesque.[13]

Persuasive though this argument is, Mark Twain's form
rules out the possibilities which Marx insists on. Since
Huck's entire identity is based upon an inverted order of
values just as his style is based upon "incorrect" usage,
he cannot have any recognition of his own virtue. Failure
to acknowledge this necessity causes Marx to see the
journey as a quest, whereas it simply is not at any time
a quest. A quest is a positive journey, implying an effort,
a struggle to reach a goal. But Huck is escaping. His

[12] Bernard De Voto, *Mark Twain at Work* (Cambridge, Mass.,
1942), p. 92.
[13] Leo Marx, "Mr. Eliot, Mr. Trilling, and Huckleberry Finn,"
American Scholar, XXIII (Autumn, 1953), 423-39.

journey is primarily a negation, a flight *from* tyranny, not a flight toward freedom.

In fact, Huck's central mode of being is that of escape and evasion. He forgets much more than he remembers; he lies, steals, and in general participates in as many confidence tricks as the King and the Duke. But the two cardinal facts—that he is a boy and is involved in helping a runaway slave—serve endlessly to sustain the reader's approval. It is precisely this approval which, putting the reader's moral censor to sleep, provides the central good humor pervading the incongruities, absurdities, and cruelties through which the narrative beautifully makes its way. The vernacular inversion, which so surely evokes the feeling of approval and indulgence, is narratively embodied in the very drift of the great river on which the raft miraculously rides.[14]

To be sure, at the fateful moment when Huck determines to set Jim free, he finds himself in open rebellion against Negro slavery. But he comes reluctantly, not gloriously, forward; even as he makes his famous declaration to go to hell, he is looking for a way out. He is certainly not a rebel; he is in a tight place and does the *easiest* thing. The role of Abolitionist is not comfortable nor comforting to him and in turning over to Tom Sawyer the entire unpleasant business of freeing Jim, Huck is surely not acting out of but remarkably *in* character.

Marx's inversion of Huck's escape into a quest drives him to the position of saying that Mark Twain could not "acknowledge the truth his novel contained" and thus evaded the central moral responsibilities of his vision. Yet for Marx the "truth" amounts to nothing more than Huck's perceiving that Negro slavery is wrong and in-

[14] The perfect integration between this drift and the river's motion is in part responsible for the beautiful economy with which Mark Twain treats the river. Far from needing to provide extensive descriptions and facts about the river as he did in *Life on the Mississippi*, he was able to render the river enormously real with economy of means. The reason: the fugitive boy and the river are made one through Huck's language.

volving himself in a quest for *political* freedom. In saying that the ending of the book discloses a failure of nerve and a retreat to the genteel tradition, it seems to me that Marx is completely turned around. Surely the genteel Bostonians would have applauded the moral sentiment of antislavery and political freedom which the novel entertains. They would have welcomed the quest rather than the escape. Yet if Marx is wrong, what is there to say about the ending?

To begin with, the ending is, to use Huck's term, uncomfortable. The problem is to define the source of this discomfort. Without question, there is a change when Tom Sawyer reappears. The narrative movement changes from one of adventure to burlesque—a burlesque which, in place of Huck's sincere but helpless involvement in freeing a real slave, puts Tom Sawyer's relatively cruel yet successful lark of freeing a slave already free. It is not Mark Twain's failure to distinguish between the two actions which jeopardizes his book; rather, it is his ironic exposure of Tom's action which threatens the humor of the book and produces the inharmonious burlesque De Voto regrets. Tom appears in such an unfortunate light in the closing pages that many readers of *Huckleberry Finn* can never again read *Tom Sawyer* without in one way or another holding Tom responsible for motives he had not had in the earlier book.

Tom's play seems unpardonable because he already knows that Jim is free. Yet this knowledge—which Tom withholds from Huck—finally clears up for Huck the mystery of Tom's behavior toward him. Upon at last discovering the knowledge Tom has withheld from him, Huck, who has been troubled by Tom's "badness," at last understands why his respectable companion has been able to commit such a crime. His only remaining problem is to find out why Tom spent so much effort "setting a free nigger free." This, too, is cleared up when Tom explains to the long-suffering Aunt Sally that he made his elaborate and vexing arrangements purely for "adventure."

Tom's adventures are a unique cruelty in a book which depicts so much cruelty. All the other cruelties are committed for some "reason"—for honor, money, or power. But Tom's cruelty has a purity all its own—it is done solely for the sake of adventure. After facing Tom's long play, it is possible to see Huck's famous remark about the King and the Duke in a larger perspective. "Human beings can be awful cruel to each other," Huck had said upon seeing the scoundrels ridden out of town on a rail. This statement not only points backward to the episodes with the King and the Duke, but serves as a gateway leading from the King and the Duke's departure to Tom Sawyer's performance. For Tom's pure play runs directly counter to a wish the journey has generated. That is the frustration of the ending—the inversion. Having felt Huck's slow discovery of Jim's humanity, the reader perforce deplores Tom's casual ignorance and unawareness.

Yet the judgment which the last ten chapters render upon Tom is surely the judgment rendered upon the moral sentiment on which the book has ridden. If the reader sees in Tom's performance a rather shabby and safe bit of play, he is seeing no more than the exposure of the approval with which he watched Huck operate. For if Tom is rather contemptibly setting a free slave free, what after all is the reader doing, who begins the book after the *fact* of the Civil War? This is the "joke" of the book—the moment when, in outrageous burlesque, it attacks the sentiment which its style has at once evoked and exploited. To see that Tom is doing at the ending what we have been doing throughout the book is essential to understanding what the book has meant to us. For when Tom proclaims to the assembled throng who have witnessed his performance that Jim "is as free as any cretur that walks this earth," he is an exposed embodiment of the complacent moral sentiment on which the reader has relied throughout the book. And to the extent the reader has indulged the complacency he will be disturbed by the ending.

To be frustrated by the ending is to begin to discover the meaning of this journey, which evokes so much indulgence and moral approval that the censor is put to sleep. Beneath the sleeping censor, the real rebellion of *Huckleberry Finn* is enacted. For there must be a real rebellion—a rebellion which cannot so easily be afforded—else Mark Twain is guilty of a failure far greater than the ending. If the "incorrect" vernacular of *Huckleberry Finn* is to be more than décor, it must enact an equally "incorrect" vision. Otherwise, the style becomes merely a way of saying rather than a way of being. It is not simply the "poetry" or "beauty" or "rhythm" of Huck's vernacular which makes his language work, but the presence of a commensurate vernacular vision. The reason that imitators of *Huckleberry Finn* fail—the reason that Mark Twain himself later failed—is that they lack the vision to match their style, and thus their language is merely décor. One has but to read Edgar Lee Masters' *Mitch Miller*—which is a "modern" attempt to show what the childhood of Huck and Tom was really like—to know how sentimental such language can be unless it is sustained by a genuinely radical vision. Even Sherwood Anderson's "I Want to Know Why," in many ways the finest example of vernacular vision directly derivative from *Huckleberry Finn*, falls far short of Mark Twain, because its end, though finely climactic, is unfortunately sentimental. The young boy's anguished appeal upon discovering the Jockey with the whore is, after all, just the same old truth we knew all the time.

What then *is* the rebellion of *Huckleberry Finn*? What is it but an attack upon the conscience? The conscience, after all is said and done, is the real tyrant in the book. It is the relentless force which pursues Huckleberry Finn; it is the tyrant from which he seeks freedom. And it is not only the social conscience which threatens Huck, but *any* conscience. The social conscience, represented in the book by the slaveholding society of the Old South, is easily seen and exposed. It is the false conscience. But what of the true conscience which the reader wishes to project upon Huck and which Huck himself is at last on the threshold of accepting? It, too, is finally false. Although the book plays upon the notion that all conscience is finally social, it does not stand on that line; for the action is not defining the conscience so much as rejecting it. Whether the conscience is "lower" social conscience or the "higher" inner conscience, it remains the tyrant which drives its victims into the absurd corners from which they cannot escape. Thus on the one hand, there is the "law" or "right" of slavery from which Jim is trying to escape and against which Huck finds himself in helpless rebellion. But there are then the "inner" codes which appear as equally absurd distortions. There is Pap's belief in freedom; there is the code of the feud which the Grangerfords and Shepherdsons hold to; there is the "honor" of Colonel Sherburn; and finally there is the "principle" of Tom Sawyer who rises proudly to the defense of Jim because he "is as free as any cretur that walks this earth." In every case the conscience, whether it comes from society or from some apparent inner realm, is an agent of aggression—aggression against the self or against another. Either the means or the excuse by which pain is inflicted, the conscience is both law and duty, erasing the possibility of choice and thereby constraining its victims to a necessary and irrevocable course of action.

From the "Southern" conscience, Huck first attempts to flee. But even in flight from it, borne southward on the great river, his "Northern" conscience begins to awaken. This is the apparently internal conscience—the Civil War he finds himself engaged in on the raft as it glides deeper and deeper into the territory of slavery, not of freedom. Our moral sentiment approves his flight from his Southern conscience, but with the approval comes the hope that he will discover his Northern conscience. But it is just here that Huck will not accept the invitation. For chapter after chapter he remains the fugitive—in flight from the old conscience and evading the development of a new one.

And the reason he evades it is clear—the conscience is *uncomfortable*. Indeed, comfort and satisfaction are the value terms in *Huckleberry Finn*. Freedom for Huck is not realized in terms of political liberty but in terms of pleasure. Thus his famous pronouncement about life on the raft: "Other places do seem so cramped and smothery, but a raft don't. You feel mighty free and easy and comfortable on a raft."[15] And later, when the King and the Duke threaten to break the peace, Huck determines not to take a stand against them, observing, "What you want above all things, on a raft, is for everybody to be satisfied, and feel right and kind toward the others."[16] In almost every instance Huck projects the good life in terms of ease, satisfaction, comfort. A satirist would see it in terms of justice; a moralist would have it as a place of righteousness. But a humorist envisions it as a place of good feeling, where no pain or discomfort can enter. This is why Huck does not see clothes, which figure so prominently as the garments of civilization, as veils to hide the body, or as the false dress whereby a fiction of status is maintained. This would be the satiric vision. As far as Huck is concerned, clothes and civilization itself are undesirable because they are essentially *uncomfortable*. "But I reckon I got to light out for the territory," he says as he departs, "because Aunt Sally she's going to adopt me and sivilize me, and I can't stand it."[17] When Huck says he "can't stand it," he is literally referring to the cramped discomfort of submitting to the clothes and quarters of civilization. To be sure, the phrase suggests a vastly wider range of significances, but significances

[15] *Writings*, XIII, 162. The conscience, on the other hand, is the source of discomfort. As Huck says, ". . . it don't make no difference whether you do right or wrong, a person's conscience ain't got no sense, and just goes for him *anyway*. If I had a yeller dog that didn't know no more than a person's conscience does I would pison him" (*Writings*, XIII, 321).

[16] *Ibid.*, p. 174.

[17] *Ibid.*, p. 405.

that are inexorably rooted in a logic of feeling, comfort, and bodily satisfaction. The significances are *our* discoveries, which are at once made possible by and anchored to the concrete image of the raft, the boy, and the Negro. The good feeling, comfort, and ease dominating this journey which makes its way through a society of meanness, cowardice, and cruelty are perfectly embodied by the raft adrift upon the river.

This logic of pleasure at the heart of the book must also be at the heart of any "positive" value we may wish to ascribe to the experience of reading it. Most criticism of *Huckleberry Finn*, however, retreats from the pleasure principle toward the relative safety of "moral issues" and the imperatives of the Northern conscience. This flight is made because of the uncomfortable feeling relating to Huck's "evasion," his "escape," and finally his "rejection" of civilization. What Huck is rejecting is, of course, the conscience—which Mark Twain was later to rail at under the name of the "Moral Sense." The conscience, the trap of adult civilization which lies in wait for Huck throughout the novel, is what he is at such pains to evade. It is his successful evasion which we as readers cannot finally face. The reader who rejects the paradox usually does so on the grounds that the book is "just" a humorous book. The one who detects and is disturbed by it is more likely to follow William Van O'Connor's pronouncements about the "dangers" of innocence and the "failure" of moral vision. A weakness in Huck—pontificates O'Connor in his attempt to prove that the book is *not* a great American novel—is that he does not "acknowledge the virtues of civilization and live, as one must, inside it."[18] Huck does acknowledge the virtues, of course, and upbraids himself for being uncomfortable with them.

But far from relying upon such cozy affirmations as O'Connor longs for, the book moves *down* the river into

[18] William Van O'Connor, "Why *Huckleberry Finn* Is Not The Great American Novel," *College English*, XVII (October, 1955), p. 8.

the deeper repressions of slavery, enacting at every moment a conversion of morality into pleasure. Extending the range of humor through the ills, the agonies, and the cruelties of civilization, it shows how much the conscience—whether Northern or Southern—is the negative force leading to acts of violence upon the self or upon another. Huck's "escape" is of course an escape from violence, a rejection of cruelty—his instinct is neither to give nor to receive pain if he can avoid it.

The prime danger to his identity comes at the moment he chooses the developing inner or Northern conscience. This moment, when Huck says "All right, then, I'll *go* to hell," is characteristically the moment we fatally approve, and approve *morally*. But it is with equal fatality the moment at which Huck's identity is most precariously threatened. In the very act of choosing to go to hell he has surrendered to the notion of a *principle* of right and wrong. He has forsaken the world of pleasure to make a moral choice. Precisely here is where Huck is about to negate himself—where, with an act of positive virtue, he actually commits himself to play the role of Tom Sawyer which he *has* to assume in the closing section of the book. To commit oneself to the idea, the *morality* of freeing Jim, is to become Tom Sawyer. Here again is the irony of the book, and the ending, far from evading the consequences of Huck's act of rebellion, realizes those consequences.

Mark Twain's real problem—his real dilemma—was not at all his inability to "face" the issues of slavery; certainly it was not a fear of the society or a failure of moral and political courage which brought Mark Twain to the tight place where Huck had to decide forever and ever. Rather, it was the necessities of his humorous form. For in order to achieve expression of the deep wish which *Huckleberry Finn* embodies—the wish for freedom from any conscience—Mark Twain had to intensify the moral sentiment. The moment there is any real moral doubt about Huck's action, the wish will be threatened. Yet

when Huck makes his moral affirmation, he fatally negates the wish for freedom from the conscience; for if
his affirmation frees him from the Southern conscience,
it binds him to his Northern conscience. No longer an
outcast, he can be welcomed into the society to play the
role of Tom Sawyer, which is precisely what happens.
When he submits to Tom's role, we are the ones who become uncomfortable. The entire burlesque ending is a
revenge upon the moral sentiment which, though it
shielded the humor, ultimately threatened Huck's identity.

This is the larger reality of the ending—what we may
call the necessity of the form. That it was a cost which
the form exacted no one would deny. But to call it a
failure, a piece of moral cowardice, is to miss the true
rebellion of the book, for the disturbance of the ending
is nothing less than our and Mark Twain's recognition of
the full meaning of *Huckleberry Finn*. If the reader is
pushed to the limits of his humor, Mark Twain had
reached the limits of his—he had seen through to the end.
The disillusion begins not when Tom returns to the stage,
but when Huck says "All right, then, I'll *go* to hell"—when
our applause and approval reach their zenith. At that
moment, which anyone would agree is Mark Twain's highest achievement, Huck has internalized the image of Jim;
and that image, whose reality he has enjoyed during the
fatal drift downstream, becomes the scourge which
shames him out of his evasion. The whole process is disclosed in the lyric utterance leading to his decision. Having written the note to Miss Watson telling where Jim is,
Huck feels cleansed and at last able to pray:

> But I didn't do it straight off, but laid the paper
> down and set there thinking—thinking how good it
> was all this happened so, and how near I come to
> being lost and going to hell. And went on thinking.
> And got to thinking over our trip down the river;
> and I see Jim before me all the time: in the day and
> in the night-time, sometimes moonlight, sometimes
> storms, and we a-floating along, talking and singing

and laughing. But somehow I couldn't seem to strike no places to harden me against him, but only the other kind. I'd see him standing my watch on top of his'n, 'stead of calling me, so I could go on sleeping; and see him how glad he was when I come back out of the fog; and when I come to him again in the swamp, up there where the feud was; and such-like times; and would always call me honey, and pet me, and do everything he could think of for me, and how good he always was; and at last I struck the time I saved him by telling the men we had smallpox aboard, and he was so grateful, and said I was the best friend old Jim ever had in the world, and the *only* one he's got now; and then I happened to look around and see that paper.

It was a close place.[19]

This lyrical rehearsal of the journey is also the journey's end. And the decision which ends it is cast in the positive locution of Tom Sawyer, not in Huck's essentially negative vernacular.[20] When Huck says he will go to hell, in five minutes of reading time he is there. For in this novel, which constantly plays against superstitious hereafters, there is no fire-and-brimstone hell but only civilization—which is precisely where Huck finds himself as a consequence of his own determination.

This dilemma and disillusion are what Mark Twain would not shrink from, but carried through, though it cost him almost everything—which is saying it cost him his good humor. In the burlesque chapters, he understandably though precariously turned upon his invention, upon his reader, and upon himself. Yet even here he did not

[19] *Writings*, XIII, 296-97. Although Huck's language constantly describes his feelings and thoughts, they are so directly wedded to external action and dependent on it that he seems to have no independent "thought." This passage is the only extended narrative of such an inner life. Once the decision is made, he hardly reflects upon his past. If he remembers, he keeps it to himself.

[20] Huck's most characteristic errors of grammar are, significantly enough, his constant use of the double negative and his persistent confusion of verb tense.

entirely abandon the pleasure principle, but left his "serious" readers pleased with themselves instead of the book,
their moral complacency ruffled by nothing more than
comfortable indignation at the evasions of humor.

As for Mark Twain, he had seen through to the end,
and it almost killed him. He never would have so good
a humor again. His despair, having set in at the moment
of Huckleberry Finn's affirmation, never really let up.
The only way he could survive was to try to swallow the
joke which became more and more sour the rest of his
embattled way. Having seen the limits of his humor,
he turned upon them and railed at the conscience and
the need for self-approval, the twin human characteristics which seemed to make the human race utterly
ridiculous and damned.

And what of Huck? As Nick Carraway said of Gatsby,
he turned out all right. He went to the territory because
he was true to himself and to his creator. He didn't go
there to lead civilization either, but to play outside it.
Refusing to grow up and tell the lie of the conscience,
he left behind him a novel for all time. It was truly a
novel of reconstruction. First, it had brought into fiction
not the Old South but an entirely new one which the
Northern conscience could welcome back into the Union.
And in the process of its humor, it reconstructed the
psyche, following the pleasure principle as far as it would
go to discover in the southern reaches of the Great River
the tyranny of the conscience which keeps the adult in
chains and makes his pleasure the enactment of greater
and greater cruelty. He had not reached childhood's end,
but had disclosed the lie of the adult world. In his last
moment he said, "so there ain't nothing more to write
about, and I am rotten glad of it, because if I'd 'a'knowed
what a trouble it was to make a book I wouldn't 'a'tackled
it, and ain't a-going to no more." We of course constantly
lecture Mark Twain about having turned away from his
true vein of ore. The fact is, however, that he could not

turn away but kept trying to do just what we want of him. He kept trying to call Huck back to tell another story. But Huck, though he came docilely, could never tell the truth. He had told all the truth he had to tell in one glorious lie.

CHAPTER
VIII

THE CAMPAIGN
THAT FAILED

ALTHOUGH he did not know it at the time—perhaps he could not have afforded such knowledge—Mark Twain had reached the high-water mark of his career with the publication of *Huckleberry Finn*. Everything he was to do would mark a falling away from the flood tide of imaginative energy which had lifted him buoyantly to the peak of his power in art. Nor is it surprising that this peak was also the zenith of his fortunes in life. Throughout his career there had always been a vital link between art and fortune in his creative enterprise. In the very beginning of things, "Mark Twain" had been discovered in the Nevada silver fields, and the first great story which began to make his fortune—"The Celebrated Jumping Frog" —was the nugget of imaginative experience he had salvaged from an abandoned mining camp. The figures of the miner, the pilot, and Tom Sawyer are invariably linked with glamor, capital, and treasure. Their dream of striking it rich not only reveals their creator's involvement in capitalistic society; their stature as great inventions reflects the intense imaginative effort which went into their making. Mark Twain was himself an embodiment of the twin activities of investment and invention, and the remarkably intimate relationship between the two makes it possible to define his genius as essentially speculative. This does not mean that the invention and the investment were always in harmony. Like those extraordinary Siamese twins who preoccupied Mark Twain from the beginning to the end of his career, they were often in direct conflict. When, for example, Mark Twain was riding the creative tide of *Huckleberry Finn*, he wrote on June 29, 1883, in heat and haste to his nephew Charles L. Webster:

> I cannot answer letters; I can ill spare the time to read them. I am writing a book; my time is brief; I cannot be interrupted by vineyard business or any *other*. . . . You are my business man; & business I myself will *not* transact, neither will I write letters or consult about it. . . . I *won't* talk business—I will perish first. I hate the very idea of business, in all its forms.[1]

Such outbursts against the harassments of the business world, frequent enough to be considered characteristic, resemble his repeated attacks upon the life and act of lecturing. Yet just as he instinctively went back to the platform, he again and again involved himself in the life of business. All his attacks upon these modes of life were assaults which one-half of his creative self levied against the other half. Such fulminations led Van Wyck Brooks, and critics who followed him, to lament Mark Twain's involvement in the business world, but the intensity of Mark Twain's invective and the clarity of his style in such moments confirm how much art and business were for him a single creative enterprise.

He had from the beginning of his career been interested in investment and speculation. Literature itself was a business for Mark Twain, a means of converting his imaginative inventions into capital. More than the artist, soldier, or politician, the inventor was to him the hero; he often saw himself as an inventor and guarded his discoveries accordingly. All his life he fought for copyright

[1] *Mark Twain, Businessman*, ed. Samuel Charles Webster (Boston, 1946), pp. 216-17.

laws which would afford authors more protection, for he viewed the copyright as a patent. Regretting that copyrights expired after a period of time, he sought in later life to circumvent such an eventuality by incorporating himself, thereby converting his pseudonym from mere pen name to a formidable trade-mark which would hold his copyright in perpetuity.

In the early years of his career, Mark Twain was so busy trying to make literature a successful venture that he could not give full play to his business ambitions; but by the time he was engaged in the final phase of *Huckleberry Finn*, he was almost equally engaged in speculative ventures beyond the world of art. He had shown interest in everything from vineyards to history games and had actually made extensive investments in a steam generator, a steam pulley, a new method of marine telegraphy, a watch company, an insurance house, and in a new process of engraving—the kaolotype. All these investments, though significant, were but preliminaries for his involvement in two huge projects: the Webster Publishing Company in which he was chief investor and senior partner; and the Paige typesetting machine. There is no more graphic way of disclosing how inseparable the careers of art and business were for Mark Twain than by remembering that *Huckleberry Finn* was the first book published by the Webster Publishing Company.[2]

Huckleberry Finn, though financially a success, seemed but to prepare the way for Mark Twain's ultimate triumph as a businessman. It was as if his triumph in language and art gave him new power and left him free to deal with forces he had either evaded or submitted to in his struggle to make a fortune. Thus, in November of 1884, at almost the same moment *Huckleberry Finn* was to be published serially in the *Century*, Mark Twain deserted the Republican party to vote for Grover Cleveland. In declaring his independence from the party he had conspicuously supported since returning from his Western

[2] Paine, *A Biography*, II, 723-31, 771-73, 903-14.

sojourn, he was turning away from the approved politics of the Reconstruction era. His Mugwumpery was the political gesture accompanying his imaginative triumph. The one was the novel of Reconstruction, freeing him both from the guilt of the Southern past and from the moral tyranny of Radical Reconstruction; the other freed him from the approved politics of Reconstruction. Having conquered and reconstructed his own and the nation's past, he now occupied a position of command and power in the present.

Nowhere was Mark Twain's new power more apparent than in his determination to publish Grant's *Memoirs*. The assurance with which he secured and executed the Grant contract shows more clearly than anything else how, at the precise moment he had become a master of his art, he had also become a master of business. He not only had to know Grant; he had to know the world of publishing. Although he overrated the literary merit of the *Memoirs*—though simply and lucidly direct, Grant's style lacks the power Mark Twain claimed for it—he nevertheless gauged with precision the immense popularity Grant's book would have. Having been born out of the Civil War and having himself touched the heart of a mass audience, he understood, in a way that none of his contemporaries could have, the power of Grant's appeal. Both men had learned to command a multitude—the one upon the field of action, the other through the written language and the spoken voice. If Mark Twain the writer saw the force of Grant's style, Mark Twain the publisher instinctively recognized that the triumph of Grant's book lay not only in its style but in the fact that the old warrior was dictating it in the face of imminent death. The book was in effect a last act of heroism by the man who, having been so paralyzed in the White House, was, in the ordeal of his last battle, once more the great commander.

Mark Twain the publisher also knew that in publishing, as in lecturing, timing was everything and he wasted no time in taking full advantage of the moment when Grant was, by virtue of his death, once more in the minds and hearts of his countrymen. The publication of the book was as successful as his contract with Grant had been generous, and Mark Twain was able to pay Grant's widow a check for $250,000—probably the largest single royalty check issued in the nineteenth century. The whole venture was characterized by a bold audacity and supreme confidence on the part of the new publisher, and in the throes of his unparalleled success he had ample reason to believe that he was indeed gifted with the Midas touch.

The publication of the Grant *Memoirs* was much, much more than a mere financial *coup* in the life of Mark Twain. For in negotiating the contract with Grant, Mark Twain was quite consciously "saving" General Grant from the financial ruin to which Grant's presumable naiveté had exposed him. In Mark Twain's own version of the episode—and he lavished great attention upon it in his autobiographical dictations[3]—he had heard that Grant had been deceived and defrauded by a trusted associate, one Ferdinand Ward. This arch villain had mercilessly absconded with every dollar of Grant's he could lay hands on, leaving the ever-unsuspecting and innocent General at the point of bankruptcy. In speeding to the aid of the endangered Grant, Mark Twain was not only offering Grant much more advantageous terms for his *Memoirs* than those he was about to accept from another publisher; he was in effect coming to the rescue of the man who, as his tall tale would have it, had pursued him through the forests of Missouri during those two hectic, rainy weeks of his enlistment in the Confederate Army. As a former Southern soldier, a traitor no less, he was in a position to offer his old antagonist terms as liberal as those Grant had given at Appomattox. In the summer of 1884, Mark Twain had succeeded in converting his desertion to the Western territory into the triumphant

[3] *Mark Twain's Autobiography*, ed. Albert Bigelow Paine (2 vols.; New York, 1924), I, 13-70.

closing paragraphs of *Huckleberry Finn*, in which Huck lights out for the territory in a grandiose evasion of civilization and conscience. A year later, he was appearing as the knight in shining armor to rescue from imminent ruin the dying warrior who had once defeated him.

Mark Twain's "victory" over General Grant was thus a kind of victory over his past, and he may have felt during that buoyant period that he was ready to face, not obliquely through the displacements and guises of fiction but garrulously through the form of humorous autobiography, his Civil War past.[4] Robert Underwood Johnson, editor of the *Century*, had heard Mark Twain tell the story of his two weeks as a Confederate; at about the time Mark Twain closed the contract with Grant, Johnson persuaded him to contribute a written account of these two weeks for the *Century*. The article, tentatively entitled "My Campaign against Grant," seized immediately upon the fact that Grant and his future publisher had almost met in battle in the early spring of 1861. Of course, the supposed meeting had not really taken place, but Mark Twain's tentative title and his determination to disclose Grant as his old nemesis give indication enough of his ebullient confidence in the wake of the Grant contract.[5]

But this "Private History of the Campaign that Failed"—as Mark Twain happily chose to call the piece—was much more than an assimilation of the Grant contract. For the

[4] Mark Twain's first account of his war experience occurred in October, 1877, in a speech given to the Putnam Phalanx of Hartford. This account, much briefer than "The Private History," evades all explosive or touchy issues by concentrating on the antics of Ben Tupper, an orderly sergeant incapable of and impervious to military behavior. Even so, it constitutes an interesting moment in that period when Mark Twain was growing more and more hostile to the literature and morality "above" him. The speech, published in the *New York Times*, Sunday, October 7, 1877, was followed two months later by the Whittier Birthday Speech.

[5] For a full account of the origins, writing, and publication of "The Private History," see John Gerber, "Mark Twain's 'Private Campaign,'" *Civil War History*, I (March, 1955), 37-60.

"history" of the "Private History" is precisely that part of his past which lay unwritten and unreconstructed between *Roughing It* and "Old Times on the Mississippi." In the wake of *Huckleberry Finn*, his Mugwumpery, and his contract with General Grant, however, he turned to that long-evaded episode.

Under the pseudonym of Mark Twain, the Civil War experience of Samuel Clemens assumed the form of a tall tale. There was, first of all, the familiar burlesque perspective. At the time the article appeared, the *Century* and a host of other periodicals were inundating the public with a flood of articles by generals and other war worthies recounting the public histories of campaigns that succeeded. The *Century* itself, under Johnson's direction, was running "Battles and Leaders of the Civil War"—a series of just such accounts. Mark Twain hovers throughout his sketch between an attitude of justification and self-defense on the one hand, and burlesque aggression on the other. Thus, he begins with a mock apology for bringing to the public eye his inglorious war record; goes on to observe that at the outset he was for the Union but was in effect driven to the Southern cause by an abolitionist pilot from New York who insulted and belittled his Southern origins; then launches into the narrative of the adventure, occasionally pausing to document seeming absurdities with allusions to similar occurrences at other places in the South. The war itself, insofar as it is delineated, is presented as a rumored, offstage, unseen force pressuring a group of naïve recruits into various postures of absurdity. Instead of being brave, they invariably are cowards; instead of advancing, they master the art of retreat; instead of acquiring respect for discipline, they display total confusion. They instinctively avoid the enemy, fall back persistently through a series of deeper evasions and futilities, disobey their officers, reject all aspects of military order and procedure, and generally flout the war. To state the essence of the matter, instead of being willing to become soldiers—which is to say, men

—they insist on remaining boys. To emphasize the fact, Mark Twain repeatedly refers to the company, in which he had been a twenty-four-year-old man, as having been composed of "boys." As boys they play at war, treating the Civil War as a joke, as child's play. All the young soldiers are either youthfully incompetent or boyishly vain, either incapable of marching and shooting or childishly dreaming of glory.

The humor of the sketch, however, lies in neither the burlesque aggression nor the apologetic defense but in the genuine merger of the two. For the apologetic defense, which was the ostensible motive for the narrative, becomes the narrator's extravagant narrative of his own innocent and incompetent participation in the private history. If his friends were green and raw, so was he, and his imagination is as involved in elaborating his own misadventures as theirs. By just such elaboration, the apologetic defence of not having been a good soldier is transformed into the humorous offense of displacing the public history of the Civil War with his private history. This intention is not implicit but manifest. Thus, after being girded for battle and "invested in the cause of the Southern Confederacy" by Colonel Ross, a "practised politician and phrase juggler,"

> . . . we formed in line of battle and marched four miles to a shady and pleasant piece of woods on the border of the far reaching expanses of a flowery prairie. It was an enchanting region for war—our kind of war.
>
> We pierced the forest about half a mile, and took up a strong position, with some low, rocky, and wooded hills behind us, and a purling, limpid creek in front. Straightway half the command were in swimming and the other half fishing.[6]

But the old serious Civil War will not be displaced by such boyish antics or pastoral style and at the climax of

6 *Writings*, XXI, 262.

the sketch it intrudes to destroy their innocent pleasure. Hearing the report of an enemy approaching in the night, the recruits at first believe themselves victims of one more rumor and settle complacently into the comfort of their fortified corn crib, until the prolonged silence makes them uneasy. Their apprehension becomes terror when the sound of hoofbeats breaks upon the quiet night. Overmastered by fear, six of the recruits fire almost simultaneously upon a single horseman who appears in the moonlight and bring him down:

> When we got to him the moon revealed him distinctly. He was lying on his back, with his arms abroad; his mouth was open and his chest heaving with long gasps, and his white shirt-front was all splashed with blood. The thought shot through me that I was a murderer; that I had killed a man—a man who had never done me any harm. That was the coldest sensation that ever went through my marrow. I was down by him in a moment, helplessly stroking his forehead; and I would have given anything then—my own life freely—to make him again what he had been five minutes before. And all the boys seemed to be feeling in the same way; they hung over him, full of pitying interest, and tried all they could to help him, and said all sorts of regretful things. . . . Once my imagination persuaded me that the dying man gave me a reproachful look out of his shadowy eyes, and it seemed to me that I could rather he had stabbed me than done that. . . . In a little while the man was dead. He was killed in war; killed in fair and legitimate war; killed in battle, as you may say; and yet he was as sincerely mourned by the opposing force as if he had been their brother. . . . The man was not in uniform and was not armed. He was a stranger in the country; that was all we ever found out about him. The thought of him got to preying upon me every night; I could not get rid of it. . . . And it seemed an epitome of war; that all war must be just that—the killing of strangers against whom

you feel no personal animosity; strangers whom, in other circumstances, you would help if you found them in trouble, and who would help you if you needed it.[7]

The approvable sentiment of the passage has easily gained the praise of critics in search of serious values. Bernard De Voto, for example, has this to say about "The Private History":

There is more of the war in these youngsters, subject to glory and panic, than in most of the heroics that the *Century's* War History reveals. No glamour clouded Lieutenant Clemens' vision as he looked back over a quarter-century to that herd of cattle; and happily no typical impulse toward burlesque marred his writing. The sketch remains a lonely realism about the gathering of the militia clans in the confused days of '61, a perfect expression of Missouri's Civil War.[8]

The "lonely realism" which De Voto finds so compelling could only have been evoked by the passage in question. But is such power really present in the style? The entire texture of the passage is given over to all the stock responses of the most maudlin melodrama. The single horseman, the moonlight, the "white shirt front . . . all splashed with blood," the "cold sensation" passing through Mark Twain's "marrow," the helpless stroking of the forehead, the "pitying interest," the guilt fantasy in which the dying man's "reproachful look" and "shadowy eyes" haunt the murderer, and finally the utterly complacent and genteel little moral at the end—surely these blatant aspects of style hardly add up to the lonely realism De Voto praises. There is not one vivid image or vigorous perception in the entire passage.

Such a patchwork of clichés gains power only when seen as an impersonation embodying an element of the

[7] *Ibid.*, pp. 277-78.
[8] De Voto, *Mark Twain's America*, p. 114.

burlesque which De Voto rejoices is absent. But this passage lacks the kind of effective impersonation which Mark Twain had managed in *The Innocents Abroad* or *Roughing It*. It discloses instead the same weakness evident in the genteel description on art and the river in "Old Times on the Mississippi." The passage is actually weaker than the poetic outburst about the river, for in the earlier work Mark Twain's relation to the river had been buoyant. There was both inventiveness and authority in the elevated description comparing the river with a book. But in the passage on the soldier's death, the clichés and melodrama are evident from the beginning. The passage, more than merely impersonating the clichés, is appealing to the sentiments which they express.

The presence of this appeal is not so much an intrusion of a new element as it is the emergence of an element incipiently present from the beginning of the sketch. Unable to commit himself fully to the tall tale of his Civil War experience, Mark Twain is constantly at the threshold of pleading for his reader to understand his former folly. In *The Innocents Abroad*, he had been able to utilize reverent passages and retain his humor. Thus, even the most serious apostrophes to the monuments, the ruins, and the past invariably exposed the sentiment to the play of impersonation. But in "The Private History" the irreverence fails largely because the older Mark Twain —the "experienced" figure—is more given over to justifying his past than to making humor out of it. He could confidently impersonate the piety of the pilgrims and the reverence of the guidebooks, but against the reverence of the Civil War he restricted the play of his humor to Tom Sawyer romance, enlarging his sentimental appeal into a "serious" revelation about the senseless brutality of war. The result of this twin process amounted to a reduction of Mark Twain. Unable to realize the humor of his exaggeration, he fell back upon the "truth" of his sentiment, thus reducing his tall tale to a mere tale.

The failure of "The Private History" reveals much about

Mark Twain. It came at the height of his career, before the abrupt decline began. Until it appeared, the Civil War had been the great unwritten experience in the tall tale of his past. Moreover, it had been not simply forgotten, but evaded—and evaded from the very beginning. The discovery of "Mark Twain" in the Nevada Territory in 1863, while it had been Samuel Clemens' discovery of his genius, had quite literally been a way of escaping the Civil War past which lay behind him in Missouri. In effect, the humorous identity and personality of "Mark Twain" was a grand evasion of the Civil War. His form, the tall tale, was a means of converting all the evasions and failures of Samuel Clemens into the invasions and excursions of Mark Twain. Thus, aspects of the innocent, the gullible, the foolish, and the incompetent "young" Mark Twain are rehearsed by the experienced and "old" Mark Twain. Omitted in this humorous strategy is the transition between youth and age, failure and success, innocence and knowledge. Instead of telling how he at first failed as a pilot but gradually learned the river to become the experienced master pilot, he *stages* the failure all over again from a perspective of safety.

The humor required the margin of safety as much as the substance of failure, and a major part of Mark Twain's career is a long display of innocent poses against parties and ideas relatively safe to ridicule. That is why the "Europe" of *The Innocents Abroad*, and the pious pilgrims who visit it, are fair and easy game for innocence. The same is true of the Congressman, the spoils, the speculation, and the Washington of *The Gilded Age*; the small-town society of *Tom Sawyer*; the monarchy and social ills of *The Prince and the Pauper*; and finally the apotheosis of all safe subjects to attack—the slavery of *Huckleberry Finn*. Insofar as Mark Twain ridiculed any of these aspects and issues of his culture, he was not with the minority but with the majority; he had not chosen the unpopular but invariably the popular cause. That was, as he came increasingly and hostilely to know, one of the costs of being a humorist.

The *real* sacred cows of Mark Twain's time—as indeed they seem to be of our whole history—were the Civil War and its heroes. The great generals of the war were revered in a way that no other members of the society were. Whatever guilt Mark Twain may have felt about his Civil War experience depended for its intensity on the reverence in which the Civil War was held—and that reverence was high. To talk about one is necessarily to talk about the other. It was one thing to make fun of strait-laced preachers, newly rich businessmen, and ambitious politicians. It was quite another to belittle the achievements of the illustrious warriors who had saved the Union. One might laugh at God—Col. Robert Ingersoll made a livelihood out of that—but let him laugh at General Grant. The bloody shirt was still waved in every campaign, and though secret alliances were formed in 1877 between the Republicans and the old Whig faction in the South, the compromise *was* secret.

These public necessities were slow to give way, for the North was as slow to reconstruct itself as the South was to be reconstructed. If the writing of *Huckleberry Finn* was an act which liberated Mark Twain to desert the Republican Party and empowered him to negotiate the contract with General Grant, it is also true that the same failure he encountered in *Huckleberry Finn* he faced in an even more disconcerting way in the "Private History." For in order to convert slavery and the Civil War into the forms of humor, he had to rely more and more heavily upon moral sentiments in an effort to secure approval for his humor—so heavily in fact that his whole humorous identity was threatened. In confronting that past in which the nation had reached its limits and been rent asunder, Mark Twain reached the limits of his humor, which is to say he reached the threshold of his disillusion. In *Huckleberry Finn* he had come as near —and as far—as he was ever to do in reconstructing the Civil War past. The "Private History" marked a second effort to encounter that past, but it was a smaller, safer effort. It was indeed a campaign that failed.

CHAPTER

IX

YANKEE SLANG

A Connecticut Yankee in King Arthur's Court holds much the same position in Mark Twain's career that *Pierre* occupies in Melville's. Before both books stand single masterpieces; after them comes work of genuine merit, work of a higher order than they themselves represent, but work more quietly desperate, as if the creative force behind it had suffered a crippling blow. Moreover each book displays its author's ambitious effort to scale heights hitherto unattempted. Finally, the books share a similarity of substance, reaching resolutions involving self-destruction for the artist-hero. Melville's Pierre is a writer so caught in the involutions of love and creativity that suicide becomes a last refuge. Mark Twain's Hank Morgan, a brash superintendent of a Hartford Machine Shop transported into a sixth-century feudal world, assumes the role of a superman inventor in an effort to revolutionize the Arthurian world by accelerating the course of history. He does revolutionize it, only to destroy his technological marvels and defeat himself. Despite a certain audacity of conception, however, both works disintegrate into extravagant failures. Each involves an excess of energy, as if the energy invested had not been fully assimilated, leaving the author to force his way toward a destructive ending which would perforce break the identification between himself and the artist-hero.

Such a struggle is particularly evident in *A Connecticut*

Yankee. The most revealing comment on the unfulfilled effort is Mark Twain's reply to Howells' praise of the novel: "Well, my book is written—let it go. But if it were only to write over again there wouldn't be so many things left out. They burn in me; & they keep multiplying & multiplying; but now they can't ever be said. And besides, they would require a library—& a pen warmed-up in hell."[1] This humorous exaggeration rests on two central assumptions: that the book is an incomplete expression of suppressed attitudes, and that the suppressions are self-generatively threatening the writer's personality. The entire passage points to the final incompleteness of *A Connecticut Yankee*, corroborating the incompleteness of the novel; or—to put it inversely—the novel realizes the sense of incompleteness which the remark suggests. In this respect it is a new kind of failure for Mark Twain. He had failed before, and failed often, but usually in the midst of successes. For example, there is the failure of *The Innocents Abroad*—a failure of concentration and economy. And there is the failure of *Roughing It*, a failure to realize the true structure of the book. And even in *Huckleberry Finn*, there is, after everything one can say about the ending, a failure of proportion. But in all these instances the failure is directly related to and defined by a discovery in form.

In *A Connecticut Yankee*, however, the failure is as central and pervasive as it is in *The Prince and the Pauper*. Moreover, it is of greater magnitude for the simple reason that *A Connecticut Yankee* pretends to be more than *The Prince and the Pauper*. The earlier book had been addressed to a juvenile audience on the one hand and to a respectable audience on the other. It was a book which could be read aloud in the parlor to all the family. If it seemed tame, Mark Twain could rest in the solace of not having claimed it was profound, and also in the knowledge of having subtly conveyed the impression that the book had been written to please the respectable world

[1] *Mark Twain-Howells Letters*, II, 613.

in which he found himself. *A Connecticut Yankee* was a different thing. It was not peripheral but central; it was not respectable but genuinely irreverent; it offered itself not as an exercise but as an experiment. Like *Huckleberry Finn*, it did not come quickly but slowly, five years elapsing between the time of his first notebook entry in the late fall of 1884 and the date of publication in December, 1889. That first notebook entry—"Dream of being a knight errant in armor in the Middle Ages"—was supposedly inspired by Mark Twain's reading of Sir Thomas Malory to whose work he had been introduced by George W. Cable on their lecture tour in the fall of 1884.

Not until a year later, in December, 1885, did he actually begin to write; by March, 1886 he had written "A Word of Explanation" and the first three chapters. Then, much as he had done with *Huckleberry Finn*, he simply let the manuscript gather dust for a year and a half before returning to write sixteen chapters at Quarry Farm during the summer of 1887. This summer burst of writing carried him into Chapter 20, where Sandy and the Boss visit the Ogre's Castle. But when he returned to Hartford and the business world, his writing stopped. Not until he returned to Quarry Farm in July, 1888 did he begin the sustained assault which carried through disappointments and frustrating delays to the end of the manuscript in the spring of 1889.[2] This brief history of the composition points up the similarity between the emergence of *Huckleberry Finn* and *A Connecticut Yankee*. In each instance there was a beginning, a long delay, a return, another hesitation, and a final sustained push to, or near to, a conclusion.

But similarities have a way of pointing up essential differences, the difference in this instance being that the creative enterprise of *A Connecticut Yankee*, insofar as it

[2] For the best account of the writing of the book, see Howard G. Baetzhold, "The Course of Composition of *A Connecticut Yankee*: A Reinterpretation," *American Literature*, XXXIII (May, 1961), 195-214.

parallels that of *Huckleberry Finn*, is on a slighter scale. The total time of its composition is shorter, the initial burst of writing is much less decisive, and the *literary* waste required to complete the book is almost minimal compared to the failures which marked the way toward the success of *Huckleberry Finn*. Yet—and here is the issue—*A Connecticut Yankee* sounds bigger than *Huckleberry Finn*. It makes more noise; it seems more aspiring; it is much more liberal; it exposes the evil as well as the folly of man and his institutions. It thus becomes the central book for those critics who want to see Mark Twain as a robust frontier spirit at war with tradition, and also for those who wish to measure literature in terms of political liberalism and social conscience. This is why Howells—whose awareness of Mark Twain was often so perceptive—singled out *A Connecticut Yankee* as his favorite book. It is why De Voto, though he thought the book a failure, followed Howells in thinking the *conception* extraordinarily bold. It is why, much more recently, Louis Budd, exposing Mark Twain's political conservatism, finds himself granting *A Connecticut Yankee* priority for its distinctly liberal views. Finally, it is why Henry Nash Smith considers the *Yankee* as the most difficult of Mark Twain's works to evaluate, yet the most necessary to understand.[3]

[3] Howells, in *My Mark Twain* (p. 44), says, "I wish that all the work-folk . . . could know him their friend in life as he was in literature; as he was in such a glorious gospel of equality as the *Connecticut Yankee in King Arthur's Court*." In his essay "Mark Twain: An Inquiry," which appeared in the *North American Review* in February, 1901, and was included in *My Mark Twain* (pp. 165-85), he insisted that the book was Mark Twain's highest achievement in the way of "a greatly inspired and symmetrically developed romance" (*My Mark Twain*, p. 174). De Voto, in *Mark Twain's America* (pp. 272-79) sees the bold satiric conception thwarted by the burlesque and frontier humor. Louis Budd (*Mark Twain: Social Philosopher* [Bloomington, Ind., 1962]) concludes his chapter on the *Yankee*: "When he snatched up the banners under which the middleclass was forcing the nobility to disgorge, he was eloquently sincere; his flaming calls to revolt against self-appointed masters are great statements of that right, and his genius at phrase-making left memorable appeals for self-respect-

Yet for all the audacity the *Yankee* seems to have, it is actually a much tamer, safer performance. This fact is immediately evident in the Preface. Whereas the Preface to *Huckleberry Finn* was defiant and nihilistic, humorously warning the reader to look for something at the cost of his life, the *Yankee* Preface begins:

> The ungentle laws and customs touched upon in this tale are historical, and the episodes which are used to illustrate them are also historical. It is not pretended that these laws and customs existed in England in the sixth century; no, it is only pretended that inasmuch as they existed in the English and other civilizations of far later times, it is safe to consider that it is no libel upon the sixth century to suppose them to have been in practice in that day also. One is quite justified in inferring that whatever one of these laws or customs was lacking in that remote time, its place was competently filled by a worse one.[4]

Already there is the fatal appeal of *The Prince and the Pauper*: the appeal to history and at the same time the apology for fiction under the assurance of exposing eternal injustices. In a word, the Preface promises satire rather than humor, seriousness rather than mere laughter. Yet the language of *A Connecticut Yankee* was apparently vernacular, not genteel as it had been in *The Prince and the Pauper*. Promising a revolutionary revision of the past it invaded, it seemed a secure armor against the sentimentality of the earlier work. Yet *A Con-*

---

ing manliness and political equality" (p. 144). Smith has dealt extensively with the novel on two separate occasions: in *Mark Twain: The Development of a Writer* (pp. 138-70) and again in *Mark Twain's Fable of Progress* (New Brunswick, 1964). In the latter book, which is devoted exclusively to the *Yankee*, Smith feels that "at some point in the composition of this fable, he had passed the great divide in his career as a writer" (p. 107), and that understanding an event so important is to understand the writer.

[4] *Writings*, XVI, vii.

necticut Yankee, for all its hardheaded irreverence, succumbed to sentimentality.

The form of *A Connecticut Yankee* is what may be called an inverted Utopian fantasy. A graphic way to see the inversion is to compare it with Edward Bellamy's *Looking Backward*, which appeared in 1887 and was a best seller by the time the *Yankee* was ready for publication. Mark Twain himself was extremely fond of Bellamy's book, though he apparently did not read it until after the *Yankee* was completed.[5] In Bellamy's dream fantasy Julian West is precipitated into the future, where, faced with the material and ideological evolution evident in the year A.D. 2000, his own nineteenth century appears meager and startlingly inadequate. Through all his experience, West remains the observer, the listener, the interrogator who assimilates the persuasive criticism which the imaginary age affords. Bellamy's central achievement is to realize the terms of the Utopian fantasy, which is to say he conveys the notion of a dream of reason. Thus his hero finds himself being constantly persuaded that truths he had believed, values he had held, and causes he had supported are nothing more than outworn attitudes and trappings of a dead age. Being reasonable in the face of the disparity, he submits to the superior argument and assents to the promise of the strange new world.

Mark Twain, however, instead of sending his hero into an imaginary future territory outside history where the terms of criticism could operate freely to create the dream of reason, plunged him into history as if to invade and reform the past. The Yankee is not the innocent interlocutor but the chief actor of his chronicle. Just as his machine-shop lingo collides with the Malory-ese of the Age of Chivalry, his democratic ideology does battle with the aristocratic and religious dogmas of the king's realm. The superintendent of a Colt Arms machine shop, he emerges into the sixth-century Arthurian world and is

---

[5] Budd, *Mark Twain: Social Philosopher*, p. 145.

able to see this feudal pastoral from the presumable advantage of democratic industrialism. Unable to resist the lure of potential power residing in his technological advantage, he finds himself "inventing" labor-saving devices, instigating reforms, and organizing the people in an effort to proclaim a republic in England. For a brief moment his regime prevails; but the Church, never quite defeated, plays upon the superstition of the populace, declares an interdict, and sends an army against the Yankee; he in turn blows up his technological world, along with the assaulting forces of Church and Chivalry. Surrounded and poisoned by the vast corpse he has made of the past, the Yankee is condemned to a thirteen-century sleep by Merlin, the old-time magician whom he initially ridiculed.

The energy generated by this incongruity between chivalric past and practical present made up—as near as one can tell—the central impulse for beginning the book. Mark Twain's letters and notebook entries say as much, and the early portions of the book itself, even after all revisions were made, are essentially built upon a burlesque contrast between two styles: Morgan's roughneck, irreverent abruptness set against the exaggerated impersonation of Malory's circumlocutive archaism.[6] There are, particularly in the early chapters and from time to time throughout the book, amusing moments when Mark Twain is able to exploit the possibilities of the contrast to genuine advantage. His mounting the knights on bicycles, for example, or forcing them to wear placards advertising such items as Persimmons Soap or Peterson's Prophylactic Toothbrushes, have the genuine force of burlesque incongruity and exceed the expectations of the situation. And his utilizing the waste power of a genuflecting ascetic in order to operate a shirt factory has about it the old reckless irreverence which still has power to shock a safe gentility.

But as Morgan gains power in the Arthurian world, the

6 Baetzhold, "Composition of A Connecticut Yankee," pp. 196-98.

democratic assumptions on which his identity rests assert themselves, causing the burlesque contrast to assume satiric form. Such a change produces a marked transformation of Hank Morgan's character. For insofar as the burlesque contrast is the dominant impulse, Hank Morgan is essentially the showman, his characterizing compulsion being his urge to gain attention. Wherever he appears, the Yankee must shine, and more than food or women or even life itself, he loves the effect. In a rare moment of insight, he observes that the crying defect of his character is his desire to perform picturesquely. His whole style—given to overstatement from the moment he appears until he finally collapses under Merlin's spell—is in large part a manifestation of his desire to show off. Even the sad-faced Mark Twain ruefully observes of the Yankee's dying call to arms, "He was getting up his last 'effect'; but he never finished it."

But as the satiric impulse comes to the fore, the surprise, bewilderment, and amusement with which Morgan had originally beheld the Arthurian world are displaced by the indignation he feels upon discovering the atrocities at the heart of chivalry. Whereas the burlesquing Morgan had been intent upon making fun of chivalry, the satiric Morgan becomes determined to make war upon it. Yet the satiric Morgan can never really be effective, because the narrow range of his burlesque style cannot tolerate enough analytic intelligence or wit to discharge his growing indignation. Instead, his outrage tends to reduce his democratic ideology to clamorous fulmination and noisy prejudice, so that he becomes an object of curiosity rather than an effective satiric agent. Constantly advertising his ideas, his mechanical aptitude, and his stagey jokes, he becomes a grotesque caricature of the nineteenth century he advocates. Prancing through every conceivable burlesque and flaunting himself before the stunned Arthurian world into which he bursts, he begins to be the real buffoon of the show he manages.

Mark Twain recognized the Yankee's limitations, going

so far as to confide to his illustrator Dan Beard, ". . . this Yankee of mine . . . is a perfect ignoramus; he is boss of a machine shop; he can build a locomotive or a Colt's revolver, he can put up and run a telegraph line, but he's an ignoramus, nevertheless."[7] Aware of Morgan's career and Twain's own statements, certain critics have maintained that Mark Twain was directing his fire upon the nineteenth century as much as upon the sixth. Thus, Parrington insisted that Twain was "trimming his sails to the chill winds blowing from the outer spaces of a mechanistic cosmos,"[8] and Gladys Carmine Bellamy has more recently observed that the book is "a fictional working out of the idea that a too-quick civilization breeds disaster."[9]

Plausible though such arguments are in the light of the Yankee's ultimate failure, the logic of the narrative and the tone which sustains it move in precisely the opposite direction. For although the Yankee finally destroys himself, Mark Twain's major investment is in the Yankee's attitudes. After all, most of those attitudes were the same ones Mark Twain himself swore by at one time or another during his public life; and the usual response to the novel has been—and inevitably will continue to be—that he was lampooning monarchy, religion, and chivalry. There is abundant evidence that Mark Twain himself intended just such criticism. As early as 1866, he was attacking feudalism in the Sandwich Islands, and his belief in the superiority of democracy to monarchy goes back to the very beginning of his career; his hatred of an established church stretches equally far back—and further forward. Ten years after the Yankee's diatribes against organized religion, Mark Twain took special pleasure in mounting a sustained, logical attack upon Mary Baker Eddy, whose Christian Science he feared

[7] Paine, *A Biography*, II, 887-88.
[8] Vernon Louis Parrington, *Main Currents in American Thought*, 3 vols. in one (New York, 1930), III, 98.
[9] Gladys Carmine Bellamy, *Mark Twain as a Literary Artist* (Norman, Olka., 1950), p. 314.

would become the official religion of the Republic. There is also clear evidence, as John B. Hoben long ago observed, that some of the Yankee's attitudes have their exact counterparts in Mark Twain's hostile responses to Matthew Arnold's strictures upon American culture.[10] Finally, Howard Baetzhold has shown that Mark Twain's picture of feudal England is at times almost a direct transcript of the elder George Kennan's lectures and writings on Russia, both of which Mark Twain particularly approved.[11]

What becomes evident is that during the composition of the *Yankee*, the hostility, anger, and indignation which were permanent aspects of his personality came into much fuller play. As he had done while writing *Huckleberry Finn*, he *gave himself up to these emotions*. To read his notebooks of either period is to come across long passages in which fury and brooding animus are often indulged, much as if the writer were cultivating those emotions in order to motivate himself to write.[12] But whereas in the vernacular of *Huckleberry Finn* he had discovered a vehicle to convert the indignation which stands behind both humor and satire into the ironic observation, apparent indifference, and mock innocence which constitute them, the vernacular of Hank Morgan lacked the inverted point of view which would convert the emotions of rage and hate into humor. Instead of being the instrument which transfers the indignation from writer to reader, as in the case of satire, or converts it to pleasure, as in the case of humor, Morgan—who is conceived as a rowdy agent of burlesque—comes to be

[10] John B. Hoben, "Mark Twain's *A Connecticut Yankee*: A Genetic Study," *American Literature*, xviii (November, 1946), 197-218.

[11] Baetzhold, "Composition of *A Connecticut Yankee*," pp. 207-11.

[12] Paine's edition of the notebooks omits most of Mark Twain's savage attacks, but in the years 1877-80 there are, in the unpublished notebooks, voluminous assaults on Whitelaw Reid and the French nation, to name but two targets. And during the composition of the *Yankee*, abuse is heaped on a variety of subjects.

invested with the indignation of his creator. He is therefore not fully dramatized and remains part of the author, who seems to struggle more and more desperately to free him into character. It is just this struggle which makes the ending seem like a fantasy in which the author is driving the mechanism of his hero faster and faster until it flies apart. Thus in the closing chapters of the book, what began as a burlesque dream assumes the character of a nightmare in which Morgan is electrocuting knights so rapidly and so thoroughly that the dead, being merely an alloy of brass and buttons, are impossible to identify. Trapped at the center of his destruction, the Yankee is condemned by Merlin to a thirteen-century sleep from which he awakens to find himself a stranger in his once familiar nineteenth century. Unmoored from space, adrift in time, he lies down at last to death.

This relatively "sad" ending to what had begun as a burlesque contrast is what makes the book seem a turning point in Mark Twain's career, embodying as it does the shift from joy to despair, from dream to nightmare. The whole nature of the enterprise, in which Mark Twain finds himself killing the character who had given utterance to so many of his own criticisms and opinions, makes biographical speculation well-nigh inevitable. It is possible, for example, to show that Mark Twain's increasing involvement with the Paige Typesetter during the years the novel took shape had much to do with his growing desperation in the *Yankee*. For it was during these years, in the wake of his success with General Grant, that Mark Twain invested all his available capital in the typesetter. There is a sense in which the Yankee's demise is both a foreshadowing and a rehearsal of the fall which Mark Twain must have begun to see awaiting him. There is even a correspondence between the Yankee —whom Mark Twain indulges and almost glorifies, then brings to grief—and James Paige, the inventor of the typesetter who, like the Yankee, worked in the Colt Arms factory and was at first Mark Twain's hero, later his devil. The intricate relationship between book and type-setter is nowhere better revealed than in a letter Mark Twain wrote to his wife's brother-in-law, Theodore Crane, when, racing to finish the *Yankee*, he was also awaiting the advent of the mechanical miracle which Paige kept toying with.

> I am here in Twichell's house at work, with the noise of the children and an army of carpenters to help. Of course they don't help, but neither do they hinder. It's like a boiler-factory for racket . . . but I never am conscious of the racket at all, and I move my feet into position of relief without knowing when I do it. . . . I was so tired last night that I thought I would lie abed and rest, today; but I couldn't resist. . . . I want to finish the day the machine finishes, and a week ago the closest cal-culations for that indicated Oct. 22—but experience teaches me that their calculations will miss fire, as usual.[13]

The process of composition as Mark Twain describes it— a dumbly driven effort going on almost outside himself— is perfectly explained by his wish to finish the book on the day the machine was to be completed. He was saying, in effect, that he was a machine-driven writer; but more important, he revealed that the novel had come to be identified with the machine. There is, however, the hint of fatal doubt about Paige's invention. To accommodate his writing to its schedule was to be anchored to perpetual uncertainty. The machine was not perfected on October 22; nor was the novel completed on that date. Not until eight months later, after seasons of ecstatic hope punctu-ated by periods of depression or anxious alarm about the mechanical marvel, did Mark Twain succeed in com-pleting his novel. As for the machine, it was never really completed. Paige, constantly taking it apart in an effort

[13] *Letters*, II, 500.

to perfect it to the last dimension of its complexity, was overtaken by the simpler Mergenthaler linotype. As for Mark Twain, he was left in bankruptcy.

That Mark Twain could bring the book to an end and break the identification discloses how much writing was his real business. It was the act he had ultimately to rely upon to recover from the financial involvements of his business ventures. Yet the recovery was as costly as it was desperate, for it required killing the Yankee. And the Yankee in the book is not simply a businessman or a mechanic in the Arthurian world, but an *inventor* as well; his power was indivisibly a part of Mark Twain's creative impulse. Killing the Yankee was symbolically a crippling of the inventive imagination, as if Mark Twain were driven to maim himself in an effort to survive. Understandably he considered this radical redefinition of himself to be the logical end of his writing life and went so far as to say jokingly to Howells that his career was over and he wished "to pass to the cemetery unclodded."[14] Of course, his career was not over. He wrote again and again, not simply because there were financial necessities which required it, but because writing was at last his life.

The priority of writing in Mark Twain's life brings us back to the matter of form in the *Yankee*. For it is finally the form—which is to say the style and character of Hank Morgan—that failed Mark Twain. Though a change in his outlook took place during the process of composition, and though this change is reflected in the book, it is difficult to say—as it was difficult to say about *Huckleberry Finn*—how much the art fed into the life and how much the life fed the art. Thus, while it can be said that Mark Twain's investment in his publishing house and the Paige Typesetter "caused" him to run into writing difficulty, it is also possible to argue that Mark Twain's increasing tendency to invest in business rather

[14] *Mark Twain-Howells Letters*, II, 611.

than in art was a result, not a cause, of a lesion in his own creative faculties.

That there was such a lesion is evident in the slender frame he cast round the *Yankee*. In that frame—appropriately entitled "A Word of Explanation"—he employed the author-meets-narrator stratagem as a device for getting into the narrative and also for introducing his narrator. Following a guided tour through Warwick Castle, itself a representative of the storied past of the tourist's imagination, the author encounters a stranger "who wove such a spell about me that I seemed to move among the specters and shadows and dust and mold of a gray antiquity, holding speech with a relic of it!"[15] Here is the familiar impersonation of the clichés of travelogue nostalgia, and throughout the introduction Mark Twain continues to portray himself as the dreamy-eyed tourist bent on caressing images of the past. In this moment of sentimental retrospection—while the guide is attempting to explain the presence of a bullet hole in an ancient piece of armor—the stranger appears, like the fabulous genie come from a bottle, and into Mark Twain's ear alone proclaims himself the author of the bullet hole. The "electric surprise of the remark" momentarily shatters the tourist's dream, and by the time he recovers, the stranger has disappeared. That evening, however, sitting by the fire at the Warwick Arms, "steeped in a dream of the olden time," Mark Twain is again abruptly confronted by the stranger, who, knocking upon the door to interrupt the dream, takes final charge of the narrative.

The frame makes clear that Morgan, instead of being a companion character, is a projection, or, more accurately, an anti-mask of the tourist Mark Twain's stock nostalgia. In the same way that Morgan has put a bullet hole in the antique armor, he punctures the sentimental dream of the past. Moreover, he comes unbidden to menace the dreamer and his retrospective vision. Speaking with casual and confident authority, he proclaims himself the

---

[15] *Writings*, XVI, 1.

antithesis of sentimentality. "I am a Yankee of Yankees—and practical; yes, and nearly barren of sentiment, I suppose—or poetry, in other words." His entire narrative, appropriately preserved on a palimpsest, is the record of an attempt to overwrite as well as override the past.

The Yankee's role, as defined in the frame, is thus one of burlesquing "Mark Twain's" tourist version of the past. Taken together in the frame, Morgan and "Mark Twain" could be considered as the essential mechanism of Mark Twain's burlesque. There are the two attitudes—nostalgia and irreverence—in collision; both attitudes are at the heart of Mark Twain's creative impulse. For in order to make the irreverence work, Mark Twain had to impersonate reverence. Even as he specialized in burlesquing the piety of retrospection, he had to cultivate his longing for the past. Sentimental as that longing could be—he speaks in his *Autobiography* of "the pathetic past, the beautiful past, the dear and lamented past"—it nevertheless inspired, at the same time it drove him back upon, his memory.

Probably his chief protection against this intense longing for the past, which he indulged as necessarily as he had to indulge anger and indignation, was his capacity for burlesque. Burlesque was the means of both mocking and checking the nostalgic impulse. In *The Innocents Abroad* Mark Twain, by discovering a perspective along the borderland between pathos and ridicule, had developed a style which contained both attitudes in a new synthesis. Yet in the frame of *A Connecticut Yankee* he reverted to the simple division of polite tourist and vulgar companion—a division he had used in his *Travels with Mr. Brown*, only to transcend it in *The Innocents Abroad*.[16] In giving over the narrative to Hank Morgan,

[16] Franklin Rogers has an excellent discussion of the refined tourist and his vulgar companion (*Burlesque Patterns*, pp. 36-61). Rogers defines Mark Twain's problem of development as the difficulty of getting a narrative plank which would release the narrative from the stasis of the burlesque division. In the early travels with Mr. Brown, he merely inserted factual chapters be-

Mark Twain attempted to transcend the essential division at the heart of the burlesque impulse; but in displacing "Mark Twain" with Morgan rather than Huck Finn, he had no way of producing the mock gravity so essential to his earlier humor. With Morgan as narrator, there was no possibility of impersonating pained seriousness or genteel piety. For Morgan is, as he proudly proclaims, a Yankee of Yankees and barren of sentiment. Instead of embodying the underside of language and experience in the manner of Huck Finn, Hank is the rowdy and irreverent genie of burlesque. Although both Hank and Huck are involved in reconstructing history, the mode of reconstruction is opposite at nearly every point. Huck is the apparently helpless figure drifting upon the current of the mighty Mississippi; Hank is both director and chief actor in his drama. Huck thinks all his heroism is wrong; Hank is sure that his revolution is right. But whereas Huck's successive evasions bring us to the awareness that a real revolution has taken place, Hank's revolutionary indignation involves him in an ever-enlarging fantasy.

All of which brings us to Hank Morgan's style, for Hank's style, like Huck's, will tell everything about the book. It is a loud and boisterous style, given to bluntness and dogmatic attitude. Unlike Huck's Southwestern vernacular, Morgan's Yankee lingo is essentially correct as far as its grammar is concerned. Though it runs toward a jaunty boastfulness and apparently reckless contempt for conventional attitudes, it does not play havoc with the proprieties of grammar. In the final analysis, Hank's vernacular is rather conventional language masquerading as burly, rough talk.

In Huck's vernacular, Mark Twain used the illusion of illiteracy to secure the impression of simplicity while at

---

tween the burlesque chapters, but in *The Innocents Abroad* he assimilated the division into a single narrator who retained burlesque characteristics yet could narrate his travels.

the same time retaining a complex syntactical structure. Set against the implications of conventional syntax, the illiteracies make possible a style capable of a vast range of expressive utterance. Take, for example, Huck's reflection upon Mary Jane Wilks's offer to pray for him:

> Pray for me! I reckon if she knowed me she'd take a job that was more nearer her size. But I bet she done it, just the same—she was just that kind. She had the grit to pray for Judus if she took the notion —there warn't no back-down to her, I judge. You may say what you want to, but in my opinion she had more sand in her than any girl I ever see; in my opinion she was just full of sand. It sounds like flattery, but it ain't no flattery. And when it comes to beauty—and goodness, too—she lays over them all.[17]

Here Huck's language defines perfectly the breach between his reality and her convention. Mary Jane can approve of him only sentimentally, only because she refuses to know the extent of his sin; and Huck can approve of her only in metaphors which are unwittingly abrasive. In a very real sense his praise of her "ain't no flattery." Yet neither Mary Jane's banality, Huck's self-depreciation, nor the implicit irony of his metaphors disturb the sentiment of his approval. Compare Huck's art of language to Hank's description of a girl he meets upon entering Camelot:

> Presently a fair slip of a girl, about ten years old, with a cataract of golden hair streaming down over her shoulders, came along. Around her head she wore a hoop of flame-red poppies. It was as sweet an outfit as ever I saw, what there was of it. She walked indolently along, with a mind at rest, its peace reflected in her innocent face. . . . But when she happened to notice me, *then* there was a change! Up went her hands, and she was turned to stone; her mouth dropped open, her eyes stared

[17] *Writings*, XIII, 265.

wide and timorously, she was a picture of astonished curiosity touched with fear. And there she stood gazing, in a sort of stupefied fascination, till we turned a corner of the wood and were lost to her view. That she should be startled at me instead of at the other man, was too many for me.[18]

This passage is as representative as it is revealing. The features which distinguish the passage as vernacular are clear—and few. First of all, there is a certain exaggeration of metaphor and figure, as illustrated by the "cataract of golden hair streaming down over her shoulders," and "hoop of flame-red poppies." This exaggeration is also present in other areas of the style. It is evident when the Yankee speaks of "astonished curiosity" and "stupefied fascination." The method here is to call into service an adjective which overlaps the meaning of the noun in an effort to intensify the description. This doubling effect, while it can produce a certain flamboyance of description, is more likely to result—as in the passage under scrutiny— in a redundancy and loss of nuance.

Aside from the exaggeration, the Yankee's style is pervaded with literary clichés. There is the "fair slip of a girl," the "golden hair," the "flame-red poppies," the "mind at rest." Then there are the elaborately stylized locutions— "Up went her hands," "her eyes stared wide and timorously," "she was a picture of astonished curiosity," and "there she stood gazing." These two tendencies—the one toward exaggeration and loud intensity, the other toward literary cliché—reach their logical end in the last sentence of the passage, where the sentence begins with the stilted noun clause as a subject and ends by veering into colloquialism. The entire passage illustrates the essential rhythm and feature of Morgan's language. Grounded in clichés and conventional syntax, its character emerges by means of exaggeration and calculated vulgarity. The exaggeration is achieved largely by relying on clichés which generalize images and impersonate Arthurian gen-

[18] *Writings*, XVI, 10-11.

tility; the slang is the means of dissociating from and exposing the overelaborate impersonation.

These revelations about Hank Morgan's style put us directly in touch with his action and his character, for Morgan's action bears the same relation to his style that Hucks action bore to his. Huck, it is worth remembering, was helplessly involved in doing the thing which his society disapproved—freeing a slave. It was an action which he himself disapproved but could avoid no more than he could avoid his grammatical blunders. Both morally and grammatically he "hadn't had no start." The humor in the book lay in involving Huck in a wrong action which his society might abhor yet the reader would heartily approve. Such a strategy required either setting the action in a primitive society and using space or geography as the point of reference; or setting the book in time and using history as the referent. The game lay in playing upon the reader's—and author's—instinctive belief in progress; and Mark Twain had played it admirably in *Huckleberry Finn.* Not only had he involved his protagonist in a revolution which his reader inexorably approved; the hero could not help himself. He simply found himself helplessly and ironically in revolution against a society which he kept thinking he should admire.

In *A Connecticut Yankee*, Mark Twain tried much the same strategy. His Yankee, finding himself in the Arthurian world, sets about revolting against the monarchy and the Catholic Church—institutions which were fairly safe game for a nineteenth-century Yankee. Certainly Mark Twain could count on a general audience approval of these aims almost as much as he could count on their disapproval of slavery. But the great difference between the Yankee and Huck is that the Yankee is a reformer whereas Huck is a helpless rebel. The Yankee acts upon principle and moral confidence; he is finally a Yankee, an abolitionist, an American, who never doubts that he is right. Huck, the fugitive and helpless outcast, acts out of a sense of being always wrong.

The Yankee's assurance that he is in the right contributes as much as anything else to alienating him from
the reader. For a real problem arises the moment the
Yankee begins to establish his republic. It is not that the
reader disapproves of the Yankee's republicanism, but
that he cannot approve the revolutionary zeal which goes
along with it. As long as he is simply amused at the contrast between his own century and the quaint absurdities
of the Arthurian world, the Yankee at least remains
plausible; but when he begins to rail at the injustice of
the past, his indignation becomes missplaced. The direction of the book discloses that the *intention* of the narrative can neither sustain nor account for the emotion of
the central figure; for the emotion—the indignation—is a
manifestation of the failure and inadequacy of the intention. The intention of the narrative is a burlesquing or
making fun of the past. But what begins as making fun
becomes making war. Insofar as the Yankee begins to
make war upon the Arthurian kingdom he loses his sense
of show and pleasure. His indignation is the index to his
capacity, not for the destruction of the past, but for self-
destruction.

Even more important, the Yankee's revolution is really
as correct as his style. It *sounds* like revolution but is actually thoroughly safe and respectable gentility. Small
wonder that Howells, who was himself at the threshold
of a great "conversion" to political liberalism, should have
congratulated his friend upon the bravery of the novel.
And so, of course, did E. C. Stedman. Actually there is
no courage about the novel. It marks a great turning back
for Mark Twain—a turning back in technique and a betrayal of humor. Worst of all, Mark Twain seems to have
been self-deceived since he apparently thought the Yankee
was a rebel. Yet the reality of the situation is that there
is scarcely anything rebellious about the Yankee. His
language, as we have seen, is the index of his tameness.
Although he sounds and thinks as if he were rebellious,
he is quite clearly echoing the sentiments of a society

fairly sunk in the complacent and institutionalized "liberalism" which had sponsored the Civil War in 1860-65.[19]

That is why the book, seen in a certain light, amounts to fighting the Civil War again. It is, after all, a tale of the Yankee doing battle with chivalry. Mark Twain himself had made it eminently plain in *Life on the Mississippi* that the South he could not abide was the South which had created itself in the image of Walter Scott and chivalry. Henry Nash Smith, in a fine discussion of Mark Twain's images of Hannibal, has shown decisively how the entire Arthurian kingdom is a thinly veiled picture of Southern regional culture which Mark Twain, as he grew older, came more and more to criticize. Smith points out that Arthur's Britain is "a projection of the benighted South," a "negative image of Hannibal, of Hannibal as Bricksville."[20]

Into this "backward" region the Yankee marches to free the people from religion, aristocracy, and slavery. It is here that he seeks to establish his republic. Insofar as the action of the book amounts to a fighting of the Civil War, Mark Twain assumes the role of the Yankee; he puts on—or better, indulges in—the Yankee conscience and commits aggression after aggression upon the South in himself. For Hank Morgan does, almost from the beginning, what Huck is finally driven helplessly to do—he commits himself to the Northern conscience. This commitment Mark Twain evidently believed was rebellious; actually it is nothing less—or more—than the *approved* action. Huck's rebellion lay not at all in his "All right, then, I'll *go* to hell," but in his rejection of conscience— of hell and heaven—altogether. Having committed himself to the "approved" rebellion, Hank Morgan sounds off louder and louder about it—and the more he commits

[19] Budd has an excellent account of Mark Twain's opinions in relation to the middle-class Liberalism of the period (*Mark Twain: Social Philosopher*, pp. 111-44).
[20] Henry Nash Smith, "Mark Twain's Images of Hannibal: From St. Petersburg to Eseldorf," *University of Texas Studies in English*, XXXVII (1958), 15.

himself to it, the less real rebellion there can be. This is Hank Morgan's and Mark Twain's self-deception—a self-deception which the style reveals. For Hank's supposed vernacular is not really vernacular at all but indulged colloquialism. It is, in a word, slang, which is to say that it is simply put-on vernacular. Mark Twain, in *A Connecticut Yankee*, succumbed to the lure of mere lingo, which so many writers since his time have done. He wanted to have a hero with an ideology *and* a vernacular. The vernacular was to ground the character in "reality" and give him a "realistic" and recognizable "social" quality. Such a hero really knows what ideas are and showily makes bright philosophical formulations in the rough and salty savor of colloquial speech. But what happens in *A Connecticut Yankee*, and in many another such attempt, is simply a faking and collapse in both directions. The ideas are so crudely simplified in Morgan's vernacular that they actually become pretentious evasions. And the vernacular is nothing but a *show*, an act. It is not necessary to the action, but simply decoration, a contrast. Nothing more than one of Hank Morgan's *effects*, it is in the last analysis an affectation.

To see this failure is to see the crucial difference between vernacular and slang. Slang is a patronizing indulgence of metaphor by someone consciously taking imaginative flights for purposes of mystification, in-group solidarity, or protective, secret communication. Vernacular, however, as we defined the term in *Huckleberry Finn*, is the "lower" or illiterate language whose very "incorrectness" at once indulgently implies a correct grammar and at the same time subverts the literary vision. The more a book is committed to a vernacular hero, the more it necessarily must produce a vision which displaces the genteel values it plays upon. *Huckleberry Finn* did carry such a vision—so much so that the vernacular and vision wait upon each other to produce a new reality of form and action. In the world of childhood which Huck's language reconstructed lay the central confrontations and discoveries which Mark Twain's humor could make. There lay the pleasure principle, which somehow gave the lie to the adult reality principle.

But in moving from Southwestern boy to Yankee adult, Mark Twain actually regressed. The Yankee is in many ways Tom Sawyer grown up—but Tom Sawyer grown up is, alas, somehow grown down. Mark Twain had refused to let Tom grow up on the grounds that he would "just be like all the other one-horse men in literature." And Morgan, if we look at him carefully, does do little but be like other one-horse men. That is why he comes to believe in himself, to take himself seriously. In *Tom Sawyer*, Mark Twain had kept Tom's speech contained within a frame—a frame half-indulgently patronizing, half-burlesque, which both indulges and exposes Tom's essential conformity with and imitation of adult ways. The indulgent narration of *Tom Sawyer* had greatly enriched Tom's reality by showing that it was somehow absurd yet pleasurably *real* in a lost nostalgic way.

When he dropped himself—the "Mark Twain" narrator—out of the action in *A Connecticut Yankee*, he could never compensate for the loss of perspective; instead, he was drawn inevitably to invest the fantasy Yankee with "serious" values. But the fate of the slang form inexorably produced a reduction in the intellectual content of Hank's "thought" and an attendant excess of emotion. The result is an increased amount of sound about ideas, yet a reduction of sense in expressing them.

The conclusion to be drawn from an examination of *A Connecticut Yankee* is that Mark Twain was deceived into believing that slang and vernacular were one and the same. But in vernacular humor, the *form* indulgently inverts conventional values, whereas in slang the *character* must attack them. The one inverts relationships and values; the other moves toward overt judgment and criticism. To realize the possibilities of slang form, Mark Twain would have had to reduce Hank Morgan's intelligence, thereby producing a burlesque, or increase his capacities of criticism and move toward satire. Yet he was able to do neither. It was as if the writer, having reached the top of his form in vernacular, was actually deceived by his masterpiece into believing that the sound of language was identical with its form. By failing to realize the necessities of his form, Mark Twain was never able to be fully responsible to the book he was making. Yet if he fatally confused vernacular and slang, he did no more than many of his successors have done. Believing that they are writing vernacular *Huckleberry Finns*, they produce instead slang *Connecticut Yankees*. Take Saul Bellow's *Henderson the Rain King* as a formidable example. Like the Yankee, Henderson speaks a salty colloquial idiom. Though much more intellectual than Morgan, Henderson nonetheless indulges language in a reckless, carefree way. Both the *Yankee* and *Henderson* try to be responsible by proposing themselves as fantasies, yet the consequences of slang indulgence take their revenge anyway. Whereas the burlesque Morgan turns serious and assaults the fantasy, the intellectual clown Henderson requires excessive folds of fantasy to make his arrantly conventional sentiments seem boldly speculative. If in the process of becoming serious Morgan negates his own burlesque identity, Henderson in the act of sustaining his fantasy more and more depletes the reality of his speculations, making them seem mere tricks of thought. Both works, in trying to give serious content to the fantasy, succeed only in becoming more and more extravagantly fantastic—and tiresome.

CHAPTER

X

THE IRONIC

STRANGER

IN RELATION to his career, *A Connecticut Yankee* is the disaster through which Mark Twain entered into the twilight of his life as a writer. It marks the division between the masterful years of 1875-85 and the long aftermath of failures, fragments, and disillusion which characterized so much of Mark Twain's later life. This does not mean that it was the turning point of his life. That point, if there is such a thing as a turning point, occurs when Huck says "All right, then I'll *go* to hell." But the *Yankee* nonetheless remains the visible shoal marking the descent from the sweeping middle passage of Mark Twain's career to the later darker stages. Although Mark Twain's fiction prior to the *Yankee* discloses foreshadowings of his later work, it is dominated by play and possibility, whereas the subsequent humor strikes stances of cynicism, savage irony, and despair. The world of Tom and Huck, after everything is said, is a world of boys. The world of Hank Morgan, Pudd'nhead Wilson, and Hadleyburg is a world of men. Though the world of boys pivots upon necessity, it continues to sustain a powerful illusion of freedom. True, pain and death are present in the idyl, but the forms which characterize and enchant the world are play and pleasure. The world of men, on the other hand, is realized in terms of death and slavery. The illusion of freedom has vanished; the reality of determinism remains.

It is upon this last period that so much speculation has been lavished. Both Brooks's and De Voto's theses largely rest in efforts to define what went "wrong" with Mark Twain. For Brooks, Samuel Clemens' disaster lay in his selling out to "Mark Twain," and the final disillusion was the lonely artist's recognition and judgment of his long self-betrayal. De Voto, on the other hand, saw Mark Twain as the incarnation of Southwest humor and tradition who finally succumbed to the gentility he had at first so brilliantly shocked. This at least was essentially his position in *Mark Twain's America* when he launched his assault upon Brooks's thesis. Later however, after becoming editor of the Mark Twain Papers, De Voto moved, though in his individual way, toward a position much nearer to Brooks's. Surveying the roomful of abortive and embittered manuscripts which Mark Twain left behind, De Voto concluded that Mark Twain's disillusion was an outgrowth of two central disasters striking upon a sensitive and already guilt-ridden soul. The first was his bankruptcy in 1894, resulting from the failure of the Webster Publishing Company in which he was senior partner and the subsequent collapse of the Paige Typesetter. The second was the death of his favorite daughter, Susy, in 1896, which occurred just as he reached England on the homeward leg of his round-the-world lecture trip undertaken to pay off his creditors.

These two catastrophes, according to De Voto, left Mark Twain with a feeling of guilt he could not bear. Unable to accept the responsibility, he came to fix the blame on a callous God and his inventor, man. Though Mark Twain sought desperately to embody his vision in literary form, all he succeeded in achieving was a long succession of false starts and futile projections, central among them a narrative of a voyage begun in a drop of water under a microscope and ending in a white and chilling arctic sea; all points of reference long since lost or abandoned, the stunned survivors look into the face of a desolating annihilation. These repeated failures—particularly the iceberg fantasy—De Voto chose to call the symbols of despair.[1]

De Voto's theory is, on the whole, the most satisfactory yet written about Mark Twain's later work—satisfactory because it makes a sustained effort to deal with a confusing and difficult period. But De Voto's speculations, and also Brooks's, rest on the assumption that the life "causes" the art, that behind the work lies the experience. Actually, an artist's art is so much a part of his experience that it is indeed difficult to say that one exclusively causes the other. The longer one surveys the life of art the more one inclines to reject H. G. Wells's conclusion that life makes art in favor of Henry James's counter thesis that art makes life. Certainly James's contention seems particularly applicable to Samuel Clemens, whose "Mark Twain" was a cause as much as it was a result of experience. De Voto's notion that the bankruptcy of 1894 and Susy's death in 1896 produced Mark Twain's despair is difficult to believe for anyone who has read *A Connecticut Yankee*, which was completed five years before the bankruptcy.

For Hank Morgan's collapse, more than being a prevision of coming disasters, is a disaster itself. Doubting his burlesque impulse, Mark Twain had tried to make his book serious; determining to write a satire, he had destroyed his humorous genius; seeking for truth and ideology, he had deserted the pleasure principle. His Hank Morgan—who embodies so much of the inventive, speculative, and performing aspects of Mark Twain's humorous genius—is trapped and destroyed in his effort to be a serious revolutionary. He is the unconverted indignation, and he proves that vernacular is no more proof of genuine protest than it is an assurance of an escape from gentility.

The measure of Mark Twain's confusion is evident from his inability to move forward from the disaster of

[1] De Voto, *Mark Twain at Work*, pp. 105-30.

A Connecticut Yankee. As if instinctively aware of being crippled and unable to move forward, he fell back upon characters he had created in the past, attempting to invoke through their voices, which is to say their *form*, an action which would complete itself. Thus, before he would fully discover *Pudd'nhead Wilson*, he had attempted to revive Colonel Sellers in *The American Claimant* and had called upon Huckleberry Finn in *Tom Sawyer Abroad*. He had also contracted to write a series of European travel letters for the New York *Tribune*. All of these productions have some interest as writings of Mark Twain, but none represents any discovery. Little more than reflexive attempts to activate achieved forms, they are not so much experiments as exercises. Their failure gives the lie to those who lament Mark Twain's inability to understand his true strengths and achievements. His difficulty once again stemmed from his instinctive tendency to fall back upon discovered forms, not from his incapacity to recognize their power.

He finally managed, amid the collapse of his fortunes, to break away from his gallery of achieved characters and strike out toward a new form. The book, *Pudd'nhead Wilson*, was written in a desperate effort to stave off the financial disaster engulfing him. His responses to the financial crisis were these. First he moved to Europe in an effort to economize his depleted capital and to escape the chaotic demands the business world was making upon him. Second, he wrote doggedly to make money to feed the faltering typesetter. Third, he vainly tried to keep a hand upon his projects, frantically corresponding, telegraphing, and even coming in person from Europe, to the Hartford world of enterprise. But for all the urgency of that period, *Pudd'nhead Wilson* evolved slowly and was extensively trimmed and concentrated before Mark Twain released it.

Written in Europe, *Pudd'nhead Wilson* was Mark Twain's last American novel—the final volume in what we may justly call his Mississippi trilogy. It deserves the central position it occupies in the Author's National Edition of Mark Twain's works, immediately following *Tom Sawyer* and *Huckleberry Finn*. Not that it approaches the greatness of *Huckleberry Finn* or matches the discovery of *Tom Sawyer*. Cast in the cramped mold of that sentimental Victorian closet drama *The Prince and the Pauper*, the plot of *Pudd'nhead* greatly inhibits the possibilities of episodic freedom which the other two books so amply embody. An innocent reader, seeing Mark Twain turn his plot upon the mechanical changeling device, inevitably expects the novel to demonstrate how the Negro, given the advantages of white status, will prove himself worthy of his opportunity in the manner of Tom Canty. Yet having seen the ultimate direction of the action, one can hardly imagine Olivia Langdon Clemens adapting *Pudd'nhead*, as she adapted *The Prince and the Pauper*, and presenting it—with the Clemens girls in the major roles—as a Christmas surprise for her husband.

No, *Pudd'nhead Wilson* is of a different order. Hemmed in though it is by its mechanical form, its action achieves a significance which belies the flimsy superstructure of the plot. For in moving from the class lines of Tom Canty's England to the racial barriers of *Pudd'nhead Wilson*, Mark Twain left the dead world of monarchy for the world of slavery where he once had lived. In *Pudd'nhead Wilson*, he came to grips with the animating issue of slavery in a sustained effort which, challenging him more deeply as he wrote, called upon the deepest resources of his imagination. In a prefatory note to "Those Extraordinary Twins," the slender farce from which *Pudd'nhead* evolved, Mark Twain left a humorous record of the birth of his novel. Having begun, he tells us, with the notion of chronicling the adventures of Siamese twins—one virtuous and fair, the other vicious and swarthy—who are perpetually and absurdly at cross-purposes, he found himself suddenly confronted by strange intruders who seized the foreground of the stage:

> Among them came a stranger named Pudd'nhead
> Wilson, and a woman named Roxana; and present-
> ly the doings of these two pushed up into prom-
> inence a young fellow named Tom Driscoll, whose
> proper place was away in the obscure background.
> Before the book was half finished those three were
> taking things almost entirely into their own hands
> and working the whole tale as a private venture of
> their own—a tale which they had nothing at all to
> do with, by rights.[2]

Seeing the emerging story as a tragedy, Mark Twain
solved the problem of his hybrid form by extracting the
farce from the story which had grown around it—an act
which he called a "literary Caesarian operation."

The terms of the account deserve emphasis—not because the account is necessarily accurate, but because it
discloses how Mark Twain was dramatizing the act of
writing at this juncture of his career. First of all, he saw
his chief character as a stranger—not simply within the
framework of the novel, but to himself as writer. Second,
the entire narrative is seen as an unwilled action which,
intruding from the background into his creative consciousness, comes to dominate the conscious narrative
which evoked it. Third, this unconscious narrative is
termed a tragedy, not a comedy, not humor. Finally, the
novel is curiously and strikingly figured not as the child
of the farce but as the *mother* from whom the child—the
farce—is forcibly extracted. Thus the unconscious, expressed "mother" is left intact and "natural," while the
conscious, unnatural story of freak twins is arbitrarily
removed. However, these implications become fully explicit only in the light of *Pudd'nhead Wilson* itself.

Actually, the novel which remained after the unnatural
removal of the farce is not a tragedy. It begins with a
seemingly pointless joke, chronicles the history of a crime,
and ends as Pudd'nhead Wilson, the stranger and hero,

[2] *Writings*, XIV, 209.

brings to justice the false Tom Driscoll, who has harassed the peace of Dawson's Landing. The hero's triumph over and entry into the society is in the comic rather
than the tragic mode. But the facile neatness of the ending, instead of being joyously comic, emphasizes that the
problems evoked by the novel have not really been settled
so much as swept under the carpet. The triumph of justice, the defeat of the criminal, the success of the long-
suffering hero are transparent veils which seem deliberately to expose rather than to conceal the larger doom,
the deeper crime, and the final failure of the society
which the novel scrutinizes. Coward, thief, and murderer
though Tom Driscoll is, his indictment is more disturbing
than gratifying. His sale down the river in the closing
moment of the novel is a final indictment of the world
in which he had his being, a last ironic stroke in this
savagely ironic novel. It is ironic for Tom himself, whose
career at launching had been pointed toward a raceless
utopia only to veer through a series of atrocities culminating in Tom's murder of his white foster father and
his selling his mother down the river. But the irony is
also directed at the society itself, for Tom's entire career
reveals how much he is the instrument of an avenging
justice which has overtaken Dawson's Landing.

For Tom is a marked man—a Negro. Yet how different
he is from Nigger Jim, whom Huck ultimately saw as
"white inside." Tom Driscoll is white *outside*, his white
face and white talk hiding the mark within. If Jim was
the indulgent slave who wakened Huck's sleeping conscience, Tom Driscoll is the nightmare plaguing the moral
sleep of Dawson's Landing. Only one-thirty-second black,
he is invisible to his victims, the six generations of white
patrimony contributing to his creation having physically
equipped him to assume the role of changeling which
Mark Twain assigns him. He thus stands always in the
foreground as the figure embodying the long history of
miscegenation in the background; although this background is not elaborated, the novel is nonetheless the his-

tory of a time, a place, and a crime. The narrative is, as Mark Twain insistently terms it, a chronicle.

Since miscegenation can culminate in "passing" the color line, the arbitrary changeling device functions as the comic equivalent of historic possibility and can legitimately dramatize the last phase of a society trapped by its secret history. Although the slaveholding society of Dawson's Landing is built around an aristocracy of Virginia gentlemen who worship honor, the novel discloses that across its coat of arms runs a dark bend sinister, an indelible stain disfiguring the heraldry of every member of the community's ruling class. The first families cannot, of course, see the stain, because they have conditioned themselves not to see it; but the novel exposes it in the person of the false Thomas à Becket Driscoll.

Spawned at the very center of their legalized institution of slavery, he crosses the color line in the white disguise six generations of white blood have given him. He is, after all, the son of white men's casual lust gratified by a series of aggressive sexual acts at the expense of their slaves. Although the masters may have assumed economic responsibility for these actions, their sexual willingness to cross the color line—the legal fiction they have created to define the unbridgeable gulf separating the races—merely underlines their refusal to accept any moral responsibility in the matter. The miscegenation which they have tacitly indulged within the framework of slavery is their own covert affirmation of the inexorable bond between the races. The secret channel carrying white blood steadily down into the area of human life separated and suppressed by slavery, it makes possible the emergence of the false Tom Driscoll into the white world. The dark force he possesses upon his return represents the loss of power sustained by the ruling class.

Pudd'nhead Wilson thus implies a world in which the power of those who rule has been transferred to those who serve, for if the origin of Tom's force is the lust out of which he was created, the immediate source is embodied in the personality of his mother, Roxana, who shifts him into the cradle of the white heir. One of Twain's most interesting creations, she possesses the strength, the passion, and the fertility so strikingly absent in the white women she serves; in fact, her darker, deeper beauty merely emphasizes their frigidity. Mark Twain remarks that on the same day she bore her son she was "up and around," while Mrs. Percy Driscoll "died within the week" of her childbirth confinement. The long logic underlying this chronicle explains Roxana's power, for the submerged lust transfers the passion from the white wives to the slave mistresses. If the transfer bestowed purity upon the white women, it nonetheless left them increasingly impotent. Thus, in the white South of Mark Twain's memory, the Negro women became the Mammies who were the real mothers in a society so obsessed with purity that it divested the ordained mothers of passional vitality. That is why, in the Southern gentleman's idealized version of existence, the white women of privileged classes could not nurse their children and were relieved of the obligation as soon after the travails of childbirth as possible.

In rearing the white man's legitimate children and giving birth to his illegitimate ones, Roxana bears what their honor cannot bear—*the guilt of their repressed desires.* Their guilt is objectified in her repression. Her humiliation (she has no guilt) takes the form of repressed vengeance. Thus, her release of Tom into the white society grows out of her arraignment before Percy Driscoll on the false charge of petty larceny. She acts not in overt vengeance but out of desperation to save him from the fate of being sold down the river. That her ostensibly defensive action constitutes such an aggression against the society discloses how much unconscious power and hostility she actually commands. When Tom Driscoll is finally unmasked, she is the sole person in the society who can assume inward responsibility for the crime of the society. Her cry, "De Lord have mercy on me, po'

misable sinner dat I is!" is a stricken cry of acknowledg-
ment in a world given over to repression and confirms
the nobility and responsibility she alone possesses. She
is, after all, the darkly powerful queen in the society
which Mark Twain depicts. Although the "nobles" of the
society bear the names of Elizabethan court lovers, the
white queens in the New World imitation of the Old remain as remotely in the background of the novel as the
real Tom Driscoll who shambles about the slave quarters.
Only Roxana has the power to create drama and to become the primary force in the world she serves.

The responsibilities thrust upon her become her critical force, enabling her to vitalize with certain insight
the empty illusions which she inherits from the world
above her. Reprimanding Tom for his failure to meet the
terms of the code duello, she affirms her honor and origins
with a summary of the family pedigree.

> "Whatever has become o' yo' Essex blood? Dat's
> what I can't understan. En it ain't on'y jist Essex
> blood dat's in you, not by a long sight—'deed it ain't!
> My great-great-great-granfather en yo' great-great-
> great-great-granfather was Ole Cap'n John Smith,
> de highest blood dat Ole Virginny ever turned out,
> en *his* great-great-granmother or somers along back
> dah, was Pocahontas de Injun Queen, en her husbun'
> was a nigger king outen Africa—en yit here you is, a-
> slinkin' outen a duel en disgracin' our whole line
> like a ornery low-down hound! Yes, it's de nigger
> in you!"[3]

Even as she parodies the genealogical obsessions of the
first families, she confronts the distinctive heritage of
Dawson's Landing and America, the strange and remarkable history which so much defines the New World. Her
sketch of her American family tree is the repressed genealogy which upholds the tenuous tracings educed by the
First Families of Virginia, at least insofar as the novel
implies their genealogies. The self-styled aristocrats of

3 *Ibid.*, p. 124.

Dawson's Landing, in repressing her genealogy, cut themselves off from the vitality of their own past as well as hers. Denial of their secret history is actually a denial of themselves, and their blood, flowing in that covert tradition, becomes their nemesis in the person of Tom Driscoll.

As long as Tom is ignorant of his identity, he does not direct his inborn hostilities upon his fathers but gratifies his uncontrollable temper with cruel jokes perpetrated on the slaves who serve him, particularly the unfortunate Chambers, his true master, and Roxy his mother. His brutal treatment of Roxy, however, eventually angers her into humiliating him with the facts of his lineage. His discovery of his true mother, though temporarily paralyzing, is nevertheless a self-discovery and a half-conscious realization of his destiny. His casually malevolent will, which has struck blindly downward in indiscriminate aggression, begins to find its fated target. Thus, when Roxy tauntingly asks him what his father would think of his refusal to accept the dueler's challenge, Tom "said to himself that if his father were only alive and in reach of assassination his mother would soon find that he had a very clear notion of the size of his indebtedness to that man, and was willing to pay it up in full, and would do it too, even at risk of his life. . . ."[4] At such a moment, when even Mark Twain's rhetoric assumes Faulknerian aspects, outward and inward action tend to coalesce into social and psychological reality, disclosing that the false Thomas à Becket Driscoll is the avenging agent who carries back across the color line the repressed guilt which has gathered at the heart of slavery. Although he withholds his terrible intention from Roxy, Tom willingly seizes upon his fated mission: the murder of Judge Driscoll. For the Judge, who harbors within his walls the invisible assailant, is not only Tom's foster father and inevitable target of his malice; he is also the living symbol of law and order in the community, and

[4] *Ibid.*, p. 123.

his murder suggests the anarchy which the white society has by its own action released upon itself.

This, then, is the crime which strikes at the heart of Dawson's Landing. The man who finally "sees" Tom Driscoll and restores a semblance of honor and order to the community is quite appropriately the rank outsider, Pudd'nhead Wilson—the stranger who first intruded into Mark Twain's farce about the Siamese twins. Having wandered West from his native New York to seek his fortune, Wilson comes into the community a free agent. His "freedom" places him at the opposite extreme from the fate in which Driscoll is caught. So far apart are they—Wilson on the periphery of the society, Tom at the center—that Mark Twain resorts to arbitrary devices to draw them together. Thus, there is the weakly plotted series of accidents upon which the novel turns: Pudd'n-head arrives in Dawson's Landing during the month in which Tom is born; he is rejected by the society at almost the same time Tom enters it; his rise to fame begins the same moment Tom's honor is questioned. Pudd'nhead even shares character traits with his opposite number. Both are notorious idlers, both are collegiately sophisticated, both are given to droll and cutting irony. Finally, both share a desire for the limelight, and when Wilson exploits the drama of the final courtroom scene, he is merely usurping the role of showman which Tom has played in society. At opposite points on the wheel of fortune, the destinies of the two figures are fatally related, the ascending fortune of Pudd'nhead coming necessarily at the expense of Tom's fall. The novel predictably ends with Wilson standing above his cowering antagonist to pronounce his doom.

In order to show how and why this plot machinery fails to rise above the level of mere mechanical contrivance, it is necessary to recognize the real relationship between Tom Driscoll and Pudd'nhead Wilson which is implied by Mark Twain's insistence on plot symmetries.

Wilson's first act upon entering Dawson's Landing is to mutter the joke which isolates him and launches the novel. Hearing an "invisible" dog barking behind the scenes, he expresses to a group of loitering citizens the wish that he owned half the dog. Upon being asked why, Wilson rejoins, "Because I would kill my half." The only response the literal-minded inhabitants can make to this sally is summed up by one of the gullible bystanders, who inquires of his comrades, "What did he reckon would become of the other half if he killed his half? Do you reckon he thought it would live?" Jay B. Hubbell, in a penetrating objection to the novel, contends that the joke is typical of small-town humor and that "the village yokels would have yelled with delight when they heard it."[5] Hubbell feels that at this point in his career Mark Twain had lost his sense of connection with the village of his memory and thus was becoming cut off from the reality of his humor.

In a very particular way Hubbell is right. The joke, an old chestnut in the provinces, should have evoked a warm response. Yet, coming from a total stranger, Pudd'nhead's wisecrack reveals a discomforting familiarity and at the same time betrays a veiled threat. Given the particular province, there is a certain realism in the instinctive withdrawal of the village idlers and their rejection of the strange humorist as a "pudd'nhead." Wilson's subsequent behavior lends a measure of justification to their puzzled distrust, for although he ultimately discloses the invisible assassin in their midst, he is also the one who plants in Roxy's mind the possibility that her son is indistinguishable from the legitimate Driscoll heir. "How do you tell them apart, Roxy, when they haven't any clothes on?" he asks with innocent amusement.[6] Remembering Wilson's observation, and assuming that if one so intelligent cannot distinguish the children neither can the dull-

---

[5] Jay B. Hubbell, *The South in American Literature* (Durham, 1954), p. 835.
[6] *Writings*, xiv, 13.

witted villagers, Roxy decides to shift her son into the cradle of the legitimate Tom Driscoll.

If Wilson is capable of suggesting the possibility of mistaken identity in the village, he is also visibly engaged in erecting a system of detection which will expose the possibility. Thus, his casual observation to Roxy reveals that personal identity in Dawson's Landing is a matter of mere appearance; and his reliance upon fingerprints as a means of criminal detection undercuts the whole structure of familial identity on which the society stands. His effort to establish a complete fingerprint file of every member of the community is a stratagem for checking personal identity against the one unchanging characteristic of human physiology. Trusting only these "natal autographs,"[7] as he calls them, Wilson refuses to rely on names and faces, the conventional hallmarks of identity. His arduous "hobby" is, in fact, based on an essential distrust of the identity of the entire village.

Having precipitated the crisis which only his system can resolve, Wilson's final apprehension of the criminal merely completes and closes the circuit of the plot. For all the detached curiosity with which he surveys the village, he remains singularly blind to the series of incidents set in motion by his own idle remark to Roxy; and although he holds Tom Driscoll's true signature within arm's reach, he is almost as bewildered by the murder case as the dullest citizen in Dawson's Landing. The fatal attraction between detective and criminal is the only thing that finally saves him from failure, despite his foolproof system. For Tom compulsively seeks Wilson out to taunt him for failing to solve the murder of the Judge, only to leave his telltale print on one of Wilson's glass slides. Seeing Wilson's shocked countenance and unaware of his crucial error, Tom grants his host's request to be left in peace but cannot resist a parting jibe: "Don't take it so hard," he says; "a body can't win every time; you'll

[7] *Ibid.*, p. 193.

hang somebody yet." Wilson's reply is a mutter to himself: "It is no lie to say I am sorry I have to begin with you, miserable dog though you are!"[8]

More than being a silent retort to Driscoll's taunt, Wilson's remark is an oblique answer to the joke which initiated his isolated career, for in addition to finding the "invisible dog"—or, as Roxy puts it, the "low down hound"—which disturbed the peace of the community, he has indeed come to own half of it and is ready to assume the role of killer which he first proposed for himself. He demands in the courtroom that Tom make upon the court-room window the fingerprints which will hang him. But the society into which Wilson is about to be accepted owns the other half and determines not to destroy such a valuable property. The terms of the joke thus become the terms of the novel, and Wilson's casual wish to own half of the unseen dog is realized at the moment he estab-lishes Tom's identity and guilt. As a result of Wilson's detection, Tom reverts from his role of secret agent to the status of property "owned" by the society at the same instant Wilson's twenty-three-year period of rejec-tion is ended and he is welcomed into the community of owners as a reward for his achievement. As the two figures "enter" the social order at the conclusion of the narrative, it becomes evident that they are the *real* twins in this novel which grew around a farce about Siamese twins.

Yet the book does not reveal so much as it implies the ligature connecting the two figures. It pursues their ca-reers at the embarrassing cost of ignoring the true Tom Driscoll, who humbly keeps his place in the slave quar-ters—outside the action of the drama. The life of this neglected figure would, announces Mark Twain just be-fore the conclusion of his book, be too long to pursue.[9] Thus the narrative excludes the legitimate Driscoll,

[8] *Ibid.*, p. 184.   [9] *Ibid.*, p. 202.

brings in a stranger who saves the community, and concentrates on an irony directed against the monstrosity of slavery. As the curtain falls on the problem comedy, Pudd'nhead has convinced the townspeople that honor is restored and the blot removed from the community escutcheon. By discovering the false Tom Driscoll, however, Pudd'nhead has actually exposed the flaw of the entire society, for Tom is, under the terms of slavery and by virtue of the final court decision, irrevocably the living property of the community. Moreover, he has not simply been brought into the society; he has been created by it. That is why the honor of Dawson's Landing is defined as mere respectability.

This is not to say that Mark Twain hated the Virginia gentlemen who bestrode the world of Dawson's Landing. Wilson the stranger sides with them and struggles to protect them from the criminal they have fathered. But to say, as F. R. Leavis has said, that "Mark Twain unmistakably admires Judge Driscoll and Pembroke Howard"[10] is to forget that the irony of this chronicle takes the measure of the honor they uphold. If York Leicester Driscoll's only religion was "to be a gentleman—a gentleman without stain or blemish," the narrative exposes the religion to be as false a front as the whitewash which hides the dark reality of the sleeping village. Although Mark Twain does not portray the white patriarchs as vicious, the narrative judges them; they are, after all, the ones indicted before the bar when the false Thomas à Becket Driscoll is brought to justice. [11]

[10] F. R. Leavis, Introduction to Grove Press edition of *Pudd'nhead Wilson* (London, 1955), p. 21.

[11] Not only are these patriarchs exposed by the ultimate irony of the novel; their sense of honor is often broadly burlesqued. Upon hearing that Tom has failed to challenge Luigi to a duel, York Driscoll swoons into the arms of his F.F.V. compatriot, Pembroke Howard:

Presently the old Judge came out of his faint and looked up piteously into the sympathetic face that bent over him.

"Say it ain't true, Pembroke; tell me it ain't true!" he said in

This indictment within the novel leads to the larger indictment reflected in Pudd'nhead's calendar maxims which constitute epigraphs for each chapter and provide an ironic commentary upon the action. Thus, in the chapter which details Roxy's richly statuesque beauty, Pudd'nhead's calendar entry reads:

> Adam was but human—this explains it all. He did not want the apple for the apple's sake, he wanted it only because it was forbidden. The mistake was in not forbidding the serpent; then he would have eaten the serpent.[12]

But these aphorisms stand above and beyond the narrative, lending a final perspective upon the world of the novel. Delivered as if from a timeless moral realm, they are not simply Wilson's brief against the society of Dawson's Landing but against the world. They summarize the ironic tone within the novel and at the same time provide a series of generalizations upon time and man. They are the voice of "experience," the wisdom saved up from the expense of success, and present themselves as the disillusioned vision of a man who has seen through the pretentious lie of the world. Cast in the form of calendar maxims, they make up a broad antithesis to all of Poor Richard's wisdom. Poor Richard had defined the ways to wealth and success; Pudd'nhead drolly observes that all success is a failure.[13]

---

a weak voice.

There was nothing weak in the deep organ tones that responded.

"You know it's a lie as well as I do, old friend. He is of the best blood of the Old Dominion" (*Writings*, xiv, 104).

[12] *Ibid.*, p. 8.

[13] The extremity of Pudd'nhead's disillusion is reached in his final maxim, commemorating Columbus' discovery of America (heading the chapter in which Pudd'nhead becomes the hero: "October 12. The Discovery. It was wonderful to find America, but it would have been more wonderful to miss it.") The experience of the novel enables one to see beyond Pudd'nhead's dry observation that it would have been remarkable for the old explorer to miss a continental land mass the size of America. For

Thus the character of Pudd'nhead is the "way" or means by which Mark Twain realized his disillusion. He had begun to realize it in Hank Morgan, the stranger whose emergence into the sleepy world of Camelot forecasts Pudd'nhead's entry into Dawson's Landing. But two things caused Mark Twain to lose control over Morgan. First, Morgan's unconverted indignation manifested itself in increasingly bad humor. Second, Morgan's slang could not assimilate the "thought" which Mark Twain increasingly tried to give it. But in the character of Pudd'nhead, Mark Twain solved both these problems. Pudd'nhead is not a vernacular character but a college man and thus can legitimately "say" any thought Mark Twain can give him. More important, the indignation which in effect blows up Morgan, is economized in *Pudd'nhead Wilson* by means of a radically disjunctive irony.

To achieve this irony, Mark Twain moved away from vernacular and back to plot—in the manner of *The Prince and the Pauper* and *Tom Sawyer*. Both these earlier books contain irony, but the emotion on which

---

both Mark Twain and Pudd'nhead have made a newer discovery. Columbus' new world has become an old one. For Mark Twain, this novel was, to all effects, his last *American* novel. His major work after *Pudd'nhead* was to be set in Europe. In his humorous foreword to the novel, aptly entitled "A Whisper to the Reader," Mark Twain, in vouching for the authenticity of the legal chapters in the book, "sealed" the chronicle with these words: "Given under my hand this second day of January, 1893, at the Villa Viviani, village of Settignano, three miles back of Florence, on the hills—the same certainly affording the most charming view to be found on this planet, and with it the most dreamlike and enchanting sunsets to be found in any planet or even in any solar system—and given, too, in the swell room of the house, with the busts of Cerretani senators and other grandees of this line looking approvingly down upon me as they used to look down upon Dante, and mutely asking me to adopt them into my family, which I do with pleasure, for my remotest ancestors are but spring chickens compared with these robed and stately antiques, and it will be a great and satisfying lift for me, that six hundred years will." The six hundred year "lift" would, of course, take him back behind Columbus' discovery and into Dante's world, where a radiant Beatrice reigned, not a dark queen.

the irony rests is essentially indulgent. The world depicted is a world of boyhood—particularly is this true in *Tom Sawyer*—and the relationship established between narrative consciousness and action is one of ultimate approval. Even in *Huckleberry Finn*—despite all the bitter knowledge and experience which go into the book—the emotions upon which the humor rides are indulgence and approval. In *A Connecticut Yankee* irony gives way to direct expression, outbursts of anger and spleen, and to a sarcastic tone. In *Pudd'nhead Wilson* a genuine irony is restored—but it is irony without indulgence. Scorn and contempt are the emotions at the heart of this irony. The perspective upon the world of Dawson's Landing is as remote as it was in *Tom Sawyer*, but the world is a world of men, and the narrative consciousness, instead of approving the antics on stage, evokes disapproval of the entire world. There is only one "actor" held in affection by the narrative consciousness: Roxana. The others, even Pudd'nhead, are either held in check or exposed by the sardonic eye of the chronicler.

The strength of Mark Twain's irony is particularly evident in the light of Hank Morgan's slang fiasco; it is a means of keeping the action in focus and control. While its fine edge noticeably diminishes the possibility of "good humor," it nevertheless prevents the intrusion of Mark Twain's anger and bad temper; it is a way of controlling them from the beginning. Speaking from the vantage point of the historian, the chronicler chooses a perspective which allows him to see the events of his history as fatal—to see that the relationships between man, society, and history take precedence over man's individual desires and ambitions. Viewed from such a perspective, man is at once the creator and the creature of fate; he carries out and is the victim of destiny. But in order to achieve this perspective, the plot must be made to *seem* like a part of the destiny. This does not mean that the plot has to be "invisible." Instead, it must be extremely visible, its absolute visibility disclosing that the entire order of the action is an expression or symbolic enactment of fate itself.

It is precisely in this realm that *Pudd'nhead Wilson* fails. The best way to see the fundamental weakness of Mark Twain's plot is to compare *Pudd'nhead* with *The Scarlet Letter*. The two books are remarkably similar, and it is surprising that, in an age of comparisons, they have not been associated. First of all they are novels of adultery, but the adultery has happened before the novels begin and is in each instance the unseen cause of the novel. The action of each novel is the unfolding consequence of the adultery, centering upon the birth and identity of the child. The offspring of the adultery is not therefore repressed, but emerges into the foreground as both projection and definition of the *act* of adultery which remains veiled in the background. For Hawthorne, the act is essentially natural in a world where civilization is itself a process of subduing nature. Consequently, Pearl is alien from society. Because her identity is defined by the natural act which "conceived" her, she is not rebelliously but irrevocably anti-social. For Mark Twain, however, the act is social—a liberty taken by one person at the expense of another. The false Thomas à Becket Driscoll becomes the instrument of vengeance, his very hostility being an unwitting response to the sexual aggression which begot him.

Each novel thus depicts a repressive society under attack from the very consequences of its repression—and in each instance the repression is dramatized in terms of adultery. But the adultery is not the climax of the action, as in the traditional novel of adultery; it is the origin. Thus the erotic motive, which constitutes so much of the suspense in the traditional novel, is forced into the background and supplanted by its consequences. Both novels invite the reader to act in the role of judge upon the action of repression. This does not mean that the books champion adultery or condemn it; rather they use it as a means of exposing and bringing their societies to *trial.* Instead of engaging the reader in the lure and expectation of sexual gratification, they involve him in meting out judgment upon the society punishing the sexual offense. Hawthorne exposes for indictment the gloomy Puritan society, Mark Twain the slave society of the Old South—two societies which Democratic America had to invalidate. Both books—and this is the remarkable aspect they share—raise the issue of adultery and repressed love, yet by diverting attention toward judgment and consequences, they succeed in freeing themselves from the erotic stigma on which they depend. In doing this, both writers are open to the charge of being squeamishly unable to "face" the very realities they evoke. This is particularly true of Hawthorne, who is often seen as old-maidishly "afraid" of Hester Prynne. Yet clearly Hawthorne's great force in *The Scarlet Letter* lies in his ability to censor his heroine in just such a way as to enhance her power. Thus he casts himself as a *fifth* character in *The Scarlet Letter*—the *editor* of Old Surveyor Pue's manuscript which he finds in the Custom House. Standing directly between the reader and the Puritan world of the novel, this editor evokes sympathy for the persecuted Hester and at the same time constantly moralizes upon her crime. His moral resistance, instead of reducing Hester's stature and dark power, greatly enriches them, making her the only genuinely passionate woman in American literature.

To see Hawthorne's achievement is to see Mark Twain's failure—a failure to be measured by comparing Hester to Roxana. Hawthorne succeeded in intensifying Hester's sexual power by resisting, judging, and even disapproving of it. The action of the novel moves inexorably toward the forest scene in which Hester's restrained sexual identity powerfully asserts itself in such a way as to threaten Dimmesdale's very masculinity. Every move which the editor Hawthorne makes in "resisting" Hester's sexuality becomes a means of defining her power as something far beyond that of a mere adulteress or *femme fatale*. Her force as woman is at once natural and primal. Regal in its power, it underlies at the same time it threatens the foundations of society.

Roxana occupies a position remarkably similar to Hester's. She too is an adulteress whose action threatens the society. Moreover, her appeal rests heavily upon sentimental grounds. If Hester Prynne's punishment evokes the reader's pity for a woman at the mercy of a ruthlessly masculine society, Roxana's apparent helplessness in a slave society blinds the reader to the vast potency of her action in the novel. But whereas Hawthorne's plot drew the action inexorably back upon Hester's sexual identity, Mark Twain's Negro vernacular concealed Roxana's sexuality. Her language actually unsexed her, forcing Mark Twain to explain the situation in the following terms:

> From Roxy's manner of speech, a stranger would have expected her to be black, but she was not. Only one-sixteenth of her was black, and that sixteenth did not show. She was of majestic form and stature, her attitudes were imposing and statuesque, and her gestures and movements distinguished by a noble and stately grace. Her complexion was very fair, with the rosy glow of vigorous health in the cheeks, her face was full of character and expression, her eyes were brown and liquid, and she had a heavy suit of fine soft hair which was also brown, but the fact was not apparent because her head was bound about with a checkered handkerchief and the hair was concealed under it. Her face was shapely, intelligent, and comely—even beautiful. . . . To all intents and purposes Roxy was as white as anybody, but the one-sixteenth of her which was black outvoted the other fifteen parts and made her a negro.[14]

Although the language here is extremely conventional, every adjective being designed to mitigate with polite

[14] *Writings*, XIV, 11-12.

gentility Roxana's direct sexual force, it nonetheless directly identifies Roxana's sexuality. But Roxana's speech, as the opening sentence of the passage makes clear, literally represses this entire aspect of Roxana's identity, displacing her sexual power with humorous power. Yet in so doing, Mark Twain dissociated her from her primal action—the action of adultery from which the entire plot originates. Since her speech *is* her character, the dissociation means that character is dissociated from plot. That is one reason why the plot is not integrated with the characters, why it seems like an arbitrary mechanism designed to regulate and manipulate the action. That is also why the plot capriciously disposes of the real father, Cecil Burleigh Essex. It is also why Roxana, though she functions as the queen in the novel, ultimately fails to transcend the sentimentality she evokes. Hawthorne had actually enhanced his heroine's power by dramatizing and objectifying himself in the role of censoring her, and his style and plot were the embodiment of just this dramatization. But Mark Twain's plot, even though it bitterly exposed the repression of slavery, was an agent of repression itself. Instead of dramatizing his role of censor, Mark Twain was actually censoring himself by means of Pudd'nhead and his plot machinery.

For Pudd'nhead and his plot are themselves the apparatus of censorship. He is the stranger who would "have expected" Roxana to be black, and his expectations are nothing less than the repressive plot of the novel. They are the machinery by which "order" is kept. Whereas *Huckleberry Finn* expressed and enacted freedom through the metaphor of slavery, Pudd'nhead and his plot enact a slavery under cover of an antislavery sentiment. Thus Pudd'nhead ultimately upholds the slave society by avenging the murder of the charitable foster father. He is not only the prosecuting son in the process of becoming the ironic father. He is also the sole surviving member of the Freethinker's Society.

(244)

In the light of *Pudd'nhead Wilson* it is possible to trace as well as define the evolution and impact of the ironic stranger upon Mark Twain's imagination during what we may call the years of disillusion and despair. The stranger is, after all, the embodiment of the disillusion which came to have such dominion over Mark Twain's inventive life. First appearing as Hank Morgan, he reached full stature as Pudd'nhead Wilson. As Hank Morgan, the stranger had appeared in the form of a Yankee inventor whose desire to reform the past had ultimately become an impulse to destroy it. As Pudd'nhead Wilson, the stranger dropped his Yankee slang and burlesque in favor of epigram, wit, and irony; in this role he was capable of releasing an ironic "philosophy" of despair.

He appears in relatively quiet and complacent communities, bringing with him private technological knowledge which is the source of secret power. At first scoffed at and rejected by the community, he ultimately returns to save it and in the process succeeds in exposing the shabby moral structure of the society he somewhat contemptuously protects. He himself is finally disillusioned by the discrepancy his superior intellect perceives between the fatal disease he exposes and the superficial cure he offers. His disillusion hardens into the conviction that man in general is not worth saving—that indeed man is damned by his own inability to speak out. Man is, in other words, a slave—a slave to his community and to himself. Mark Twain was himself to say during this "dark period" that "the skin of every human being contains a slave."[15] Fatally bound to his past, every man's identity—which is to say his very name—designates his slavery. This discovery is the bitter knowledge which informs the irony of *Pudd'nhead Wilson*.[16]

[15] *Mark Twain's Notebook*, prepared for publication with comments by A. B. Paine (New York, 1935), p. 393.
[16] The profound relation between the character of Pudd'nhead and the subject of slavery is shown by the fact that Mark Twain used maxims from Pudd'nhead's *new* calendar for chapter headings in *Following the Equator*. That last, and interesting, travel

Yet the ironic stranger, whose very irony was a means of releasing order into the chaos left in Hank Morgan's wake, was also repressive—and repressive in two ways. First, his role in the novel is repressive, not liberative. Thus, although his irony ultimately indicts the society his detection has exposed, his immediate concern is to indict the false Tom Driscoll and restore the status quo. But Pudd'nhead is not only repressive within the novel; he is repressive upon it. This would not be true if his character were fully realized, for then his repressive tendencies would be dramatized as character trait. But he is not so realized, and it is just this failure which accomplishes what can be called a completion of the central weakness of the book. For whereas Roxana's character denied her original relation to the plot, Pudd'nhead's plot keeps him from ever really becoming a character. He remains instead little more than a massive plot device. Neither he nor his "twin," the false Tom Driscoll, is ever freed into character; rather, they function as dominant parts of the plot machinery.

Even though Mark Twain confidently asserted that Pudd'nhead came unbidden and "freely" into his creative consciousness, the form which the character imposed upon the action was extremely constrictive—so constrictive that Mark Twain was ironically right in calling the book a tragedy. For the bitter plot of Pudd'nhead overrides the character of Roxana, reducing her vernacular to dialect and severing her humor from the sources of her instinctive power. Exposed by Wilson's detection, that power is reduced to a mere guilty minstrel cry: "De Lord have mercy on me, po' misable sinner dat I is!"

---

book records Mark Twain's trip around the equatorial black belt of the world, where he saw in colossal dimension the white man's repression of the black.

CHAPTER

XI

THE MYSTERIOUS

STRANGER

THE extent to which Mark Twain was being threatened
by the repression implicit in the dominant figure of the
ironic stranger becomes fully explicit in the direction
he took upon completing *Pudd'nhead Wilson*. His next
book was *Joan of Arc*. It is inaccurate, however, to say
simply that *Joan of Arc* was "by" Mark Twain, for not
until after the book was serialized was Mark Twain's
authorship acknowledged. This hesitation is the central
fact about *Joan of Arc*, revealing more, perhaps, than
the entire two volumes which chronicle the history of the
saintly maid. For Samuel Clemens' reluctance to acknowledge Mark Twain's authorship was not a mere modest
withdrawal but an almost total denial of his humorous
genius and was inseparably related to the very conception
of the pure and white Joan of Arc.

The terms under which Mark Twain was being stifled
were as clear as they were simple. *Joan of Arc* was to be a
"serious" book. The whole project had about it a fatal
reverence perhaps best figured forth in Paine's unctuous
account of his master's transition from Pudd'nhead to
Joan. "With [*Pudd'nhead Wilson*] out of his hands,"
averred Paine, "Clemens was ready for his great new undertaking. A seed sown by the wind more than forty years
before was ready to bloom. He would write the story of

Joan of Arc."[1] The wind to which Paine referred was that which, blowing along the main street of Hannibal in 1849, supposedly wafted a leaf from a book about Joan of Arc in the path of the highly imaginative thirteen-year-old Samuel Clemens. This event, according to the sixty-year-old writer, marked the beginning of his *literary* ambition. Ever since that memorable day, he maintained, the figure of Joan of Arc had stood like a beacon in his imaginative landscape—a light which at once signified the source as well as the goal of his inspiration.

The entire story of the wind, the leaf, the book, and the fledgling author is every whit as conventional in conception as the *Personal Recollections of Joan of Arc*, whose advent it presumably foretold. Moreover, no direct evidence exists to prove that the episode transpired. Although both Paine and Dixon Wecter cite it prominently in the life of Samuel Clemens, there is no reason to believe in it any more than in any of the other dubious memories of Mark Twain.[2] The story gives every evidence of having come to prominence after the writing of the book and is but one more of Samuel Clemens' testimonials to his lifelong faith in the maid whose history he had written.

The story is a fabrication, not a tall tale. Instead of reconstructing the past of Samuel Clemens under the humorous exaggeration of Mark Twain, this anecdote set about transforming the tall tale of Mark Twain into the invention of the boy-author Samuel Clemens. As the story was designed to present the emergence of literary ambition in the untutored but sensitive boy, so *Joan of Arc* was to be the ultimate fruit borne from the chance seed planted so long ago. The book was to be, above everything else, serious literature. Once again, Paine's nar-

---

[1] Paine, *A Biography*, II, 957.

[2] *Ibid.*, I, 81-82. Dixon Wecter, *Sam Clemens of Hannibal* (Boston, 1952), p. 211. But Wecter notes (p. 309n) that Mark Twain failed to mention this supposedly significant turning point in his sketch "The Turning Point of My Life" which was written long after *Joan of Arc*.

rative sets the tone admirably, revealing the particularly decorous scene in which the genteel undertaking was conceived.

> Walking the floor one day at Viviani, smoking vigorously, he said to Mrs. Clemens and Susy: "I shall never be accepted seriously over my own signature. People always want to laugh over what I write and are disappointed if they don't find a joke in it. This is to be a serious book. It means more to me than anything I have ever undertaken. I shall write it anonymously."
>
> So it was that that gentle, quaint Sieur de Conte took up the pen, and the tale of *Joan* was begun in that beautiful spot which of all others seems now the proper environment for its lovely telling.[3]

Securely located in a picturesque Italian villa, surrounded by wife and daughter, the humorous artist piously announces his intention of embarking upon a work which will be the culmination of a lifetime ambition, heretofore rendered impossible by his impure and worldly journeywork. He is, in other words, undertaking to write a literary "masterpiece"—a work which, identified with the very birth of literary ambition, is to be triumphantly serious in intention and executed in an idealized and sequestered setting. It was not enough that the book be serious; it must be unstained with commerce—a labor of pure love, untouched by money. Writing to Henry Huttleston Rogers, the Standard Oil tycoon who was mightily assisting him through his financial crisis, Samuel Clemens could note with pride: "Possibly the book may not sell, but that is nothing—it was written for love."[4]

He went out of his way to insist that it had been in the process of creation longer than any of his other productions. On his seventy-third birthday when, as Paine observes, "all his important books were far behind him, and he could judge them without prejudice," he announced with finality:

[3] Paine, *A Biography*, II, 959.   [4] *Letters*, II, 624.

> I like the *Joan of Arc* best of all my books; & it *is*
> the best; I know it perfectly well. And besides, it
> furnished me seven times the pleasure afforded me
> by any of the others: 12 years of preparation & 2
> years of writing. The others needed no preparation,
> & got none.[5]

This proclamation was no casual verbal aside to be quoted by his biographer, but a formal note left by its author as an unmistakable testimonial to his most serious literary effort. Paine dutifully reproduced the facsimile of the document in his biography as incontrovertible evidence of Mark Twain's preference.

Such high esteem for the work and its saintly subject did have some basis in Mark Twain's imagination. That Joan of Arc may have long been a subject of interest to him is revealed in a love letter he wrote his wife during their courtship. There he specifically linked Olivia with Joan, observing that though his frail lady might not lead men into battle, she would, in her own exquisite way, command all the power of Joan of Arc. Yet there are by no means enough references to Joan in Mark Twain's earlier letters or other writings to warrant the passionate involvement with her story he later professed to have had. Moreover, a scrutiny of his account of the birth and progress of the book tends to disclose the slightness rather than the profundity of his engagement. When he said much later that the book was twelve years in preparation and two years in the writing, the point to remember is that *Huckleberry Finn* was eight years in the writing. Despite his insistence that he began the story five times, even Paine could find no direct evidence that he had done enormous work on the project before he actually began the book.[6] In the preface of *Joan of Arc*, eleven sources are cited, all of which, Mark Twain says, were carefully "examined in verification of the truthfulness" of the narrative.[7] This is hardly the extensive

[5] Paine, *A Biography*, II, 1,034.
[6] *Ibid.*, p. 959.   [7] *Writings*, XVII, vi.

bibliography that either Mark Twain or Paine thought it was. Furthermore, the whole notion of a bibliography was but one more way of puffing *Joan* as a serious book resting upon solid literary scholarship. Actually the scholarship amounted to little more than a dependency: the books, rather than proving a stimulus for narrative discoveries, provided an arrangement of events on which Mark Twain's torpid imagination could rely. And rely he did. Having invented the Sieur Louis de Conte as his narrator, he could let this invented voice move easily along the ready-made sequence of events which the previous histories recorded. Such a procedure relieved him of the burden of conceiving a plot. Instead of reconstructing the past, as he had done in his great narratives, he was actually leaning upon it.

If his insistence upon the length of time and amount of research devoted to *Joan of Arc* actually conceals how modest were his endeavors, what of his claim that Joan was not commercially tainted? Here again there is every indication that Mark Twain did not lose sight of the commercial possibilities of his great, pure project. When the book was finished and being serialized in *Harpers*, he disclosed his usual determination to exploit the financial possibilities of the book. In 1895, writing from Vancouver to J. Henry Harper—he had just undertaken his world tour to pay his way out of bankruptcy—Mark Twain expressed the wish that his identity as author of *Joan* be revealed. He thought it would help the lecturing tour by keeping his name before the public. He wrote later, however, that Olivia was troubled about the matter and wanted Harper to decide when the time was right. Harper decided that the time to capitalize on Mark Twain's name was when the book was to be published.[8]

These conflicting responses disclose that Mark Twain's elaborate statements about the birth and writing of *Joan* hold no more weight—possibly even less—than his casual dismissals of his humorous productions. Both attitudes

[8] Paine, *A Biography*, II, 1,005-1,006.

were in a sense lies, but the humorous attitude exposed
the truth, whereas the serious attitude denied the character and concealed the truth. Yet they are attitudes, not
facts, and primarily lead us to demand the truth concealed behind them. If this truth is concealed, it is by no
means buried. Indeed, the facts concerning the writing
of *Joan of Arc* are, like Poe's purloined letter, remarkably
evident, and they confirm the course Mark Twain's repression of himself was taking as he made his way from
Pudd'nhead Wilson toward *The Mysterious Stranger*.

Although the primary fact about *Joan* is Mark Twain's
attempt to deny his identity as its author, there are two
other facts which stand out in the history of his writing
during this period. First, throughout the entire time following *A Connecticut Yankee*—the time during which
Joan was written—Mark Twain was heading into bankruptcy, a shameful experience for anyone who has taken
pride in his rise from poverty and obscurity to wealth
and prominence. For Mark Twain it was much more
than business failure. His discovery of his genius in Virginia City had literally been a substitute for the silver
he could not find, and all his life he tended to see his
creative productions in terms of the capital into which
he could convert them. Possessed of a truly speculative
imagination, he invariably saw his literature as invention and enterprise.

Just as his literary efforts were related to speculative
enterprise, his speculative enterprises became concentrated upon two ventures intimately related to the act
of writing: the Webster Publishing Company and the
Paige Typesetter. Into the publishing concern and the
Paige Typesetter Mark Twain literally poured all his available capital, and by 1892 he had actually put his own
capacity for invention in the service of Paige's machine.
He was, as he himself once said, a slave of business, for
his books were being written to obtain immediate capital
to sustain his sinking projects. Mark Twain, investor in

the automatic writer, was converting himself into a writing mechanism in an effort to satisfy the appetite of what he came to call the "diabolical machine."

But there was a second major fact of this phase of Mark Twain's career. The seminal story of this entire period—the story which in effect generated all the others—was "Those Extraordinary Twins." Mark Twain clearly explained how the farce released *Pudd'nhead Wilson*. He did not make clear how much it had to do with the other two major productions, *Tom Sawyer Abroad* and *Joan of Arc*. His letters of the period cast interesting light on the relationship between the sketch and all his work during the years his fortunes were failing.

On August 10, 1892, he wrote to Fred J. Hall, who had assumed direction of the Webster Company after Charles L. Webster had died:

> I have dropped that novel I wrote you about, because I saw a more effective way of using the main episode—to wit: by telling it through the lips of Huck Finn. So I have started Huck Finn and Tom Sawyer (still 15 years old) and their friend the freed slave Jim around the world in a stray *balloon*, with Huck as narrator, and somewhere after the end of that great voyage he will work in the said episode and then nobody will suspect that a whole book has been written and the globe circumnavigated merely to get that episode in in an effective (and at the same time apparently unintentional) way.[9]

The novel he had dropped was, according to Paine, "Those Extraordinary Twins."[10] His turning toward Huck Finn becomes apparent later in the same letter when he casually observes that when he had been in New York "the other day," Mary Mapes Dodge, editor of *St. Nicholas*, had offered him $5,000 for a boys' story of 50,000 words. What he had evidently done was to fall back into the capital style of Huckleberry Finn, with the intention

[9] *Letters*, II, 565.   [10] *Ibid.*, p. 566.

of converting what he had already written on the "Twins" into Huck's narrative.

But Tom Sawyer's adventures apparently would not sustain his imagination, and on September 18—five weeks later—he wrote Mrs. Theodore Crane, his wife's adopted sister,

> I have been driving this pen hard. I wrote 280 pages on a yarn called "Tom Sawyer Abroad," then took up the "Twins" again, destroyed the last half of the manuscript and rewrote it in another form, and am going to continue it and finish it in Florence. "Tom Sawyer" seems rather pale to the family after the extravagances of the Twins, but they came to like it after they got used to it.[11]

This indicates that his original work on the "Twins" had been extensive and that he could not manage or did not wish to integrate it into Huck Finn's narrative. During the ensuing weeks—amid moving to the Villa Viviani above Florence, collecting fugitive tales for a volume, and taking care of Olivia—he not only finished *Tom Sawyer Abroad* but continued to make headway with the "Twins." And on December 12, 1892, he was able to write to Hall:

> I finished "Those Extraordinary Twins" night before last—makes 60 or 80,000 words—haven't counted.
> The last third of it suits me to a dot. I begin, today, to entirely re-cast and re-write the first two-thirds—new plan, with two minor characters, made very prominent, one major character cropped out, and the twins subordinated to a minor but not insignificant place.
> *The* minor character will now become the chiefest, and I will name the story after him—"Pudd'nhead Wilson."[12]

He had thus managed to capitalize on *Tom Sawyer Abroad* and was in the process of realizing *Pudd'nhead*

[11] *Ibid.*, p. 568.   [12] *Ibid.*, p. 574.

Wilson, which was evolving from the farce of the twins. On January 28, 1893, he wrote to Hall:

> My book is type-written and ready for print— "Pudd'nhead Wilson—A Tale." (Or, "Those Extraordinary Twins," if preferable.)
>
> It makes 82,500 words—12,000 words more than Huck Finn. But I don't know what to do with it. Mrs. Clemens thinks it wouldn't do to go to the Am. Pub. Co. or anywhere outside of our own house; we have no subscription machinery, and a book in the trade is a book thrown away, as far as money-profit goes. I am in a quandary. Give me a lift out of it.
>
> I will mail the book to you and get you to examine it and see if it is good or if it is bad. I think it is good, and I thought the Claimant bad when I saw it in print; but as for real judgment, I think I am destitute of it.
>
> I am writing a companion to the Prince and Pauper, which is half done and will make 200,000 words; and I have had the idea that if it were gotten up in handsome style, with many illustrations and put at a high enough price maybe the L.A.L. [Library of American Literature] canvassers would take it and run it with that book. Would they? It could be priced anywhere from $4 up to $10, according to how it was gotten up, I suppose.
>
> I don't want it to go into a magazine.[13]

This letter discloses—in a way that no amount of Mark Twain's testimonials can—that if "Those Extraordinary Twins" was the seminal book of the period, it was *Pudd'n-head Wilson* and not *Joan of Arc* which demanded all his resources as a writer. It emerges as *the* book of those difficult years. But it is upon *Joan of Arc* that the letter throws most light. First of all it shows that both *Joan of Arc* and *Pudd'nhead Wilson* had sprung into life at the time Mark Twain was working on "Those Extraordinary Twins." The letter further discloses that *Joan*, as orig-

---

[13] *Ibid.*, p. 579.

inally conceived, was a companion piece to *The Prince and the Pauper*, which amounts to saying it was a genteel historical narrative designed to make money. He makes no mention of its having been a lifelong ambition; rather, he sees it as a book which will have "handsome style," be published in an expensive edition, and be included in the Library of American Literature, that heavy-weighted "set" which was dragging the Webster Publishing Company toward bankruptcy. Finally, the letter indicates that the writing was proceeding apace. *Pudd'nhead Wilson* might be a struggle, but *Joan* was coming into being with facile and remarkable ease. That it came with ease is by no means a sign of its inadequacy, for some of Mark Twain's best work came with ease. But its ease is most significant in relation to Mark Twain's determined effort at a later time to insist upon the pains with which it was constructed.

Even so, Mark Twain did not sweep through to the conclusion of *Joan* in one sustained burst—and for a reason. He was not through with *Pudd'nhead Wilson*. Not only was he not through; he became involved in another complete revision of the book. Whether this revision was prompted by Hall's objection to the January 28th version or whether Mark Twain had found himself answering his own question is a matter of speculation. In any event he was able to write Hall on July 30, 1893:

> This time "Pudd'nhead Wilson" is a success! Even Mrs. Clemens, the most difficult of critics, confesses it, and without reserves or qualifications. Formerly she would not consent that it be published either before or after my death. I have pulled the twins apart and made two individuals of them; I have sunk them out of sight, they are mere flitting shadows, now, and of no importance; *their* story has disappeared from the book. Aunt Betsy Hale has vanished wholly, leaving not a trace behind; Aunt Patsy Cooper and her daughter Rowena have almost disappeared—they scarcely walk across

the stage. The whole story is centered on the murder and the trial; from the first chapter the movement is straight ahead without divergence or side-play to the murder and the trial; everything that is done or said or that happens is a preparation for those events. . . . When I began this final reconstruction the story contained 81,500 words, now it contains only 58,000. I have knocked out everything that delayed the march of the story—even the description of a Mississippi steamboat. There's no weather in, and no scenery—the story is stripped for flight![14]

He went on in this letter to tell Hall that he intended to complete a travelogue of a raft trip down the Rhone and to return to his Adam's diary.

All of this writing constituted Mark Twain's valiant attempt to secure enough capital to float his foundering business. Yet for all his effort, eighteen months after writing this letter to Hall, his publishing house had failed and his typesetter project had disintegrated despite his frantic battle to stem the tide of misfortune sweeping toward him. He was engulfed in business much of that time, spending the winter of 1893-94 in New York, where he could keep in touch with the ebb and flow of his fortunes. That same winter he met Henry Huttleston Rogers, the man he thought would save his business life. As Rogers firmly took the financial helm, Mark Twain was able to write Olivia of his plans to return to Europe and of his intentions of quitting business:

When the anchor is down, then I shall say: "Farewell—a long farewell—to *business*! I will *never* touch it again!"

I will live in literature, I will wallow in it, revel in it, I will swim in ink! Joan of Arc—but all this is premature; the anchor is not down yet.[15]

But the manner in which Rogers was to save Mark Twain's business life was actually to kill his businesses, thereby ending the deceptions of an illusory future. He

[14] *Ibid.*, pp. 590-91. [15] *Ibid.*, p. 607.

first closed out the publishing house in April, 1894, enabling Mark Twain to return to Europe early in the summer of 1894, apparently believing that Rogers would pull the typesetter through. Evidently with such a belief in mind he returned to work on *Joan* later that summer, for on September 9, he wrote to Rogers that he had driven himself too hard on the book and had been forced to rest. His taking up the book was by no means a purely literary venture. The letter to Rogers makes clear that he was determined to make a big book out of *Joan*.[16] If he had trimmed *Pudd'nhead* with a fine economy, he was expanding *Joan* into a work big enough to occupy handsome space in the literary world.

Mark Twain's reckonings on putting *Joan* into the service of the typesetter failed to take into account the actions of the remarkable Rogers, who, after giving the typesetter as much chance as he thought wise, determined to get Mark Twain completely out of business. By the middle of December he had all but accomplished the fact and wrote Mark Twain of the imminent failure of the machine. Even in face of the end, Mark Twain not only continued to concoct schemes to save the business, but turned instinctively to writing in an effort to raise capital. Thus in a calm postscript to his letter replying to Rogers' staggering news he wrote:

> I am going right along with Joan, now, and wait untroubled until I hear from you. If you think I can be of the least use, cable me "Come." I can write Joan on board ship and lose no time. Also I could discuss my plan with the publisher for a *deluxe* Joan, time being an object, for some of the pictures could be made over here cheaply and quickly, but would cost much time and money in America.[17]

As long as there was the remotest hope for his business enterprise, it did not occur to Mark Twain to insist that

[16] *Ibid.*, p. 616.   [17] *Ibid.*, p. 618.

Joan must not be converted into literary capital. But his business world was nonetheless collapsing. Under the astute—Paine always assures us that it was astute—direction of Rogers, Mark Twain was masterfully put out of business and all his finances put in Rogers' expert hands.

If *Joan* had formerly been the book which Mark Twain had seen as a way to keep in business, it now became a means of getting out of business, and Joan herself became the figure who could be seen as "purely" literary—so literary, in fact, that Mark Twain was able to write Rogers that the book was written for pure "love." The book itself became the means by which Mark Twain could at one and the same time put his business troubles out of mind and surrender to the financial acumen of Rogers—who efficiently saw to it that Mark Twain's affairs were brought to order.

The cost of the surrender can best be measured by seeing what the settlement was. First of all, Mark Twain declared bankruptcy—which was in effect a full recognition of the failure of his speculative imagination, that imagination which had from the beginning identified art and fortune. Second, he lost possession of his works. By Rogers' astute management, his copyrights were transferred to his wife's name to prevent creditors from gaining possession of what Rogers shrewdly realized was Mark Twain's most valuable property. The transfer of copyright had its fatal significance, however. If it meant that the property would not be lost, it also meant that Olivia—who had been his play censor—now assumed outright ownership of copyright. Her emergence as independent owner of the copyright symbolized what had happened to Mark Twain. He had lost possession of his name, and his benign censor, who had hitherto been straight man to his humorous genius, was now given legal right to his name in order to protect his family from being thrown utterly upon the mercy of his creditors. Finally, Rogers took absolute charge of Mark Twain's money until the creditors were paid off.[18] During the whole of Mark Twain's round-the-world lecture tour—which he undertook in order to pay one hundred cents on the dollar and thus show himself a man of honor in the manner of Sir Walter Scott—he sent all his proceeds directly to Rogers, who saw to it that the money was applied to the debts. Though Rogers was kind and though Olivia changed no whit toward the man whose copyright she now owned, the decisions of the period disclose the surrender of Mark Twain's creative force. It was as if Jervis Langdon, in the person of Henry H. Rogers, had returned to protect his daughter and her children from his son-in-law's irresponsibilities.

These failures in the life of Samuel Clemens did not "cause" the despair and failure in the work of Mark Twain; they are instead the disasters which corresponded to the failure of *Joan of Arc*. Thus, at the same time that Samuel Clemens was losing control of his copyrights, Mark Twain was denying his identity as a writer. The ultimate irony lay in the serious lie he invented to celebrate his own self-effacement.

Against the background of *Pudd'nhead Wilson*, the figure of Joan of Arc assumes a strikingly meaningful identity. *Pudd'nhead* ironically chronicled the secret history of miscegenation; *Joan of Arc* reverently recounted a life of purity and inviolate maidenhood. In viewing these two books which literally accompanied each other in emerging from Mark Twain's imagination, the two women, Roxana and Joan, stand like contrasting sculptures on the landscape. The one—dark, voluble, and comical—who, though her sexuality is not dramatized, is nonetheless the sexual object at the mercy of a society of gentlemen; the other—pale, chaste, and serious—whose martial power and childlike purity bring her into power over a society of rude and barbarous soldiers.

[18] Paine, *A Biography*, II, 983-87. See also Ferguson, *Man and Legend*, pp. 258-59.

The sharp contrast between the dark, humorous mother and the serious, radiant maiden goes far toward defining Joan of Arc. She is the visionary embodiment of all the utterly conventional, utterly somber, utterly reverent attitudes and language upon which Mark Twain's humor had played through all the years of his career. She is the absolute epitome of the reverence against which the irreverent Mark Twain had defined his identity in *The Innocents Abroad*. More than that, she is a stranger—but not an ironic stranger, for no genuine irony can penetrate her reverent identity. She is rather the mysterious stranger —the first authentic one to appear in Mark Twain's world— and she is quite appropriately given an angelic identity.

The surest way to see her is to define Mark Twain's point of view upon her. In that point of view lay whatever particularity, whatever signature, he was able to infuse into the legend and history he inherited. He left the legend and history largely intact, showing remarkably little tendency to analyze or explore its dramatic possibilities. His attitude toward the Middle Ages, particularly toward Catholicism, was one of almost undisguised contempt—so much so that he saw Joan's entire pilgrimage in extremely melodramatic terms. Because he could not see her rebellion as dangerous and perplexing, and because he would not see the churchmen as anything other than ignorant asses or hopeless devils, he could imagine no genuine resistance which would have in turn given Joan stature and complexity. He lacked the kind of dramatic intelligence by means of which Shaw was able to endow Joan's interlocutors with the wit which in turn gave Joan power. Compared to Shaw's intense Joan, Mark Twain's conception is, as Shaw himself shrewdly observed, peculiarly sterile.[19]

[19] Shaw says in his preface to *Saint Joan*: "Mark Twain's Joan, skirted to the ground, and with as many petticoats as Noah's wife in a toy ark, is an attempt to combine Bayard with Esther Summerson from *Bleak House* into an unimpeachable American school teacher in armor. Like Esther Summerson she makes her creator ridiculous, and yet, being the work of a man of genius,

Yet Mark Twain did have a point of view. It involved the intrusion of a fictional narrator, the old Sieur Louis de Conte, who would relate the events of Joan's life, transforming the chronicle into a kind of pleasant firsthand view of remote history. The narrator's vantage point is one remote in time from the events he chronicles, for he is an old man recollecting the life of the marvelous girl. Yet his chronicle is personal, for his youth and young manhood were spent serving as her page.

The best way to see the old Sieur's failure as a narrator is to compare it with Huckleberry Finn's success. Both books portray a child acting "wrongly" in an evil world. Huck is confronting the evil of slavery in the Old South and Joan is struggling against the impotence and corruption of the clergy and aristocracy in the bygone medieval world. Both are involved in actions which presumably are one hundred per cent approvable. What then is the difference between them? Joan, like Hank Morgan, is a conscious rebel, approving of her own actions. Huck Finn, however much he might rebel, could never win his own approval. Joan is never the bad girl in her own eyes, but the good girl consciously doing the worthy bidding of her voices. Presumably in an effort to "humanize" this coldly angelic good girl, Mark Twain put her story in the mouth of the old Sieur. But in the process of the telling, he simply managed to transfer Joan's self-approval into the old Sieur's indulgent adoration of the child he had served. Instead of personalizing Joan, the narrative merely sweetens her all the more, and what was once her bold rebellion becomes in Mark Twain's point of view an old man's tiresome reverence. Indeed, the old Sieur embodies the emotion of reverence better than any of the pious pilgrims on the *Quaker City*.

It is just this reverence which, since it is the emotion

remains a credible human goodygoody in spite of her creator's infatuation. It is the description rather than the valuation that is wrong" (*Saint Joan* and *The Apple Cart*, Standard Edition [London, 1933], p. 26).

of the narrative, inevitably suppresses Mark Twain's humor. In fact, all the forms of Mark Twain's humor literally appear as characters serving the martyred maid. There is first of all the Paladin, the liar Mark Twain who must exaggerate all experience into a tall tale; there is La Hire, the profane Mark Twain who cannot forswear swearing; there is Noel Rainguesson, the mimic Mark Twain who cannot resist impersonating the Paladin. Significantly all these characters are expended in Joan's high mystic mission. They are the humorist's sterile gestures in a world given over to propagating the reverent image of Joan. Their intended function in the narrative is clear. They are there to provide an earthy touch to the reverent narrative, thereby brightening up with a kind of comic relief the pathetic history of the martyred maiden. But their presence in the narrative confirms rather than threatens the essential gentility of the Sieur's reverent pose, giving his unctuous tale at best a proper whimsicality—something in the nature of a minister's anecdote to salt the sermon.

The whole performance is so dismal as to make one wish it were a parody, yet clearly it is no parody. Mark Twain is obviously serious—so serious that he cannot be Mark Twain. Which brings us back to Joan's identity. The embodiment of all the conventions which Mark Twain had humorously subverted during his career, she clearly and completely represses his humor. The end of the Sieur's story makes clear the meaning of Joan:

> I have finished my story of Joan of Arc, that wonderful child, that sublime personality, that spirit which in one regard has had no peer and will have none—this: its purity from all alloy of self-seeking, self-interest, personal ambition. In it no trace of these motives can be found, search as you may, and this cannot be said of any other person whose name appears in profane history.[20]

[20] *Writings*, XVIII, 287.

This image, which evoked the pathetic old narrator to adore it, all but denied the identity of Mark Twain in the process. Huck Finn had been the narrator who at once had extended and realized Mark Twain's range of humor—he had even humorously pushed Mark Twain aside in the first paragraph to write his own book. The Sieur does not push Mark Twain aside; he does not even acknowledge his existence. His story *is* the very image of Joan which he evokes. She is not the play censor who releases Mark Twain but the serious muse who does indeed censor, enslave, and finally deny the humorist; and she appears at the precise moment when Mark Twain was releasing his copyrights to the possession of his wife. Paine, with that typical unconscious irony which makes the biography at once annoying and formidable, completed his praise of the book by observing:

> It was the only book of all he had written that
> Mark Twain considered worthy of this dedication:

> 1870 · TO MY WIFE · 1895
> OLIVIA LANGDON CLEMENS
> This Book
> is tendered on our
> wedding anniversary in
> grateful recognition
> of her twenty-five years
> of valued service as my
> literary advisor and
> editor.
> THE AUTHOR[21]

Joan of Arc was thus the total embodiment of the conventional values and the emotional reverence against which Mark Twain's humor hitherto played. Mark Twain's identity was threatened in direct proportion to the autonomy she preempted. It is just this threat which accounts for the dramatic division of Mark Twain's later work into the sentimental on the one hand and the ironic on the

[21] Paine, *A Biography*, II, 1,033;

other. In the sentimental category, there are "A Horse's Tale," "A Dog's Tale," and "The Death Disk"—all more or less nauseating shorter fiction following the lines of *Joan of Arc*. All these stories, interestingly enough dominated by girls, deploy the same unctuous tone of the Sieur Louis de Conte. They foreshadow that turn in Mark Twain which brought him, near the end of his life, to form the Angel Fish Club, made up of girls of school age whose central function was to cast their doting gazes upon the club's founder and chief member. Mark Twain's grief over the death of Susy Clemens is usually cited as the essential motive behind the sentimental stories. But *Joan of Arc* preceded the death of Susy by more than a year, once more emphasizing how often in Mark Twain's career literature and style take precedence over life.

In contradistinction to the sentimental and conventional tales featuring juvenile heroines, there is the ironic fiction which continues the march of the ironic stranger. Chief among such tales are "The Man That Corrupted Hadleyburg," "The £1,000,000 Bank Note," and "The $30,000 Bequest," all of which hinge upon a stranger's intruding into a complacent society and, by tempting the community with money, subverting the entire social order. "The Man That Corrupted Hadleyburg" is preeminent among such stories and could well be called the furthest extension of all the tendencies of *Pudd'nhead Wilson*. It is a story of total irony, total plot. The epigrams which stood above the fiction in *Pudd'nhead Wilson* have been assimilated into the searing conciseness of the taut, arbitrary plot and the triumphant bitterness of tone which characterize the story.

What becomes evident in considering this pronounced division between the ironic and the sentimental is that it began in "Those Extraordinary Twins." That story first set in motion the threat of absolute division between angelic and diabolic, light and dark, ironic and sentimental. For the body joining the original twins did not bind them together so much as it defined their mortal opposition to each other. Only by severing the twins could Mark Twain pursue the divergent channels this opposition heralded—which is precisely what he did, thus releasing himself from the paralysis and structural impasse represented by the antithetical impulses. From Angelo, the blond, angelic twin, he went toward *Joan of Arc*; from the dark, conscienceless Luigi toward the false Tom Driscoll and the world of Pudd'nhead Wilson. The point of such a division is not that the sentimental represses the ironic, but that the division itself is the repression. The very emergence of the opposing twins is the signal not of unity or complexity, but of division and simplification in matters of characterization, plot, and style. To be sure, the ironic dimension of Mark Twain's writing was the more basic and represented the area closest to the world of humor; not surprisingly, the ironic narratives were the ones which exacted the greatest struggle from their divided author. Yet they too involved a repression of his humorous genius, directed as they were toward serious goals. The ironic, purged of the sentimental, involved a reduction, a loss, a maiming, an incompleteness for Mark Twain—an incompleteness absolutely embodied by the fragmented and abortive seminal burlesque of "Those Extraordinary Twins," which had in effect fathered the birth of the division. Thus Mark Twain, whose very identity and name designated a union of the two worlds, was faced with the task of bringing the two worlds back together in a new union. His effort to do just that was the last great struggle of his career—the writing of *The Mysterious Stranger*.

The apparent story of how *The Mysterious Stranger* came to be is well known by Mark Twain devotees. Like Melville's *Billy Budd*, the story was found among its author's papers. And if there has been difficulty in obtaining a reliable text of *Billy Budd*, the problems attaching to *The Mysterious Stranger* are even more disconcerting. For years there seemed to be no problem, because Paine, who published the story six years after Mark Twain's death, told such a beguiling story about discovering the cache that only chronic skeptics had cause to doubt. The story of little Satan, according to Paine, was one which Mark Twain had worked on intermittently for years and had said on one occasion was complete, aside from a brief ending which he could write at any time. But the ending had apparently not been written—or such seemed the state of affairs—when, long after Mark Twain's death, Paine came across the concluding chapter, happily preserved among the papers. What Paine did not say was that Mark Twain had made three separate and distinct attempts to write *The Mysterious Stranger* between 1897 and 1905, and that the concluding chapter which he, Paine, attached to the published version was clearly intended to be the conclusion of another version of the story. Paine was of course aware of the three attempts to write the story, but preferred to perform concealed editorial transitions and changes of names so that the true identity of the concluding chapter would be undetected.

For Bernard De Voto, who succeeded Paine as editor of the Mark Twain Papers, the closing years of Mark Twain's life came to seem the years which held the real secrets of his genius, and he determined to wrest order from the chaos of unpublished manuscripts Mark Twain had left behind him. He knew, as Paine had known before him, that there were three manuscript versions of the story of little Satan coming to a world of children to perform his miracles. The three versions were, as De Voto was to term them, the "Hannibal" version, a short and relatively unsuccessful beginning in which the action takes place in Hannibal. In this version Tom and Huck find the boredom of the schoolroom suddenly relieved by the miraculous presence of Satan, who in this version of the story goes by the name of "44." However, the story does not progress beyond exploiting "44's" magic tricks. A second version of the story, the "Eseldorf" version, is the story essentially as Paine published it, with the exception of numerous excisions and with the addition of the missing last chapter, which Paine so fortuitously "found." Finally, there is the "Print Shop" version, the longest of the three, in which Satan is once more named "44," but is by no means the boyish miracle worker of the Hannibal version. He is, instead, the dream self of August Feldner—who takes the place of Theodore Fischer—and he sets about to free August from the illusions which enslave him. But in the process, the action becomes involved in a mélange of philosophic and burlesque additions to the plot and loses the simplicity and economy of the Eseldorf version.

Whereas Paine had simply chosen to exploit the papers for publication and conceal difficult discrepancies which from his point of view did seem minor, De Voto was concerned to develop a theory of Mark Twain's despair. He intended to write a book disclosing the way in which Mark Twain arrived at his last testament. He did not live to write the book, but in the last essay of *Mark Twain at Work*, "The Symbols of Despair," he set forth the shape of his theory. As De Voto saw it, the disasters of bankruptcy, the death of his favorite daughter Susy, the discovery that another daughter Jean was an epileptic, and the acute invalidism and approaching death of Olivia, impaired Mark Twain's image of himself. Faced with the sense of responsibility for the disasters which involved his family, Mark Twain's guilt subjected his ego to a severe assault during the years of failure and grief. At the same time, however, his imagination was struggling to find a form which would bring the disasters of experience under control. For years no such form was forthcoming. Instead, there were a series of fascinating but abortive attempts at stories which came to nothing. The most powerful of these stories—stories usually involving a man in the throes of family disaster, financial ruin, or self-accusation—projected a dream fantasy of a polar voyage which began in a microscopic drop of water and ended in the desolation of an unspeakably remote and icy sea. This and similar fantasies haunted Mark Twain's imagination between 1896 and 1905. In De Voto's eyes,

The Mysterious Stranger was the narrative by means of which Mark Twain recovered his balance at the edge of insanity—and saved himself both as man and writer. Such a theory required that the Eseldorf version be the final of the three versions, and such was the conclusion to which De Voto duly came.

In a recent study of the three versions of the story, John S. Tuckey, availing himself of all possible evidence and making intelligent speculations where necessary, has conclusively shown that De Voto's guesses are untenable.[22] Rather than being the last version of the three, the Eseldorf version was, according to Tuckey, the first—except for what he terms a "pre-Eseldorf" fragment evidently incorporated into the Eseldorf manuscript.[23] Begun in the fall of 1897, when Mark Twain was in Vienna, and continued until January, 1898, the Eseldorf version was resumed from May until October of 1899, dropped, and again taken up from June to August of 1900, before being finally abandoned.[24] All work on the Hannibal version was done in November and December of 1898.[25] The Print Shop version was not begun until November of 1902, was pursued intermittently until October, 1903, intensively from January to June of 1904, and again in June and July of 1905.[26]

[22] John S. Tuckey, *Mark Twain and Little Satan* (West Lafayette, Ind., 1963). This excellent book not only describes what Paine did and De Voto thought but offers the best account to date of Mark Twain's work during this final phase of his life as an active writer.

[23] *Ibid.*, pp. 24, 51.

[24] *Ibid.*, pp. 25-40, 43-53. Tuckey believes that Mark Twain intended the Eseldorf version to end with the happy insanity of Father Peter following the trial scene, but that satiric impulses toward particular events in the summer of 1900 led him to carry the story beyond his intended conclusion.

[25] *Ibid.*, pp. 41-42.

[26] *Ibid.*, pp. 54-61, 68-70. Mark Twain wrote a small, but significant, episode in 1908 (Tuckey, pp. 72-73). This portion—in which "44" shows August Feldner a ghostly procession of the dead of all the past, then waves it away in oblivion leaving the two alone in a soundless world—could have been intended as a conclusion for the Print Shop version, but Tuckey believes that

The six-page chapter which Paine discovered as a "con-conclusion" to the Eseldorf version was, according to Tuckey, written between February and June of 1904—when Olivia Langdon was in her last illness—and was clearly intended to be a conclusion for the Print Shop version. To make it seem a part of the Eseldorf version, Paine and F. A. Duneka, both of whom edited the story, had to change the name of "44" to Satan. This was not all. They had to write the initial paragraph of the chapter in order to link the fragment with the earlier manuscript. They also borrowed the name "The Mysterious Stranger" from the Print Shop version.[27] Yet all the editorial changes cannot make the "44" of the last chapter identical with the Satan of the first ten chapters. Satan had been bodied forth as an angel, but "44" had been narratively defined in the Print Shop version as the dream self of August Feldner. Thus his announcement that he is a dream, which comes as a revelation to both Theodore Fischer and the reader in the published story, was, in its original context, to have been a revelation only to August.

Tuckey's findings do not invalidate so much as they define Paine's text of *The Mysterious Stranger*. Though clearly edited by Paine, that text just as clearly is not going to be superseded by any future text. In one sense, Tuckey is right in concluding that Paine's version "does not represent Mark Twain's intention,"[28] since Paine

---

the episode would have brought the story into line with the conclusion written in 1904.

[27] They took even further liberties. Mark Twain had, in the original manuscript, pursued what for him was a familiar plot device—the presence of a good priest (Father Peter) and a bad one (Father Adolf). But Duneka, a Roman Catholic, strongly objected to the bad priest, and he and Paine invented the astrologer to serve as villain of the published version, leaving Father Adolf precariously present but detached from the plot—resembling in this respect the twins Angelo and Luigi whom Mark Twain left in *Pudd'nhead Wilson*. According to Tuckey, Paine and Duneka cut out about one-quarter of the wordage of the manuscript—sometimes as many as forty pages of manuscript in sequence—to give the reader a coherent tale.

[28] Tuckey, *Mark Twain and Little Satan*, p. 77.

played fast and loose with the versions of the story. Yet the point remains that there is *no* text of the story—that, far from finding his intention as he proceeded from version to version of his story (as De Voto wished to believe), Mark Twain clearly lost it. What he found instead was a new editor to replace the lost Olivia Langdon Clemens. If, as Tuckey believes, he wrote the ending of his book at the time of her death, he found in Albert Bigelow Paine the man who would and could take upon himself the "liberty" of editing his remains. Considered from the point of view of "principle," Paine took outrageous freedoms. But given the state of the three versions which lay before him, Paine's edition was clearly a brilliant performance. Choosing the Eseldorf version was not difficult, since it was obviously the most sustained and coherent of the three, but the changes, excisions, and transitions Paine made required a presumptuousness bordering on audacity. Finally, Paine's "discovery" of the ending was in its way a genuine discovery. Whatever inconsistencies existed as a result of the transposition, the consistencies were far more striking. By the time Paine had completed his operation, the lesion had been concealed so remarkably as to leave but a gliding, almost imperceptible trick of transformation at the story's end, as if the movement were indeed a dream. And so the Print Shop ending turned out to be an Eseldorf ending after all; for if Satan's angelic identity in the Eseldorf ending was explicit, his dream identity was clearly implicit, thus allowing Paine's transposed ending to work in its new context.

That Paine's edition should be "doubted" is only true to Mark Twain's identity. But like his *Biography*, which—for all its censorship, protection, and concealment—has proved more and more difficult to supersede, his edition will, when the last word of each unpublished version has been duly edited and published, be more, not less, formidable.[29] In the last analysis, Mark Twain discovered in

[29] The published version of *The Mysterious Stranger* represents a wholeness unapproached by such unpublished manuscripts as

Paine the editorial intention which he had lost; thus Paine's posthumous edition of Mark Twain's last work is the closest thing to Mark Twain's intention that we shall ever have. Paine was, in fact, able to do precisely what Mark Twain could not do—integrate and coordinate the dissipating impulse of Mark Twain's final effort as a writer.[30] That is why *The Mysterious Stranger*, even with our added consciousness of the editorial process which brought it to conclusive form, remains Mark Twain's last written work. It is what we may call the essential form of Mark Twain's "despair," and deserves analysis as such.

Perhaps the most illuminating approach to *The Mysterious Stranger* is to see it in the light of *Joan of Arc*. Joan is the good, good girl—the epitome of conventional purity, the object of the reverent style, the human saint in the process of being translated into an angel. Philip Traum, on the other hand, is the *little* Satan come down to inhabit the world of the three boys. The quality of that world is immediately defined in the opening paragraphs of the story:

> It was in 1590—winter. Austria was far away from the world, and asleep; it was still the Middle

---

"Statement of the Edwardses," "The George Harrison Story," or "3,000 Years Among the Microbes." All of these share the thematic drift of the three versions of *The Mysterious Stranger* and show the same tendency of inventive impulse dissipating into indulgence. There is, as a matter of fact, a character named Doangiveadam who threatens at one point to take over the action of the Print Shop version. The character's name reveals nothing so much as Mark Twain's actual relationship to his story. Hopefully all these manuscripts will one day be edited and published, not only for the interest they inevitably have but also to dispel the myth, so energetically fostered by Mark Twain, that the powerful work is still to come.

[30] Having completed his biography of Mark Twain, Paine may very well have felt that his massive editorial work on the book was not really a violation of any principle but "only" what Mark Twain would have wanted anyway, in which case his fiction about the ending may not have seemed at all a fiction.

Ages in Austria, and promised to remain so forever. Some even set it away back centuries upon
centuries and said that by the mental and spiritual
clock it was still the Age of Belief in Austria. But
they meant it as a compliment, not a slur, and it
was so taken, and we were all proud of it. I remember it well, although I was only a boy; and I
remember, too, the pleasure it gave me.

Yes, Austria was far from the world, and asleep,
and our village was in the middle of that sleep,
being in the middle of Austria. It drowsed in peace
in the deep privacy of a hilly and woodsy solitude
where news from the world hardly ever came to
disturb its dreams, and was infinitely content. At
its front flowed the tranquil river, its surface
painted with cloud-forms and the reflections of
drifting arks and stone-boats; behind it rose the
woody steeps to the base of the lofty precipice;
from the top of the precipice frowned a vast castle,
its long stretch of towers and bastions mailed in
vines; beyond the river, a league to the left, was a
tumbled expanse of forest-clothed hills cloven by
winding gorges where the sun never penetrated;
and to the right a precipice overlooked the river, and
between it and the hills just spoken of lay a far-
reaching plain dotted with little homesteads nested
among orchards and shade trees.[31]

Here is one of Mark Twain's finest impersonations of the
style of juvenile romance—it is so good that it seems
better and "richer" than anything Charlotte Yonge, Kate
Douglas Wiggin, or Frances Hodgson Burnett might
achieve. It is a highly stylized set piece of description,
carefully wrought to convey a miniature and picturesque
idyl in which pastoral and historical past are fused in a
dreamy setting. All movement is stabilized as in a tableau,
and all tendencies of the prose are directed toward indulging the landscape by removing it from motion. Thus, the
river is tranquil, its surface is painted with cloud forms

[31] *The Mysterious Stranger and Other Stories* (New York, 1922),
p. 3.

and reflections. The sky and the moving boats are not perceived directly but pictured in a reflective scene. The castle, perfectly conventional, frowns from the top of its precipice, its bastions "mailed" in vines. The "tumbled expanse of forest-clothed hills" are "cloven by winding gorges," and the homesteads "dot" the plain. The entire passage seeks to evoke the indulgently picturesque scene of a literary fairy tale.

The intention of this first passage is more to set the convention than disclose the character of the narrator. That is why Theodore Fischer, the narrator, seems always more conventional than individual. His individuality can scarcely be felt against the pressure of the convention his language impersonates—the convention of juvenile romance, with its indulgent reverence for the olden time. Theodore is, in fact, an almost exact parallel of the old Sieur Louis de Conte who narrated *Joan of Arc*. His entire stance, especially the reverent, oversweet, and somewhat effeminate tone, echoes the Sieur's voice.

There is, of course, one touch of irony in Theodore's opening passage, when he observes that those who said the Age of Belief still prevailed in Austria "meant it as a compliment, not a slur." The irony here, though brief, is clearly intended as an intrusive, almost sardonic observation of the experienced narrator's wry comment upon the particular innocence of his past; it is at the same time a stylistic grimace at the particular complacency the idyl indulges and sustains. At first glance such irony might seem to distinguish Theodore's style from the old Sieur's, yet the same kind of irony is present in *Joan of Arc*. For the old Sieur, having seen Joan killed by the world, possesses such a contempt for humanity that he frequently releases a scornful generalization about the nature of man.

But there is a deployment of ironic effect in *The Mysterious Stranger* which makes it a direct antithesis of *Joan of Arc*. The antithesis is produced not by a change of tone or narrative consciousness but by a change of mysterious strangers. Joan had been the mysterious stranger of her village who, possessed by angelic voices, defied the despair and complacency which gripped the people she was to save. However rebellious she was, however scathingly she exposed the folly of the Church and government, she was the pure and martyred maid of Orleans whom Mark Twain, through the recollections of the Sieur, was joining history to revere. Little Satan is different. To be sure, he is an angel, but his name discloses his relationship to the darker powers. Not a devil or even diabolical, he is a bad boy angel come to earth for two reasons. As bad boy, he has come to please himself with the same kinds of showmanship that Tom Sawyer had sprung upon the bored community. As angel, however, he aspires to do more than engage in boyish pranks. He means to expose the paltry human scene in which his miracles are to be enacted and at the same time please himself.

And he does please himself with every exposure. Philip Traum is, after all, a kind of genie who appears to conduct the children on a series of remarkable adventures. The magician possessed of the greatest tricks, he enters the sleepy village to inject a sense of excitement and glamor into the lives of the bored boys who live there. The dream of possibility long since surrendered by the adults yet still visible to the children, he represents nothing less than the creative imagination. This symbolic status is at the core of the satiric conception of the book. For the book is satiric, and not humorous, in intent, which is to say that the impulse to expose reality dominates the impulse to play upon it. The pleasure of judgment thus supersedes the pleasure of play. Whereas Huck had rejected civilization in order to play in the territory, Satan rejects it because it is contemptible. The intent of Philip Traum's final speech is to illuminate Theodore's—and the reader's—mind by confronting him with a shocking revelation:

"It is true, that which I have revealed to you;
there is no God, no universe, no human race, no
earthly life, no heaven, no hell. It is all a dream—
a grotesque and foolish dream. Nothing exists but
you. And you are but a *thought*—a vagrant thought,
a useless thought, a homeless thought, wandering
forlorn among the empty eternities!"

He vanished, and left me appalled; for I knew,
and realized, that all he had said was true.[32]

Theodore's concluding word is the key term of the passage; it not only echoes Satan's contention in the immediate context, but provides a possible termination of
the entire narrative, thereby making the chapter seem,
even if it is not, the logical conclusion which Paine pre-
tended it was. This does not mean that the book is truer
than *Huckleberry Finn* or any of Mark Twain's earlier
works, but that it is committed to a conceptual rather than
a narrative substance. This tendency toward disclosure
and concept shifts the emphasis from Satan's action to
his thought. To see just how the form of the book con-
spires toward this end, one has but to see the nature of
Satan. He is seen from the beginning to be an extension
of the boys' wishes and thoughts. Thus he can both read
their minds and enliven their somnolent lives. Yet he is
by no means an hallucination of Theodore. He can be
seen by the select society of the three boys and, under
the name of Philip Traum, he has objective existence in
the village. He is, and is clearly meant to be, not a
private projection of the narrator but an embodiment of
the creative imagination itself, affording the children
excitement and adventure, even as it frees them to see the
truth.

And what is the truth which Satan reveals? It is that
man is a slave. His argument hinges on two revelations.
First, man is a slave of circumstance; his life is a fatally
fixed chain of acts brought about not by God—interestingly enough—but by his own first act.

[32] *Ibid.*, p. 140.

"You see, now [says Satan to Theodore], that a man will never drop a link in his chain. He cannot. If he made up his mind to try, that project would itself be an unavoidable link—a thought bound to occur to him at that precise moment, and made certain by the first act of his babyhood."

It seemed so dismal!

"He is a prisoner for life," I said sorrowfully, "and cannot get free."

"No, of himself he cannot get away from the consequences of his first childish act. But I can free him."[33]

Although Satan's philosophical exercise need not be perfect, this one is clearly so inadequate that it fails to sustain the illusion of philosophical thought. Theodore never questions and Satan never defines what he means by *act*, though presumably he means not a child's conscious choice but a baby's uncomprehending gesture; the first act is thus rooted not in the mind but in the identity. Yet Satan insists that this first act is more original than fatal. The point is not that the idea is false but that it is so sketchily presented as to fail to meet the demands it evokes. This failure causes action to evade the thought it provokes and drift toward a miraculous demonstration of each inadequately stated proposition. Thus when Satan says that he can free man from his slavery, he proceeds to show how he, as an angel, is able to change a link in the chain and alter the lives of men.

But man is not only in metaphysical chains, he is also morally a slave—a victim of the Moral Sense. The Moral Sense is, of course, the faculty enabling men to distinguish good from evil. Satan first calls the faculty into question when he creates a tribe of little men before the boys' astonished eyes, then pleasantly annihilates them as if they were no more than ants. Confronted by the children's horror at his action, he almost laughingly avers that men are unspeakably inferior to angels by

[33] *Ibid.*, p. 83.

virtue of possessing the Moral Sense. Discomfited by Satan's revelation, the children seek illumination from the benign Father Peter:

> There was a question which we wanted to ask Father Peter, and finally we went there the second evening, a little diffidently, after drawing straws, and I asked it as casually as I could, though it did not sound as casual as I wanted, because I didn't know how:
> "What is the Moral Sense, sir?"
> He looked down, surprised, over his great spectacles, and said, "Why, it is the faculty which enables us to distinguish good from evil."
> It threw some light, but not a glare, and I was a little disappointed, also to some degree embarrassed. He was waiting for me to go on, so, in default of anything else to say, I asked, "Is it valuable?"
> "Valuable? Heavens! lad, it is the one thing that lifts man above the beasts that perish and makes him heir to immortality."[34]

Between the innocence of childhood and Father Peter's reverence comes Satan's relentless exposure. The force of his argument lies not so much in his irreverent inversion of genteel values as in the radical orthodoxy of his position. For little Satan has the angelic, not the diabolical, point of view. Though his name suggests the experience of his old Uncle, this little Satan is unfallen. It is the children, oddly enough, who have fallen—and not into original sin but into the fatuity of adulthood. Theodore is finally just what his stilted and nice language discloses him to be—a reverent little man.

Surely Mark Twain's triumph in *The Mysterious Stranger* is the play upon this double inversion, in which Satan's apparent diabolism is actually prelapsarian innocence and the children's seeming innocence is nothing less than a complete Fall. Satan's line of logic on this

[34] *Ibid.*, pp. 33-34.

score is as relentless as the series of illuminations by means of which he proves his propositions. He shows with ironic innocence how man's belief in the Moral Sense inevitably manifests itself as an action of brutality. Why? Simply because the Moral Sense makes possible the identity of good and evil, right and wrong, thereby enabling man to subvert the pleasure principle. Whereas the angel—and by implication the child—knows no wrong and gains pleasure from an instinctive and instinctual relation to life itself, man gains pleasure by inflicting pain on others. In one of Satan's finest moments, he upbraids Theodore for referring to a particularly sadistic inquisitional torture as *brutal*.

> "No, it was a human thing. You should not insult the brutes by such a misuse of that word; they have not deserved it. . . . It is like your paltry race—always lying, always claiming virtues which it hasn't got, always denying them to the higher animals, which alone possess them. No brute ever does a cruel thing—that is the monopoly of those with the Moral Sense. When a brute inflicts pain he does it innocently; it is not wrong; for him there is no such thing as wrong. And he does not inflict pain for the pleasure of inflicting it—only man does that. Inspired by that mongrel Moral Sense of his!"[35]

Satan is not here defending animal innocence, but indicting the Moral Sense which enables man to enjoy inflicting pain, thereby exposing him as the sole creature who gains pure pleasure from hurting his fellow man.

Not only does Satan's most effective criticism of man hinge upon his exposure of the Moral Sense; his chief force of character—his effective identity—resides in his being without it. What sustains the narrative more than any other factor is the inverted or contradictory emotional response to experience which Satan and the children have. The climax of the episode in which Satan creates

[35] *Ibid.*, pp. 50-51.

the race of little men occurs when he casually and innocently annihilates them before the appalled eyes of the children. And at every point in the narrative Satan's particular emotional freedom from grief and guilt is exploited. He cannot die and he cannot do wrong; he can only expose man's absurd moral sense to the children. His whole pleasure is to laugh at the pathetic figure of man, whose moral sense epitomizes the absurdity and futility of human existence. It is the sum and summary which, in the angelic view, makes man a grotesque and foolish joke.

In the face of such folly, Satan takes upon himself the burden of initiating the children into the double awareness that life is not worth living—that Death is the blessing and not the curse of man. For Death is the event which frees man from the shackles of determinism. In a dramatic demonstration of the full import of his philosophy, Satan indicates to Theodore his regard for the three children and speaks of his intention to release Nikolaus from the chain of events which await him. Certain that Satan will do generously by one whom he likes, Theodore is delighted to hear of the decision, only to be desolated by Satan's disclosure that Nikolaus, who would have lived sixty-five years under the old dispensation, will live but twelve more days under Satan's new order. Satan blithely reassures Theodore and soothes his grief by revealing that Nikolaus "had a billion possible careers, but not one of them was worth living."[36] And so Nikolaus dies with his companions' foreknowledge grieving them at every approaching moment, yet leaving them powerless in the face of the inexorable plot which Satan has devised. Through all this section, Satan affects an innocent pleasure which at once frees him from the sentiment the little men continually indulge and dramatizes his radical innocence.

Mark Twain's success in exposing the Moral Sense brings us back to his failure in the matter of determinism. He is never able to integrate the two concepts. For the Moral Sense has to do with man's pride, folly, and self-

[36] *Ibid.*, p. 86.

deception, whereas the deterministic thesis rests upon the undefined concept of a "first" act which determines the rest of man's existence. The Moral Sense is calculated to expose the folly of man; the deterministic thesis, on the other hand, must—if it is to be effective—be the plot of God.

But precisely here the book is reticent; hence Satan's statement that the primal act is by man, not by God. Yet if man is responsible, why is the deterministic thesis necessary? Why not simply let the Moral Sense bear the satiric burden? In a certain sense, the book does point toward an attack on God; Satan places the first act in infancy, making it a product of the instinctive rather than the conscious will, thereby implicating God more than man in the chain of events. Such, at least, is the implication when Satan says that of a billion possible careers for Nikolaus none was worth living. Even so, the book evades this issue and pursues a delaying line of action. The question comes to be: why did Mark Twain avoid the real necessity of the deterministic thesis? One possibility is that he was afraid to make the direct charge against God; yet he had said things equally "dangerous" and had made jokes equally if not more irreverent.

The real reason—or at least a more relevant reason—for Mark Twain's inability to meet the necessity of the deterministic thesis has to do with the character of little Satan; he cannot really attack God directly without losing his angelic identity. If he rebels, he inevitably becomes diabolic and takes upon himself the role of the avuncular Satan. As fallen angel he could no longer blithely ridicule the Moral Sense, for he himself would be in hot-hearted rebellion against it. Instead of laughing at Man, he would perforce have to free him from his chains. His satanic identity indicates the eternal presence of the impulse to rebel against God and thus makes necessary the deterministic thesis. But just as surely, the fact that it is *little* Satan and not the Old One keeps Mark Twain from being able to carry out the attack upon God. This inability to coordinate the two lines of criticism—the one against man, the other against God—produces the real hiatus in the book.[37]

This central problem could well have been what drove Mark Twain to his repeated efforts to finish the manuscript. With every appearance of little Satan, whether the scene was Hannibal or Austria, Mark Twain was back in a new version of his old dilemma: what to do with little boys about to grow up. Yet if the dilemma forced him into greater and greater efforts to breach or camouflage the division in his conception, it must have made him more and more certain of his ending. For the ending which he confidently left for Paine to find was a way out of the dilemma. It was like a goal which he could see but could not reach. In it, Satan does attack God, but only at the moment of his disappearance. Visiting Theodore for the last time, he explains that everything is a dream, that he himself is but a dream and Theodore but a thought wandering alone in shoreless space. "I am perishing already—I am failing—I am passing away," he announces, whereupon he delivers his assault upon God:

> "Strange . . . that you should not have suspected that your universe and its contents were only dreams, visions, fiction! Strange, because they are so frankly and hysterically insane—like all dreams: a God who could make good children as easily as bad, yet preferred to make bad ones; who could have made every one of them happy, yet never made a single happy one; who made them prize their bitter life, yet stingily cut it short . . . who gave his angels painless lives, yet cursed his other children with biting miseries and maladies of mind and body; who mouths justice and invented hell— mouths mercy and invented hell—mouths Golden Rules, and forgiveness multiplied by seventy times seven, and invented hell; who mouths morals to

[37] This failure of coordination may very well have been at the heart of Mark Twain's failure during this entire phase of his career.

> other people and has none himself; who frowns
> upon crimes, yet commits them all; who created
> man without invitation, then tries to shuffle the re-
> sponsibility for man's acts upon man, instead of
> honorably placing it where it belongs, upon him-
> self; and finally, with altogether divine obtuseness
> invites this poor, abused slave to worship him!"[38]

This ending has the kind of perorational finality so lacking in *Huckleberry Finn*. Moreover, it has a logic in relation to the book, for it releases Satan's attack at the moment of his dissolution, in effect enabling him to destroy his own identity by delivering his pent-up attack on God. Yet the inevitability of the ending does not keep it from being a way out rather than a way through the dilemma which caused it. For little Satan's attack is what it reveals itself to be—an outburst of the pent-up indignation which the structure and style of the book could not discharge. More important, Satan's solipsism constitutes a decisive weakening of the criticism produced by his ironic innocence. Finally, the ending gives the lie to the identity of the book, for Satan in his act of departing actually acquires the Moral Sense he has been remark-ably and effectively free of in the successful moments of the narrative. The truth is that Satan must forego the emotion of indignation if he is to be free of the Moral Sense. There can be no hostile rebellion based on prin-ciple without acquisition of that abhorred faculty.

Mark Twain had evidently seen and understood the problem. After all, he had written the ending as a goal to be reached. Moreover, he had envisioned little Satan's dissolution in the act of releasing his pent-up indignation. What he had not been able to do was to unify the division in his conception—the division between the angelic and the diabolic Satan. That division had both plagued and motivated him from the time it formally announced itself in the seminal farce of "Those Extraordinary Twins." The writing of *The Mysterious Stranger* was his prolonged

[38] *The Mysterious Stranger*, p. 139.

struggle to breach the division and achieve the kind of wholeness which had eluded him in his waning years. But though he had seen his ending—something he had not been able to do so well in *Huckleberry Finn*—the merciless division could neither be healed nor concealed. It was there from the beginning in the very seed of the conception, making the narrative connections more and more tenuous even as the ending became more and more inevitable. Though he could end the story, he could not finish it. Instead, it finished him as a writer.

CHAPTER

XII

EXTRACT

IN *The Mysterious Stranger*, Satan gives a celebrated definition of humor:

> Satan was accustomed to say that our race lived a life of continuous and uninterrupted self-deception. It duped itself from cradle to grave with shams and delusions which it mistook for realities, and this made its entire life a sham. Of the score of fine qualities which it imagined it had and was vain of, it really possessed hardly one. It regarded itself as gold, and was only brass. One day when he was in this vein, he mentioned a detail—the sense of humor. I cheered up then, and took issue. I said we possessed it.
>
> "There spoke the race!" he said; "always ready to claim what it hasn't got, and mistake its ounce of brass filings for a ton of gold dust. You have a mongrel perception of humor, nothing more; a multitude of you possess that. This multitude see the comic side of a thousand low-grade and trivial things—broad incongruities, mainly; grotesqueries, absurdities, evokers of the horse-laugh. The ten thousand high-grade comicalities which exist in the world are sealed from their dull vision. Will a day come when the race will detect the funniness of these juvenilities and laugh at them—and by laughing at them destroy them? For your race, in its poverty, has unquestionably one really effective weapon—laughter. Power, money, persuasion, sup-

> plication, persecution—these can lift at a colossal
> humbug—push it a little—weaken it a little, century
> by century; but only laughter can blow it to rags
> and atoms at a blast. Against the assault of laughter
> nothing can stand. You are always fussing and
> fighting with your other weapons. Do you ever
> use this one? No; you leave it lying rusting. As
> a race, do you ever use it at all? No, you lack the
> sense and the courage.[1]

Almost Mark Twain's only direct definition of the sense
of humor, it has the same authoritative appeal of the
familiar passage on art in "Old Times on the Mississippi,"
and is quoted as frequently, approvingly—and uncritically.
For although the laughter here defined is associated
with the sense of humor, it is not humorous, but satiric
laughter. What Satan discloses is not a sense of humor
at all, but a sense of satire—not a joke on the self converting past humiliations or shame into totally pleasurable form which brings an audience to a helpless laughter
of affection and self-approval, but a joke on the "other"
which establishes a distinction between the audience who
is judged and the narrator who exposes.

It is not surprising that the terms of Satan's definition
of laughter actually have their origin in the world of
Hank Morgan. The metaphor of humor as a weapon for
assault which will blow the shams of the world to "rags
and atoms" has nothing to do with the laughter or the
world of Huck Finn; rather, it is a transliteration of the
very machinery of *A Connecticut Yankee.* Thus the prej-
udices of Morgan, the first of Mark Twain's alien strangers, are fulfilled in the "philosophy" of the last stranger,
Philip Traum. That is why this final passage on humor
is not so much the definition of Mark Twain's humor as
the epitaph disclosing how he had buried it.

The Mysterious Stranger thus constitutes the ironic
end of Mark Twain's writing—ironic because the characters Mark Twain invented to express and expose the

[1] *The Mysterious Stranger,* pp. 131-32.

censorship which he claimed bound the artist became the very figures who repressed and denied the humorous genius who had previously been able to pass the censor. And so the myth of the suppressed artist which Mark Twain insistently sought to develop between 1898 and 1904 became an actuality when, baffled and frustrated, he could not bring himself to finish the book intended to expose the slavery of man to the repressive Moral Sense. He could only write an ending which he more and more despaired of reaching, all the time insisting that he was a frustrated writer who could not publish the black heart's truth about himself and the world.

Significantly enough—if Tuckey is right in his excellent surmises—Mark Twain was working on the ending which he could never reach during his wife's last illness.[2] Even as she lay dying in Florence, Mark Twain's life as a writer was also being brought to a close. The play censor whom he had wooed and won at the outset of his career, she had for thirty-four years benignly presided over his literary production, "approving" each work which was to reach his vast public. From the beginning of his courtship, he had played endlessly upon her role as keeper of the proprieties and had gone upon humorous binges of abstinence in efforts to win the approval he insisted she was withholding from him. Time and again he told her that only her belief in and tolerance for him could save him from a sinner's grave. He had eagerly subjected his manuscripts to what he insisted was her superior literary judgment in order to protect himself from his own vulgarity—which had to be watched with an eagle eye. To what extent Olivia committed herself to the joke is difficult to say, for the picture we have of her is primarily supplied by Mark Twain—who presents her as the "dear little gravity" who looked upon his bad taste, his fearful blasphemy, and his dark philosophy with pained understanding yet adamant resistance. Though there

[2] Tuckey, *Mark Twain and Little Satan*, p. 65.

was no doubt a dimension of reality in Mark Twain's portrait, it is extremely likely that Olivia had a better sense of humor, which is to say a sense of her husband, than those readers and critics who have never genuinely questioned Mark Twain's exaggerated account of his wife's gravity.

Yet if remarkable gains in expression were made by means of the play censor, there was a cost in the relationship—a cost which fully manifested itself when Mark Twain lost his copyright to Olivia and wrote *Joan of Arc* for her approval. Precisely at this time Mark Twain began openly to chafe under the censorship and to lose his sense of humor, taking his wife seriously in direct proportion as he took himself seriously. Thus, directly upon the heels of the "serious" *Joan of Arc*, a reverent piece of homage to Olivia and the family, Mark Twain began to develop the myth of himself as the suppressed artist in a much more unrelenting way than he had ever presented his predicament in his earlier levity with Howells. This new Mark Twain began to assert himself in 1897-98. His letters to Howells indicate that his main efforts were being devoted to material which could not be published because of Olivia's censorship. His philosophy or "gospel," *What Is Man?*, was completed at this period; *The Mysterious Stranger* was begun, along with related "dark" manuscripts. He could write to Howells from Vienna in April, 1899:

> I suspect that to you there is still dignity in human life, & that Man is not a joke—a poor joke— the poorest that was ever contrived—an April-fool joke, played by a malicious ⟨urchin⟩ Creator with nothing better to waste his time upon. Since I wrote my Bible, (last year) which Mrs. Clemens loathes, & shudders over & will not listen to the last half nor allow me to print any part of it, Man is not to me the respect-worthy person he was before; & so I have lost my pride in him & can't write gaily nor praisefully about him anymore. And I don't intend

to try. I mean to go on writing, for that is my best
amusement, but I shan't print much. (For I don't
wish to be scalped any more than another).[3]

The letter is symptomatic of the effort Mark Twain was
making to present himself as the philosopher and writer
of truths too dark for Olivia to approve. This activity of
producing material which would not pass the censor was
not so much a way of ending his writing career as it was
a way of building up an accumulation of written matter
against two future days—the day of Olivia's death and the
day of his own.

With the death of Olivia, Mark Twain was able to
pursue the last illusion left him—the illusion that he could
begin to release to the world the material which had been
withheld from publication during her life. He did not,
of course, state the matter so simply; but once the shock
of her death passed, he began to publish the forbidden
manuscripts. Two of these are the most well-known works
of his last years: *What Is Man?* and *Extract from Captain
Stormfield's Visit to Heaven*. Both these pieces had been,
according to Mark Twain, written under Olivia's ban.

What Is Man?, the "gospel" Mark Twain referred to in
his letter to Howells, is the philosophical account of man's
fundamental helpless position in the chain of determinism. It is so essentially simple, so essentially innocuous,
that it is difficult to this day to see why either Mark Twain
or Olivia could have feared its publication.[4] Robert Ingersoll was certainly making a fine genteel reputation on
material more pungent and considerably more forthright.
Yet Mark Twain published the book in 1906, in an edition limited to 250 copies and not even under his own
signature, copyrighting it instead under the name of J.
W. Bothwell, the superintendent of the De Vinne Com-

[3] *Mark Twain-Howells Letters*, II, 689.
[4] Richard H. Powers, "To Mark Twain's Missionary Defenders,"
The University of Houston Forum, IV (Winter-Spring, 1965), pp.
10-15, makes the interesting point that Mark Twain's philosophy
was true, yet not new.

pany, which published the book.[5] The preface to the volume is worth quoting in full:

> *Feb. 1905.* The studies for these papers were begun twenty-five or twenty-seven years ago. The papers were written seven years ago. I have examined them once or twice per year since and found them satisfactory. I have just examined them again, and am still satisfied that they speak the truth.
>
> Every thought in them has been thought (and accepted as unassailable truth) by millions upon millions of men—and concealed, kept private. Why did they not speak out? Because they dreaded (*and could not bear*) the disapproval of the people around them. Why have I not published? The same reason has restrained me I think. I can find no other.

Here in succinct terms is a definition of the suppressed artist. He appears at last with a truth which he has kept secret for half his creative life because he could not face the disapproval of those around him. Yet for all the pretense of confession in the preface, the inescapable fact remains that the book was released anonymously and copyrighted under someone else's name. Thus the preface becomes the ultimate lie and the ultimate evasion.

This initial act is but an index to the kind of irony which had overtaken Mark Twain. Not only is the preface a contradiction in terms; the entire philosophic disclosure is, as Dixon Wecter rightly said, "pedestrian."[6] There is nothing secret about the thought; the kind of determinism Mark Twain was presenting had been presented many times before and in bolder form. Stripped of its transforming humor, Mark Twain's thought was as routine, tame, and dull as the sentimentality of *Joan of Arc*. More-

[5] Paine, *A Biography*, III, 1,321. But Merle Johnson in *A Bibliography of the Works of Mark Twain* (New York, 1935), notes that Bothwell was a clerk working in the law offices that handled Mark Twain's account (p. 83).

[6] Dixon Wecter in his introduction to *Report from Paradise* (New York, 1952), p. xx.

over, it had about it the same pretentiousness of the earlier work, claiming for itself an immensely extensive period of germination, meditation, and critical scrutiny. Though there is evidence that Mark Twain had brooded about determinism for some time, *What Is Man?* was written as quickly and easily as *Joan of Arc*. For all his claims that this gospel was the profound center of his imagination, the work displayed as great a repression of his humorous genius as the sentimentality of *Joan* had done. Equally serious in its particular way, it was also equally superficial.

Extract from Captain Stormfield's Visit to Heaven is an altogether different but nonetheless related matter— different because it is humorous and thus proudly exposes instead of conceals Mark Twain's authorship; related because it was presented as having been under Olivia's ban. The decisive fact of form in Captain Stormfield's adventure is that it is presented not as a complete work, but as a publishable extract from forbidden materials. The narrative drew upon experiences going all the way back to Mark Twain's San Francisco days, and in Captain Stormfield he presented a figure as irrepressible as Simon Wheeler. In light of their interminable voices, it is not surprising that at one time, early in the nineties, Mark Twain considered replacing Stormfield with the character of Wheeler.[7]

Yet Stormfield is an altogether different figure from Wheeler. Instead of being the deadpan, naïvely innocent figure who slides effortlessly through his tale, apparently unaware of the comicalities he is disclosing, Stormfield is the all-knowing figure—brash, confident, energetically reckless, and assertive—who speaks a racy slang. Far from standing in apparent confusion at the mercy of his

[7] Wecter (*ibid.*, p. xix n) quotes Mark Twain's notebook entry from November 4, 1893, "Si Wheeler's arrival in Heaven," and wonders whether Mark Twain intended to supplant Stormfield or merely imagined a narrative diversion in which Wheeler was to figure.

recollection, Stormfield confidently relates his own adventure. He is, in fine, the transcendent stranger full of himself and his journey, moving at a highhanded pace through the revered geography of heaven.

His slang and his fantasy relate his identity not to Huckleberry Finn and Simon Wheeler but to Hank Morgan. Unlike Morgan, however, Stormfield remains a "pure" burlesque figure for two reasons. First of all, by setting the scene in heaven, Mark Twain was able to maintain a balanced inversion and contrast between Stormfield's misinformed earthly expectations of a pinched Christian heaven and St. Peter's disclosure of a genuinely grand cosmic heaven. The perfect discrepancy between disclosure and expectation gives a perspective by incongruity, economizing the Captain's criticism of the puny Christian scheme and saving him from the trap of reform into which Hank Morgan's burlesque power disappeared. Moreover, there is a charge of good feeling running through the Captain's entire narrative, because St. Peter's grand disclosures amount to an expression of the Captain's own repressed hopes. The heaven to which he goes is a discovery almost too good to be true.

But there is a second reason which saved Stormfield from Morgan's fate. By posing the form as an extract, Mark Twain could not only break away from narrative responsibilities and expectations which required plot and sequence; he could hopefully convey the illusion that the extract was but the teasing surface of a forbidden reality which lay awaiting publication. The act of publication was thus an act which created possibilities offstage. Yet such a form, in order not to be the shallow evasion it played upon, had to meet one of two exacting requirements. Either it had to offer the kind of apparent fragmentation which, like the sketch, was actually the complete form; or it had to be a true extract and possess the unpublished reserve it advertised. To be great, it had to offer both. *Captain Stormfield's Visit to Heaven*—and similar extracts such as "Adam's Diary," and "Eve's

Diary"—offered the first possibility but not the second. Beautifully effective workings of limited burlesque contrasts, they were able to break off abruptly the moment the contrast was exploited and the threat of repetition loomed. But they lacked the illusion of a burden of seriousness as well as the reality of a genuinely repressed body of manuscript awaiting publication. But there was to be a work in which Mark Twain attempted to realize these possibilities: the *Autobiography*. It was his last great effort, and he quite logically came to consider the last part of his life as being identical with the book he was dictating. He even tried to tell himself and his friends that this work was what all his efforts had led toward.

In a way he was right. The autobiographical intention was deeply rooted in Mark Twain's mind. Early in his career—when he was struggling to find his way through *Roughing It*—he had written the potboiling *Burlesque Autobiography*, which he began suppressing as soon as it was published.[8] The burlesque so completely dominated the autobiography that the narrative had little to do with his character or experience and fully deserved the suppression it got. More important, he was at that moment about to succeed in inventing the tall tale of his life which, by genuinely enlarging his identity, would displace the mere reflex act of his burlesque imagination.

Not until the publication of Grant's *Memoirs* did Mark Twain return with sustained effort to the possibility of autobiography. Then, at the peak of his career, he dictated to his lecture agent, James Redpath, an extensive account of how he had secured the contract for Grant's *Memoirs*.[9]

[8] This was published in 1871 under the title of *Autobiography and First Romance*. The "First Romance" had been written in 1870. Actually, Mark Twain had written in 1870 an autobiographical fragment about the Tennessee land, and again in 1877 he wrote of his early years in Florida, Missouri. Both of these fragments are included in Paine's edition of the *Autobiography* (2 vols.; New York, 1924), I, 3-10.

[9] Paine, *A Biography*, II, 818. In his edition of the *Autobiog-*

These dictations, utterly devoid of humor, recount Mark
Twain's triumphant yet generous negotiations with General Grant—negotiations which, interestingly enough, were
begun in November, 1884, the month when portions of
Huckleberry Finn began appearing in the *Century Magazine*. Brisk and lucid though they are, these dictations are
the record of a successful venture, not the making of a
life. They are, in a word, memoirs, not autobiography.
When the story of the contract was complete, the dictations inevitably stopped.

From 1897 through 1898, while residing in Vienna,
Mark Twain once more became concerned with autobiography, this time writing instead of dictating recollections
of his childhood. Written during the period when he was
beginning *The Mysterious Stranger*, these chapters are
one more effort to mine that seemingly inexhaustible
vein of his youth. They contain the unforgettable parts of
the *Autobiography*—the description of the Quarles Farm,
the memories of slavery, the episode of Jim Wolf and
the cats, the experience of hearing ghost stories in childhood, the portraits of the slave Uncle Dan'l, of the kins-
man James Lambton, and of the philosopher Macfarlane.
These chapters are not merely memories, but powerful
recollections designed to evoke the past, to call it back
and make it "as real as it ever was, and as blessed."[10]
Yet they are not simply recollections, for they are so pervaded by the presence of the fictional past Mark Twain had
made that they seem at times to be a factual guide into the
world of Huck Finn and Tom Sawyer. Considered in
relation to his career, these chapters emphasize how much
the years between 1897 and 1899 saw Mark Twain begin
his last phase as a writer. Just as his fictive efforts attempted to draw sustenance from Huck and Tom, his
autobiography sought its inspiration in the Hannibal

---

raphy, Paine has a brief but informative account of Mark Twain's
autobiographical efforts (pp. vii-x).

[10] *Autobiography*, I, 110. The Quarles Farm is what Mark Twain
was evoking.

world of his youth. Though that world and its fictive counterpart provided impulses for autobiography and fiction, they afforded no new characters for his fiction and no narrative principle for his autobiography. If he had to relocate *The Mysterious Stranger* in the winter world of Eseldorf in order to release new characters, he had to find a "future" equivalent to the past in order to provide a reality toward which his autobiography could move.[11]

He did not find such a reality until 1904, when he once more began dictating chapters for his autobiography. Then, living in Florence in the shadow of Olivia's last illness, he found a principle of form for his dictations and felt the old jubilation of discovery. To Howells he wrote on January 16, 1904:

> I've struck it! And I will give it away—to you. You will never know how much enjoyment you have lost until you get to dictating your autobiography; then you will realize, with a pang, that you might have been doing it all your life if you had only had the luck to think of it. And you will be astonished (& charmed) to see how like *talk* it is, & how real it sounds, & how well & compactly & sequentially it constructs itself, & what a dewy & breezy & woodsy freshness it has, & what a darling & worshipful absence of the signs of starch, & flatiron, & labor & fuss & the other artificialities! Mrs. Clemens is an exacting critic, but I have not talked a sentence yet that she has wanted altered. . . . If I live two years this Auto will cover many volumes, but they will not be published independently, but only as *notes* (copyrightable) to my existing books. Their purpose is to add 28 years to the life of the existing books.[12]

[11] That "future" became in time the present moment which Mark Twain employed to release his mind into the associative channels which carried it into the past. Even in the Vienna Chapters, Mark Twain began to write portraits of present moments in Vienna.

[12] *Mark Twain-Howells Letters*, II, 778-79.

The important points to note about Mark Twain's conception of the autobiography at this time are that Olivia is still functioning as the "play" censor (Mark Twain even notes in a postscript that her health is improving), that the method of talking is releasing him from literary into natural form, and that the aim of the autobiography is to provide notes for a collected edition. There is no hint of a suppressed autobiography or of a book to be withheld from the public. Rather, the material, having passed the censor, is designed to extend the copyright of earlier writing. The whole project, as here outlined, could stand as a humorous counterpart to the New York Edition which Henry James was embarking upon at the time; whereas James's Prefaces were to be devoted purely to art and criticism, Mark Twain's dictations were to be devoted to autobiography and capital.[13] When Howells, replying to the letter, contended that not even Mark Twain would be able to tell the "black heart's-truth" about himself, the answer he received clearly showed that the book would not be suppressed but furtively expressed "truth":

> Yes, I set up the safeguards, in the first day's dictating—taking this position: that an Autobiography is the truest of all books; for while it inevitably consists mainly of extinctions of the truth, shirkings of the truth, partial revealments of the truth, with hardly an instance of plain straight truth, the remorseless truth *is* there, between the lines, when the author-cat is raking dust upon it which hides from the disinterested spectator neither it nor its smell (though I didn't use that figure)— the result being that the reader knows the author in spite of his wily diligences.[14]

Instead of being a repository of forbidden substance, the

[13] That James's New York Edition was, among other things designed to extend *his* copyright is a possibility which, though any true Jamesian would embrace it, might offend the uninitiated
[14] *Mark Twain-Howells Letters*, ii, 782.

dictations are here described as vehicles to get more truth past the censor than any other form available to a writer.

But when he resumed the dictations two years later—on January 9, 1906—conditions had signally changed. With his wife dead, he had fully emerged into the last phase of his career, the phase of the garrulous personality who, like a king, made magisterial appearances before his dutiful subjects, discoursing upon affairs of time, of state, and of eternity. The survivor of all the ravages of time, he passed judgment as from afar upon the human procession which passed in review before his remote yet curiously humorous eye. By turns the innocent angelic stranger observing human affairs and the incorrigibly experienced human being who has suffered everything, he set about making himself a fully public personage even as he prepared to withdraw from the world. This last phase officially began when Mark Twain reached seventy. To the throngs assembled to celebrate his birthday, he defined his new estate:

> Threescore years and ten!
> It is the scriptural statute of limitations. After that you owe no active duties; for you the strenuous life is over. You are a time-expired man, to use Kipling's military phrase: You have served your term, well or less well, and you are mustered out. You are become an honorary member of the re-public, you are emancipated, compulsions are not for you, nor any bugle-call but "lights out." You pay the time-worn duty bills if you choose, or decline if you prefer—and without prejudice—for they are not legally collectable.[15]

In freeing himself from the slavery of time, money, regulation, and society into the kingdom of personality, where he would wear his famous white suit, Mark Twain needed a new editor to replace Olivia. He duly found one in the person of Albert Bigelow Paine, whom he appointed official biographer and to whom he renewed his

[15] Quoted in Paine, *A Biography*, III, 1,251-52.

autobiographical dictations. No longer dictating alone to a stenographer or subjecting his dictations to the play censor who for thirty-four years had benignly edited his work, he now had an audience of two: a stenographer, Josephine Hobby, who recorded the dictation; and the shrewdly solicitous Paine, who played the dual role of admiring listener and stimulating interlocutor. The purpose was also twofold. In addition to continuing dictations for his own autobiography, Mark Twain was also supplying material and information for Paine's biography. In the admiring Paine, Mark Twain had an audience who could keep his stream of talk in motion, and the dictations proceeded at a pace and with a volume that they had never reached before.

Along with these new conditions, a new plan for the *Autobiography* was annunciated—a plan which, according to Mark Twain's account, had dawned upon him in Florence:

> Finally in Florence, in 1904, I hit upon the right way to do an Autobiography: Start it at no particular time of your life; wander at your free will all over your life; talk only about the thing which interests you for the moment; drop it at the moment its interest threatens to pale, and turn your talk upon the new and more interesting thing that has intruded itself into your mind meantime.
>
> Also, make the narrative a combined Diary *and* Autobiography. In this way you have the vivid thing of the present to make a contrast with the memories of like things in the past, and these contrasts have a charm which is all their own. No talent is required to make a Combined Diary and Autobiography interesting.
>
> And so, I have found the right plan. It makes my labor amusement—mere amusement, play, pastime, and wholly effortless.[16]

[16] This entire statement stands as a preface to the autobiographical dictations (*Autobiography*, I, 193). Paine avers that, though Mark Twain did not realize it, this had been his plan

Here is a full formulation of the method of free association. The contention is that such a free form is a full reflection of the unconscious, natural movement of the mind at play among a host of possibilities. Talent, will, and conscious form are laid by while interest and impulse take the field. And what constitutes interest, though not explicitly stated, is clearly the force and authority of the great personality in free play between the stimuli of the present and the memories of the past.

He elaborated this plan in more detail at the end of his first week's dictation with Paine.

> I am sure I have found the right way to spin an autobiography at last, after my many experiments. Years ago I used to make skeleton notes to use as texts in writing autobiographical chapters, but really those notes were worth next to nothing. . . . But by my present system I do not need any notes. *The thing uppermost in a person's mind* is the thing to talk about or write about. . . . So you see the result is that this narrative of mine is sure to begin every morning in diary form, because it is sure to begin with something which I have just been talking about. That text, when I am done with it—if I ever get done with it, and I don't seem to get done with any text—but it doesn't matter, I'm not interested in getting done with anything. I am only interested in talking along and wandering around as much as I want to, regardless of results to the future reader. By consequence, here we have diary and history combined; because as soon as I wander from the present text—the thought of today —that digression takes me far and wide over an uncharted sea of recollection, and the result of that is *history*.[17]

This emphasis on the freedom of form carried with it

---

from the beginning. Actually, this realization was a means of motivation which would release Mark Twain to talk *freely and comfortably*.

[17] *Autobiography*, I, 326-27.

the inevitable corollary that the subject matter would also be free—that this freedom from stilted literary form, with its chronology and conscious causation, would release the secret self into the light of day. Although Mark Twain was, by 1904, fully aware of the secret self to be released, his letter to Howells unmistakably discloses that at that time he was using Olivia as his play censor and was letting the secret slip through between the lines. But by 1906, with Olivia dead, the "exacting critic" had disappeared and Mark Twain, who had been intensifying the myth of himself as a suppressed writer, was a victim of his own joke. Insofar as Olivia had been a real censor, he was quite clearly now free to publish the forbidden books which would no longer offend her. Yet insofar as the books were really dangerous, he had perforce to hide them, or cast Olivia in the role of repressive rather than benign censor.

He chose to see the work as dangerous. Thus, he no longer projected a book whose truth was to pass guardedly between the lines, but one which would be frank, free, and explosive. He himself had, like a god, made a text for his autobiography.

> I will construct a text:
> What a wee little part of a person's life are his acts and his words! His real life is led in his head, and is known to none but himself. . . . His acts and his words are merely the visible, thin crust of his world, with its scattered snow summits and its vacant wastes of water—and they are so trifling a part of his bulk! a mere skin enveloping it. The mass of him is hidden—it and its volcanic fires that toss and boil, and never rest, night nor day. These are his life, and they are not written, and cannot be written. Everyday would make a whole book of eighty thousand words—three hundred and sixty-five books a year. Biographies are but the clothes and buttons of the man—the biography of the man himself cannot be written.[18]

[18] *Ibid.*, I, 2.

His autobiography was to be a release of those raging
fires which boiled beneath the crust of things. He was to
become the volcanic figure replacing, autobiographically,
the figures of Hank Morgan and Philip Traum who had
played the role in his fiction. His letters to Howells on
the 1906 dictation refer again and again to the secret
and explosive nature of the material he is accumulating.
By June, 1906, he wrote to Howells that he had dictated
since January 9 of that year 210,000 words in addition
to 50,000 words of "fat" which were in manuscript.

> The "fat" is old pigeon-holed things, of the years
> gone by, which I or editors didn't das't to print.
> For instance, I am dumping in the little old book
> which I read to you in Hartford about 30 years ago
> & which you said "publish—& ask Dean Stanley to
> furnish an introduction; he'll do it." ("Captain
> Stormfield's Visit to Heaven.") It reads quite to suit
> me, without altering a word, now that it isn't to see
> print until I am dead.
>
> To-morrow I mean to dictate a chapter which will
> get my heirs & assigns burnt alive if they venture
> to print it this side of 2006 A.D.—which I judge
> they won't. There'll be lots of such chapters if I
> live 3 or 4 years longer. The edition AD. 2006 will
> make a stir when it comes out. . . . This book is per-
> fectly outrageous, in spots, but that's nothing—
> it's going to be worse by & by if I live beyond my
> appointed date. I don't care for my other books,
> now, but I dote on this one as Adam used to dote on
> a fresh new deformed child after he was 900 years
> old & wasn't expecting any more surprises. I've
> written a short Preface. I like the title of it: "Spoken
> from the Grave." It will prepare the reader for the
> solemnities within.[19]

This letter to Howells reveals the full scope of the new
forbidden book containing past performances too profane
to pass editorial censorship as well as present vitupera-
tions too explosive for any contemporary eye.

[19] *Mark Twain-Howells Letters*, II, 811.

The Preface which Mark Twain had penned was the last word upon the kind of exposure he intended:

AS FROM THE GRAVE

In this Autobiography I shall keep in mind the fact that I am speaking from the grave. I am literally speaking from the grave, because I shall be dead when the book issues from the press.

I speak from the grave rather than with my living tongue, for a good reason: I can speak thus freely. When a man is writing a book dealing with the privacies of his life—a book which is to be read while he is still alive—he shrinks from speaking his whole frank mind; all his attempts to do it fail, he recognizes that he is trying to do a thing which is wholly impossible to a human being. The frankest and freest and privatest product of the human mind and heart is a love letter; the writer gets his limitless freedom of statement and expression from his sense that no stranger is going to see what he is writing. . . . It has seemed to me that I could be as frank and free and unembarrassed as a love letter if I knew that what I was writing would be exposed to no eye until I was dead, and unaware, and indifferent.[20]

The private love letter—secret, intimate, and serenely frank—was thus the final form to which Mark Twain likened his autobiography. To see the significance of this metaphor is to begin to understand the paradox of the *Autobiography*—the paradox that, despite Mark Twain's vast claims about the revelation he was about to make, the *Autobiography* is singularly tame. To be sure, there are attacks on certain persons—such as Teddy Roosevelt, Bret Harte, and Mrs. Thomas Bailey Aldrich—which Mark Twain understandably would not have wanted published. But the book revealed nothing about Mark Twain's mind which had not already received ample and often more powerful exposure in print. Al-

[20] *Autobiography*, I, xv-xvi.

though Mark Twain had a great deal left to *say* he had nothing left to *reveal*—nothing except the mechanism of his personality in the act of improvising a text. Thus the *Autobiography* is, as Paine rightly described it, a kind of table talk, not at all a secret revelation.[21]

The figure of the love letter as a metaphor for the form of autobiography goes directly back to the relationship Mark Twain had with his wife and censor. For he had, during his courtship in 1869 and 1870, written hundreds and hundreds of pages of love letters to Olivia. Though these letters are voluminous and easy in their flow of language, they are subjected to a much greater censorship than the manuscript of *The Innocents Abroad*, much of which was written during the same period of time. For they were directed as appeals to the reverent image of Olivia herself and thus had to pass the rigorous internal censorship of Samuel Clemens, whereas the humorous travel book was the product of the irreverent Mark Twain subjecting himself to the editorial approval of his wife. To be sure, the one manuscript was of a public, the other of a private and intimate nature, but it by no means follows from this distinction that the private document will be the more free, less guarded, or more open. In the case of the artist, the public document happens to be his art, which means that all its power is engaged in expression rather than concealment—making the public document more likely to be revealing than the private. The identification of the private with the free and the public with the suppressed, questionable when applied to any kind of document, is fatuous when indiscriminately applied in the world of art.

It was just such an identification that evidently victimized Mark Twain in his later years. He came to see his private thoughts as repressed thoughts. As this identifica-

[21] *Ibid.*, I, xi. In the sense that it was table talk, the *Autobiography* is in many ways a remarkable performance. Generally speaking, it is never dull, it is unimpeded in its movement, and it is genuinely revealing about Mark Twain's writing, speaking, and relationships with friends.

tion became a conviction, he was less able to see that it was precisely this false identification which was the repression, the delusion increasingly thwarting his artistic expression.

His fate as humorist and artist was that his public personality and art were his forms of genuine expression —they were less, not more censored—more, not less, revealing—than the unpublished letters and manuscripts which accumulated around him. As a matter of fact, Mark Twain himself could not fully resist or suppress his *Autobiography*, and within six weeks after writing the letter telling Howells that the book would not be published, he had negotiated a contract, for $30,000, which allowed Colonel George Harvey of Harpers to publish portions of the autobiography in the *North American Review*.[22]

Harvey accordingly came up to Dublin, New Hampshire, where Mark Twain was installed for the summer, made a typescript of the dictation, and made his own selection of the material. In a letter to Howells, Mark Twain proclaimed the event:

> As to the Autobiography, you're going to get it —in the neck! as the vulgar say. Harvey . . . is going to volley it at the public in the new N. A. Review, which I think is going to be the greatest of the periodicals, & the most conspicuous in America. . . . The Colonel has done some wonderful editing of this MS. He has selected five 5,000-word instalments & pieced them together so cleverly that the seams don't show, & each seems to have been written by itself.[23]

Thus it was that the great book which was not to have seen the light for a hundred years was introduced to the public in twenty-five lead installments of five thousand

[22] Paine, *A Biography*, III, 1,322. The $30,000 was used to build Stormfield. Mark Twain's last home was, in fact, tentatively titled Autobiography House (*Mark Twain-Howells Letters*, II, 817).
[23] *Mark Twain-Howells Letters*, II, 817-18.

words each, making the *Autobiography* the greatest example of Mark Twain's latest form, the extract.

The *Autobiography* really had no form except as it was
published. True, it was said to have an unpublished
"form" characterized by utter freedom of form as well as
of content. Its freedom of association *could* have had
genuine meaning in relation to the process of Mark
Twain's thought; and Mark Twain's observations on his
method indicate that he was evidently aware of such possibilities. But to have pursued them meant that the completely published dictations would provide the reader in
the far future with the opportunity and the challenge of
discovering the significant patterns of associations and
from such patterns the ultimate shape of Mark Twain's
"real" self.

But Mark Twain, for all his talk of such freedom, had
neither interest nor belief in such a form or such a self.
The freedom and the self he spoke of had meaning only
in relation to censorship and approval. Neither form nor
self even *existed*, except in relation to publication, and the
only way Mark Twain could give them reality—which is
to say form—was to publish part of his autobiographical
dictations. Hence the extract and hence the meaning of
the extract. It was a way of giving a form to chaos.
Though it presented the illusion of being a fragment released from a completed form, it actually was a completed form released from a vast chaotic fragment.

As a strategy it served two functions. It created the illusion of a complete form behind it and served as an advertisement for all the unpublished portions yet to come.
The humorous counterpart of the repressed diabolical
narratives which could not be completed, the extract
was Mark Twain's double capitalization of his expiring
genius—a publication which exploited the present and
created a future audience. It is thus a joke on posterity—
Mark Twain's final joke, one might say. By promising a
room full of forbidden surprises to readers a hundred
years hence, Mark Twain was able to bestow upon himself

a particular kind of immortality which would make him an actual literary competitor—a genuine publishing author —long after his death. Such a plan extended the capitalization of his speculative genius far beyond the goal he had originally had of dispersing the *Autobiography* through an edition of his work in order to lengthen the copyright.

There was a further dimension of the joke—how intentional it is impossible to say. For all Mark Twain's advertisements of the great disclosures for the future, there was little of a revelatory or shocking nature in all the dictations. The religious opinions, for example, which he particularly singled out as being explosive, were little if any stronger in language or opinion than he had already used in published essays and stories. The whole performance of the *Autobiography* smacked of the hoax the King and Duke had enacted in the Royal Nonesuch. Though Mark Twain's last bow was infinitely longer, it is doubtful that it was so revealing as the brief, wheeling figure of the King before his astonished, "sold" audience.

Mark Twain's last joke was not only on all the audiences his brave advertisements were to assemble; it was also on the editors the dictations required—editors who would dutifully take up the task of sifting through the mass of material, culling and arranging it according to some arbitrary principle of convenience. The nub of the joke, the snapper, is that not one of the editors of the *Autobiography* has ever followed Mark Twain's wishes. Each in his own way has violated the material. Mark Twain himself began the procession by turning over the material to Harvey to edit, and Harvey in turn simply selected material for magazine consignment. Then came Paine, whose two-volume edition in 1925 included about half of the dictations. Paine tended to omit savage passages on personalities and others on "forbidden" subjects, honoring Mark Twain's wish that much of the material be suppressed and bearing out his insistence that the real truth could not be told. But Paine, though he kept in check the outbursts and timidly respected the proprieties, assiduously followed Mark Twain's directions regarding the form, preserving the order of dictations with utter disregard for the order of chronology.[24]

De Voto, who succeeded Paine as Editor of the Mark Twain Papers, determined to bring before the world those volcanic aspects of Mark Twain's utterance which Paine's edition had suppressed. His *Mark Twain in Eruption* brought into print half of the half Paine had left untouched, releasing much of Mark Twain's humorous invective, particularly his blasts at the plutocracy. But if De Voto took pleasure in freeing the substance of the *Autobiography*, he was brought to violate the form. Considering Mark Twain's autobiographical method of free association a failure, De Voto confidently set out to replace the chaotic sequence with his own arrangement of the material, along lines of thematic order. He summed up his activity as follows:

> After determining which portions of the unpublished typescript I wanted to print, I first deleted from them interpolations, headlines and newspaper stories, and such other interruptions as I considered disfiguring, and then brought them together in a kind of order. It is a loose order but it is the tightest one that can be given the *Autobiography*; and occasionally I have chosen to let the original order stand, at some cost in incoherence. But related things have been given an explicit relationship in this book which they lack in the typescript.
>
> In brief, I have given the book a more coherent plan than Mark Twain's and I have left out what seemed to me uninteresting.[25]

De Voto's remarks—and these are by no means all he had

---

[24] Paine himself was not quite true to the form. Not only did his omissions break up the continuity of the free association, but he failed to conclude his edition with "The Death of Jean," as Mark Twain specifically directed. Believing that the *Autobiography* would have a publishing success, Paine intended to bring it out in successive stages, but the book failed as a publishing venture and Paine made no more selections.

[25] Bernard De Voto (ed.), *Mark Twain in Eruption*, pp. ix-x.

to devote to describing his editorial liberties[26]—reveal just how much of an editor the dictations had forced him to be.

Not that he should have refused to be an editor. Like Paine before him, and like Olivia before Paine, De Voto made himself formidable by taking editorial initiative. By knowing Mark Twain's work and by being assured that he knew what was interesting, De Voto was able to produce a consistently interesting volume. Yet even in his success he was caught in the toils of Mark Twain's humor, approving his own editorial performance by dismissing Mark Twain's intention. Secure in his self-approval, De Voto could abandon himself to the broadest freedoms and confidently assure his readers that remaining unpublished papers were of no real interest to anyone save scholars.

De Voto was not necessarily wrong in his evaluations, but Mark Twain has an enormous vitality, a relentless will to remain *alive*. And so, twenty years after De Voto's effort, Charles Neider produced *his* edition of the *Autobiography*. Neider's intention was twofold. First, as his title page indicated, he was releasing hitherto suppressed material in an effort to come closer and closer to the last revelation. Second, he was determined to introduce a new principle of order upon the material. That principle turned out to be the arrangement of the material in chronological order. Thus in the act of disclosing Mark Twain's most unconventional substance, Neider involved himself in absolutely conventionalizing the form. Toward Mark Twain's direct insistence that the *Autobiography* be published in the sequence dictated so as to reveal what was uppermost in the writer's mind, Neider displayed mere rhetorical astonishment: "What an extraor-

---

[26] De Voto omitted passages which he considered fantastic, injurious, or irrelevant; he did not hesitate to edit material in order to reduce its vindictiveness; and he deleted portions of typescript which he thought dropped into trivial rage; he removed particularly offensive passages, he supplied his own titles and subtitles, and he submitted his manuscript to the Mark Twain Estate for its approval.

dinary idea! As though the stream of composition time were in some mysterious way more revealing than that of autobiographical time!"[27]

If the humorist's last joke was on all the audiences who awaited revelations and on editors who were maneuvered into violating his intentions, it was also on himself. For the form of the extract, as it culminated in the *Autobiography*, was no longer a fully negotiated form subjected to the approval of a play editor. It was instead an unfinished manuscript, abandoned into the hands of a real editor to integrate and organize into coherent form. Like the successive versions of *The Mysterious Stranger*, the progress of the autobiographical dictations disclosed narrative impulse disintegrating into indulgence—but with one essential difference. The disintegration, instead of being an erosion of the creative will, as it had been in the struggle to finish *The Mysterious Stranger*, was a celebrated release from form, a freedom from the slavery of plot and pen. The editor did not have to encroach upon the manuscripts, concealing his work under the fiction of finding missing endings; he was literally evoked to *be* the missing formal principle and thereby violate the free expression of his master.

With each violation, Mark Twain's prophecy that the *Autobiography* would not be completely published for a hundred years seems more and more likely to come true. For each effort to reveal the explosive content has been accompanied by such a corresponding disregard of form that a half-century after Mark Twain's death we seem as remote as ever from the elusive reality of the *Autobiography*. More and more we shall come to ask the inevitable Editor of the Mark Twain Papers to give us the *Autobiography* exactly as it was dictated—a "true" edition. Yet whoever knows Mark Twain's achievement as a writer will have to have the sense of humor to see that when the

[27] Charles Neider (ed.), *The Autobiography of Mark Twain Including Chapters Now Published for the First Time* (New York, 1929), p. xvi.

true edition appears it may be no more authoritative than the earlier "editions." As is likely to be true of the ultimate edition of *The Mysterious Stranger*, the form will be discovered to rest not solely in the manuscripts, but in the editor—the censor—called forth by the proclaimed freedom of the dictations. At that late time, the dark and bitter truth, instead of being the substantive reality which Mark Twain's advertisements promised, is likely to be the disclosure that there was nothing left to tell. Though his voice, like Simon Wheeler's, continued into the void, Mark Twain's form had ended.

INDEX

INDEX

INDEX

INDEX

INDEX

MARK TWAIN
The Fate of Humor

Although the life of Samuel Clemens begins for the biographer in 1835, it begins for the critic on February 3, 1863, the date the name "Mark Twain" made its first appearance. With that name, Samuel Clemens had freed the genius in himself and fixed his identity as a humorist.

James M. Cox pursues the development of Mark Twain's humor through all the forms it took from "The Jumping Frog" to *The Mysterious Stranger*. Instead of concentrating on the serious elements behind Twain's style, Professor Cox focuses upon the humor itself as the transfiguring power which converted the graver issues and emotions of Mark Twain's life and time into entertaining narratives. The greatness of Twain's humor lies not in its sober aspect but in its complete and relentless invasion or subversion of all forms of seriousness and reverence. Thus, *Huckleberry Finn*, far from being a tragic or serious novel, reconstructs the tragic issue of slavery into a boy's odyssey of adventure and in the process discloses that the real tyrant which keeps man in chains, and from which not even the excursions of humor can free him, is the conscience. That discovery marked the limits of Mark Twain's humor, and for the remainder of his career it became the landmark of "truth" by which he measured the failure and folly of mankind.

"No one can afford to ignore this book. I have found it truly exciting, even where Cox is taking issue with my own previously published work."—Henry Nash Smith

"An admirable combination of biographical and literary intelligence."—*Yale Review*

JAMES M. COX is Professor of English at Dartmouth College.

PRINCETON PAPERBACKS